VIOLENCE IN THE FAMILY

KNOWLEDGE OF THE MIND

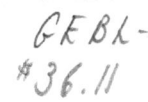

VIOLENCE IN THE FAMILY:
Social Work Readings and Research from Northern and Rural Canada

Edited by Keith Brownlee and John R. Graham

**Library Commons
Georgian College
One Georgian Drive
Barrie, ON
L4M 3X9**

Canadian Scholars' Press Inc.
Toronto

Violence in the Family: Social Work Readings and Research from Northern and Rural Canada
edited by Keith Brownlee and John R. Graham

First published in 2005 by
Canadian Scholars' Press Inc.
180 Bloor Street West, Suite 801
Toronto, Ontario
M5S 2V6

www.cspi.org

Copyright © 2005 Keith Brownlee, John R. Graham, the contributing authors, and Canadian Scholars' Press Inc. All rights reserved. No part of this publication may be photocopied, reproduced, stored in a retrieval system, or transmitted, in any form or by any means, electronic, mechanical, or otherwise, without the written permission of Canadian Scholars' Press Inc., except for brief passages quoted for review purposes. In the case of photocopying, a licence may be obtained from Access Copyright: One Yonge Street, Suite 1900, Toronto, Ontario, M5E 1E5, (416) 868-1620, fax (416) 868-1621, toll-free 1-800-893-5777, www.accesscopyright.ca.

Every reasonable effort has been made to identify copyright holders. CSPI would be pleased to have any errors or omissions brought to its attention.

Canadian Scholars' Press gratefully acknowledges financial support for our publishing activities from the Government of Canada through the Book Publishing Industry Development Program (BPIDP) and the Government of Ontario through the Ontario Book Publishing Tax Credit Program.

Library and Archives Canada Cataloguing in Publication

Violence in the family : social work readings and research from northern and rural Canada / edited by Keith Brownlee and John Graham.

Includes bibliographical references.
ISBN 978-1-55130-259-1

1. Family violence—Canada. 2. Family violence—Canada, Northern.
3. Family social work—Canada. 4. Family social work—Canada, Northern.
5. Social service, Rural—Canada. I. Brownlee, Keith II. Graham, John R. (John Russell), 1964-

HV6626.23.C3V565 2005   362.82'92'0971091734   C2004-906142-9

Cover design by George Kirkpatrick
Text design and layout by HotHouse Canada

Printed and bound in Canada

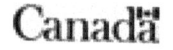

TABLE OF CONTENTS

PREFACE · vii

Chapter One · 1
EXPLORING SECONDARY TRAUMA IN SEXUAL ASSAULT WORKERS IN NORTHERN ONTARIO LOCATIONS: The Challenges of Working in the Northern Ontario Context
Diana Coholic and Karen Blackford

Chapter Two · 16
GEOGRAPHIC CONTEXT AND NORTHERN CHILD WELFARE PRACTICE
Glen Schmidt

Chapter Three · 30
INTRA-FAMILIAL ADOLESCENT SEXUAL OFFENDERS IN RURAL AND ISOLATED AREAS
Chantal Morrison-Lambert

Chapter Four · 51
SEXUAL ABUSE IN RURAL, REMOTE, AND SMALL COMMUNITIES
Michelle Aukema

Chapter Five · 61
THE EFFECTS OF A TIME-LIMITED GROUP WITH PRE-ADOLESCENT GIRLS WHO HAVE BEEN SEXUALLY ABUSED
Susan van Yzendoorn and Keith Brownlee

Chapter Six · 75
CONNECTING VIOLENCE AND CHEMICAL DEPENDENCY WITH FEMALE ADDICTS
Teresa Legowski

Chapter Seven — 90
CLIENT CONFIDENTIALITY, ANONYMITY, FACILITATOR CREDIBILITY, AND CONTAMINATION IN RURAL FAMILY VIOLENCE SELF-HELP GROUPS
Colleen Ginter

Chapter Eight — 105
BREAKING THE CONNECTION BETWEEN TRADITIONAL MASCULINITY AND VIOLENCE: Toward a Context and Gender-Sensitive Approach to Counselling Males
David Tranter

Chapter Nine — 119
GROUP TREATMENT IN NORTHERN ONTARIO FOR MEN WHO ABUSE THEIR PARTNERS
Larry Cheblovic and Keith Brownlee

Chapter Ten — 135
ADULT SURVIVORS OF CHILDHOOD SEXUAL ABUSE: A Mixed-Gender Therapy Group
Darlene Olimb

Chapter Eleven — 146
POLICE RESPONSES TO FAMILY VIOLENCE IN A NORTHERN COMMUNITY: Some Implications for Policy
Julie Woit, Keith Brownlee, Rod Brown, and Roger Delaney

Chapter Twelve — 156
HISTORICAL AND SOCIAL INFLUENCES ON VIOLENCE IN ABORIGINAL FAMILIES
Michelle Derosier and Raymond Neckoway

Chapter Thirteen — 170
MINO-YAA-DAA: HEALING TOGETHER
Cyndy Baskin

LIST OF CONTRIBUTING AUTHORS — 182

PREFACE

Writings on domestic violence have increased over the past fifteen years both nationally and internationally. But few studies, to date, consider the topic in relation to rural, remote, or northern Canadian contexts. This book is oriented to social work, and much of it to professional intervention. Most chapters are authored by practitioners with much experience in rural, remote, or northern settings. It also contributes to an emerging research literature, as few authors, to date, have considered social work and its relationship with domestic violence in northern/rural/remote Canada.

Chapter One was first published as a journal article that appeared in *Canadian Social Work* in 2003, and is reprinted here with the kind permission of the authors, the editor of the journal, and the Canadian Association of Social Workers. It provides an excellent overview of the challenges facing social workers working in rural, northern, and remote areas, and in particular the issue of secondary trauma that can occur when working with victims of sexual assault. Chapter Two examines major factors—visibility, accessibility, professional ethics, public scrutiny, and supportive practice environments—that are critical for direct and community child welfare practices in Canada's north. Several proceeding chapters consider specific practice problems and intervention solutions for rural and isolated areas, using case examples and research to highlight practice principles that distinguish rural/remote/northern intervention from what might occur in urban or non-remote settings. Chapter Three looks at practice contexts for responding to inter-familial adolescent sexual offenders in rural/remote settings, and Chapter Four addresses issues of sexual abuse. Chapter Five examines distinct issues in rural/remote contexts for providing time-limited group work with pre-adolescent girls who have been sexually abused, and Chapter Six considers the treatment of women who have experienced family violence and chemical dependency. Chapter Seven turns to rural/remote family violence self-help groups, taking into account client confidentiality, anonymity, and facilitator techniques to engender responsive delivery. Chapter Eight considers similar issues in treating men who abuse their partners in a rural/remote context, and Chapter Nine discusses mixed gender group treatment for adult survivors of childhood sexual abuse. Chapter Ten analyzes individual treatment for men involved in family violence in rural/remote communities, and Chapter Eleven focuses on the implications of police intervention on practice and policy in family violence. Chapters Twelve and Thirteen provide a perspective on family violence from the Aboriginal community. Chapter Twelve gives an historical overview of some of the factors that have contributed to high rates of family violence in First Nations, and Chapter Thirteen offers a description of a successful intervention program designed specifically for Aboriginal Peoples.

All chapters are based on current research. Taken together, we anticipate they make a contribution to the knowledge of social work practice in rural/remote/northern Canada and, by extrapolation, to family violence social work in any rural/remote jurisdiction.

Chapter One

EXPLORING SECONDARY TRAUMA IN SEXUAL ASSAULT WORKERS IN NORTHERN ONTARIO LOCATIONS: The Challenges of Working in the Northern Ontario Context[1]

Diana Coholic and Karen Blackford

The terms "secondary trauma" and "vicarious trauma" both refer to damaging effects on people who bear witness to the experience of another person's trauma, but are not themselves direct victims of that trauma. For instance, McCann et al. (1990) describe how working with trauma shifts the worker's inner experience and alters her world view. In recent years, discussions of secondary and vicarious trauma experienced by therapists have become more common in social work literature. This effect has been studied in various populations across related disciplines, in wives of war veterans, for example (Mikulincer et al., 1995), as well as partners and family members of abuse survivors (Maltas et al., 1995; Manion et al., 1996), and professionals working with survivors of abuse (Follette et al., 1994; Hartman, 1995; Schauben et al., 1995). More recently *Canadian Social Work* published an article by Regehr et al. (1999) that describes the effects of secondary trauma in working with survivors of sexual assault. These effects include a perception of the world as "evil," an increased sensitivity to reports of violence, disruption in relationships, and increased feelings of helplessness.

This research study aims to explore secondary trauma in sexual assault workers within the context of northern Ontario. While this paper contributes to our knowledge of the nature of secondary trauma, its main significance is in its discussion of the unique challenges associated with sexual assault work in northern Ontario. As Taback et al. (1992) explain, trained social workers cannot always assume that they have the "right" skills to work in any community, and certainly the northern Ontario context shapes social work and work in sexual assault in distinct ways. This paper explores some of these issues, which are certainly reflected in and shared by other rural workers and contexts (Tice, 1990; Gumpert et al., 1998; Mayer, 2001). These issues include a lack of community support for, and awareness of, sexual assault work, insufficient privacy and confidentiality, the isolation (both physical and social) of the communities, and of the difficulty of developing an understanding of the specific cultural composition of a given community.

METHODOLOGY AND STUDY SAMPLE

Letters introducing the study were sent to five community agencies that work with sexual assault survivors in five different northern Ontario locations spanning a distance of approximately 450 kilometres east to west, and 500 kilometres north to south. The letters were followed up by telephone calls from the two authors, and group meetings were arranged with these five agencies at the convenience of the participant groups. Five group interviews were facilitated by the authors with twenty-five participants in total: two groups had four participants, two groups had six participants, and one group had five participants. The duration of the group interviews was from one and a half hours to two hours in length. The authors attempted to involve the participants in a meaningful way by grounding the research inquiry in their practice experiences, and by keeping them informed of the progress of the research (participants were mailed copies of research reports and papers).

Prior to beginning the group interviews, a short demographic form and an informed consent form were completed by each participant in the group, and questions about the study were addressed. Four open-ended questions were then introduced, which addressed the workers' satisfaction and dissatisfaction with their jobs, the strategies they had employed in coping with difficulties associated with their work, and if/how the northern Ontario location affected their work. Conversations were tape-recorded and transcribed for the purposes of grounded theory analysis, except in two cases. In one instance, a participant preferred that the interviewer take written notes without a tape-recorder, and in a second instance technical problems resulted in an inaudible tape. Here the interviewer's notes and her memory served as the source of data.

Most of the participants were counsellors in community sexual assault centres. Also interviewed were two community legal clinic lawyers, one community legal clinic worker, a community legal clinic clerical worker, a counsellor employed in a women's shelter, three women's shelter workers, and one nurse doing counselling in a community-based, hospital-administered sexual assault intervention centre. All but one person interviewed were women. While the majority of the research participants were Anglophone, three were Francophone, and two were First Nations. The average age of the participants was forty-two years and most were experienced workers in sexual assault—the majority of the participants had fifteen to twenty years of experience. Finally, the highest level of education attained by participants varied from high school diploma (two), college diploma (eight), undergraduate university degree (nine), master's university degree (one) and doctoral university degree (one). Four participants did not indicate the highest level of education they had achieved.

ANALYSIS OF THE DATA

Transcriptions and notes were reviewed after the first interviews. The two authors discussed the data that emerged, and began to identify categories within the data. Impressions and categories from the first interviews and then from subsequent interviews, such as the isolation of workers, were further explored in later interviews. This repeated exploration permitted a better understanding of the elements that contributed to each category. This repetition was also a way of assessing the consistency of the information across sample groups. Additional categories such as coping strategies of workers emerged as the interviews progressed. Those categories were then added to the list of topics to be explored, and clarified in subsequent, and then final, interviews.

The two authors reviewed findings when the interviews were completed and organized the various categories of findings into major themes. The northern Ontario location was a dominant theme. Other themes that arose from discussions included the nature of secondary trauma, risk factors, coping, and the empowerment of workers. The secondary trauma experienced by the participants in the research study described in this paper share commonalities with the experiences of workers in other locations. For instance, participants reported the following effects of secondary trauma: a loss of faith in traditional institutions such as the Church, the legal system, and the traditional family; a changed world view; feeling desensitized to violence; hyper-vigilance with children; altered sexual relationships; spiritual trauma; and physical symptoms such as the worsening of allergies. However, working in northern Ontario can compound the effects of secondary trauma, and also raises unique issues of concern, including the effects of resource-based economies on the reinforcement of traditional, domestic roles for women. As Kechnie et al. (1996) argue, household routines, social relations, and economic decisions in northern Ontario have generally been shaped by the dominant masculine preoccupations with resource industries, private property, and European morality.

The following discussion focuses on the specific issues arising from the theme of the northern Ontario location, and was further separated into the following four categories: community attitudes and support; privacy; isolation; and culture. Importantly, it should be noted that the context-specific issues discussed in these four categories were perceived by the research participants to add additional stressors to the already difficult work of sexual assault, which in some cases compounded the effects of secondary trauma.

COMMUNITY ATTITUDES AND SUPPORT OF GENDER-RELATED ISSUES AND SEXUAL ASSAULT WORK

Most of the participants interviewed in this study reported that people in their local communities demonstrated little awareness of gender politics. By "gender politics" we refer to an understanding of patriarchy and women's oppression. "Red neck" was often a characterization used by participants to describe many of the attitudes they faced. One of the most difficult circumstances identified was the lack of community support and the negative perceptions of the participants by other professionals and community members. As one worker states, "When we first came here there was a big controversy. [Local people said] 'Well those are man-hating feminists who work over there, and they're all lesbians and everyone should stay away from there.'" Another participant contends that they are "always having to defend feminism, always having to defend who we are, what we do, and the way in which we do it. You know, we're always being challenged by our community."

These challenges may hamper a community's resilience, that is, their capacity to address violence against women or their ability to respond to crises in ways that strengthen communal bonds, resources, and the community's capacity to cope (Chenoweth et al., 2001). Certainly, they add a layer of tension and stress to already difficult work.

While it remains debateable whether northern Ontario communities in general are more prone to stereotypical attitudes about women and men, it has been established in other studies that women's marginalization within northern Ontario economies reinforces traditional and domestic roles for women. As Kauppi et al. (1996) contend, women who live in the north are more likely than both northern men and their southern sisters to be affected by low income, dependency, and second-class status in workplaces. They conclude that social and economic structures as well as cultural values have made independence and self-sufficiency a virtual impossibility for most women in the north. Certainly, in more populated centres, a sufficiently large feminist subculture can develop, which may influence the community, but this can be difficult to achieve in less populated northern communities. Here women's services and an organized feminist community may be non-existent or, of necessity, in hiding and difficult to access.

Another point that was raised by some participants was the lack of prominent, positive, female role models within some northern communities. Often employment in the north revolves around a male-dominated resource-based industry such as logging and mining. Members of local government tend to be men, and employment opportunities for women can be limited. As one participant notes:

> If you're a young girl growing up in a community like this, you learn who you are in this community. You're useless, you're worthless, you're not much. Where do you see your mother working? Where do you see all the other women working? You don't see them as the executive in the mining company. You don't see them making big money. It's not about you.

Thus, some women remain invisible within many of these communities by way of their relegation to the private sphere of home and family. Yet the importance for young women of visible, positive role models within their own communities cannot be discounted (Wolf, 1993). In fact, one participant reported that a relative moved to southern Ontario so that her daughter could access positive, strong female role models and friends. The lack of female role models outside the private sphere of home and family is a concern and was felt most strongly by participants in the most isolated, small communities.

ISSUES OF PRIVACY AND CONFIDENTIALITY

The lack of anonymity for counsellors working in northern Ontario exacerbates already stressful situations and work. As Delaney et al. (1997) describe, social workers in the north live as part of their community rather than apart from it, which can lead to ethical dilemmas as well. For example, often workers will come to know (through client reports) about neighbours, relatives, or prominent community people who have allegedly perpetrated sexual assault. Due to confidentiality restrictions, most times this information remains private and creates an additional form of stress for the worker, who in some cases may be forced to interact with an alleged perpetrator on a professional or personal basis. As one participant describes:

> Sometimes I may know that an offender has been named and he may never have been charged. I may know that there is not enough evidence to convict the guy—he's not going to be [charged]. So I'm left with this information. Probably 80 per cent of the time, I'm going to run into [him] one way or another.

Another participant points out, "You hear these stories and you watch people on the news and they're saying one thing, but you know all this information.

You just want to wring their neck. You can't do that. It's really frustrating." For some participants, the likelihood of having to interact with alleged perpetrators of abuse was common and created feelings of frustration, anger, and anxiety.

Lack of anonymity also limited workers' opportunities to seek professional help. Most of the research participants state that talking with peers and colleagues helped them to cope with the effects of secondary trauma, and many report seeking support and guidance on a professional level was also especially helpful, which fits with recommendations found in the literature (Briere, 1996; Kahill, 1998). However, one group of participants in particular pointed out that they felt stymied in their ability to seek this type of help in two ways. First they explained that if they sought professional help in their community they would be negatively labelled. As a consequence of this labelling, the centre where they worked would receive fewer referrals and would be damaged by an overall reputation of inadequacy. As one of these participants argued, "It's not really fair sometimes. Because I know probably the instances of burnout would not be so high if there wasn't that fear or whatever; a reflection on your workplace, a reflection on your professionalism."

Particularly troubling is the perception that other professionals in this community would negatively label these workers for seeking assistance. Engaging in professional counselling can be a worthy endeavour for enhancing one's insight and growth, and certainly should not be viewed as a sign of incompetence or weakness. Importantly, this group of participants reported that their fears are location-specific, since they perceived no barrier when they sought out counselling services in larger communities and cities. It appears that anonymity, a greater number of service options, and perceptions of increased community tolerance facilitated their participation in counselling in these larger communities.

Moreover, not only is a worker's access to other services thwarted or limited, but personal and leisure activities can also be curtailed. As one worker points out, "There's less outlets to go to. I'm single, I love to go to bars and drink which is not highly recommended in this community. Because once again, it reflects back on how I do my work. So some of my previous pastimes have been curtailed." Some participants also reported that they felt clients might be uncomfortable if they attended mutual community events or shared similar social circles. However, workers in the north are immersed in their communities in ways that are never explained or discussed in professional training (Delaney et al., 1997).

Additionally, it is important to note that the easy identification that comes with small town life can also threaten the personal safety of workers. This study uncovered two such examples. In one case a threatening letter was received by a participant when she was named in a local newspaper article, which reported on a community awareness project. In another instance a participant was stalked by a client's ex-husband. For example, he sat and watched her from his car, which he parked in her home driveway for hours. Sexual assault workers are easily identifiable in smaller communities and are then at risk of reprisals.

Finally, women seeking sexual assault services are also negatively affected by the lack of privacy and anonymity in northern Ontario communities. Participants explained how women are often discouraged from seeking help because they fear public recognition and labelling. Lack of anonymity coupled with geographical and social isolation creates enormous obstacles for many women seeking to escape violent situations. For example, the lack of local public transportation can seriously impede a woman's ability to seek help (Struthers, 1994). As Beauregard (1996) reports, the geographical, social, psychological, and economic isolation experienced by women in northern Ontario contributes both to mental health problems and the perpetuation of violence. Unfortunately, the isolation of these women and the danger in which they live is not always considered in northern Ontario services planning. This geographical and social isolation is examined further in the following section.

ISOLATION

Not only can the isolation of northern communities contribute to increased danger for women living with violence, but it also creates problems with available resources and educational opportunities, and fosters work environments where the participants are required to be highly self-sufficient. For example, some participants reported that they feel isolated from the tools that make possible healthy communities, such as technology and other communication resources. Participants spoke about how communities cocoon themselves and become self-protective and wary of outside influences. As one participant describes:

> So what happens is that you end up [with] this community bonding, and this becomes your community and you're very proud of it and nothing else. [Local people] don't care what they're doing in Toronto. [...] There's nothing to do. You can't go to the museum, there's no such thing. You can't go to the science centre, you can't really learn anything. In these communities what do women do? What do kids do?

Another participant argues, "We're isolated from learning. We're isolated from technology. We're isolated from all of those things that create sort of healthy and smart human beings."

One group of participants believed that due to their lack of local resources and facilities for education, their community did not attract the *best* or most proficient professionals. As a related example, this group notes that their community has little to encourage the best physicians to stay. This group of participants believe that if progressive professionals were available in other local health and social service agencies, they could constitute a supportive educational network. Instead, they contend that the people who work locally have been there "forever" and have little understanding of the issues associated with violence against women. One of the reasons provided for this situation includes the limited number of workplace options available in the north. Limited job opportunities perpetuate a situation where people who are employed tend to keep their jobs for long periods of time, and the lack of opportunities for continued education can impede the growth of workers and work environments.

On the other hand, expressions of dismay about insufficient professional networking are balanced somewhat by positive reports from other participants. One group of participants is situated in a community that has established university education locally. The other was a well-organized First Nations community. In these two places, workers feel a sense of satisfaction at having increased public education about violence and having been given the opportunity to build a strong community network. Continued training with experienced peers or supervisors and ongoing education are essential to the professional and personal growth of professional helpers, and are crucial to the provision of effective services. Unfortunately, most participants perceived few opportunities to educate themselves or to attend training workshops locally. A common statement was that "all conferences are in Toronto." Thus, the shortage of funding available to attend training is a problem.

Geographical isolation certainly contributes to the sense of isolation experienced amongst the participants and shapes their work. Some participants explained that they are responsible for servicing huge districts within which towns are separated by vast areas of isolated terrain. In some cases there is little or no recognition of the time needed to travel between these communities as part of their work duties. Other participants describe how women are separated from one another and often do not have the financial resources needed to travel in order to connect with services and with one another.

Additionally, the lack of other health and social services for women in northern Ontario influences the nature of sexual assault work. Sexual assault affects survivors in almost every area of their lives, and these survivors utilize a myriad of coping mechanisms to deal with their traumatic experiences and memories (Cahill et al., 1991; Beitchman et al., 1992). Consequently, survivors of abuse often require a variety of services, such as addiction treatment. Having no access locally to these services can lead to a prolonged counselling process or a less effective one. As one worker states, "Some of [the survivors'] needs are to be in [an addiction] treatment program. When it comes to referrals, it's always down south and that becomes a problem. We don't have all the places we need to refer. They're all out of town and money always seems to be a problem." Thus, workers in the north may require a broad education and training in skills related to many different fields. While some social workers may choose to work in rural settings precisely because they will be able to practice across frameworks and practice fields, the lack of available training for workers already in northern Ontario is an issue that should be addressed.

Another factor that influences the delivery of services in some northern Ontario sexual assault programs is the lack of child care resources. Again, the isolation of the north and the small size of northern communities contributes to a situation in which women must often do without child care resources. As one participant points out:

> Child care is major. It's like every second family has small kids, so those are the kinds of things our government doesn't seem to realize. The isolation and what it means in terms of getting together and working together. You may have noticed there's a lot of children around here. There usually is.

As this comment illustrates, this centre encourages women to bring their children to the service, which can sometimes lead to a work environment that is noisy and impedes the therapeutic work that workers/clients require.

Finally, isolation ultimately leads to an increased need for worker and agency self-sufficiency. Workers in the north are constantly stretching energy, knowledge, and budgets in an effort to meet the needs of assaulted women. For instance, often the sexual assault worker is the only social service resource available and, as a result, serves many functions. Indeed, the lack of local referral opportunities, limited opportunity to share knowledge with others doing similar work, the lack of public support or understanding, insufficient staff numbers, and inadequate funding for transportation and wages, all contribute to the demand on workers for an extraordinary personal investment and can compound the effects of secondary trauma. For some workers this investment quickly becomes overwhelming. One participant explains, "I think it's important to say that when you work in this type of place, a lot of times things come out of our own pockets. We don't talk about it, but if a woman is in need of food and there's no food, it's going to come from somewhere." Another worker made the following suggestion: "I would like to see for centres and for people working in this profession that they have a short-term disability plan. That's something we just don't have money for."

UNIQUE CULTURAL CHARACTERISTICS

Many rural communities are culturally homogenous (Beckerman et al., 1994). While communities in northern Ontario are not generally reflective of the multicultural diversity found in larger urban cities, many of these communities encompass significant numbers of Francophone and First Nations women in particular. As a result, these two cultures often need to be considered in the planning and delivery of culturally appropriate services.

Francophone participants in one community described a strong sense of being alone with their work. They stated that they feel little permission to acknowledge their occupation as sexual assault workers in their everyday family lives. This was attributed by these participants to the overall refusal of their community to accept the value of their work and to acknowledge violence against women. They also experienced pressure to conform to *traditional* family life—pressure that emanates in part from the patriarchal philosophies of the Roman Catholic Church, with which many Francophones are affiliated. Along these lines, one Francophone participant observes, "I think for the Francophone women it's harder for them. It's harder to reach them and it's harder for them to open up and come and see us. It's just because of their culture. Their background is just so different from an Anglophone woman." Certainly, the importance of recognizing the diversity of women's oppression and experiences is crucial to understanding how best to offer services (Valentich, 1996).

While Francophone women constitute a significant proportion of the population in many northern Ontario communities, First Nations women also represent a sizeable and important client group, whose experiences can be vastly different from both Anglophone and Francophone women. The First Nations participants reported a range of experiences as sexual assault workers. For example, one participant commented that she is known as a person doing important work within her community. However, another participant states that within her community, some members continue to view sexual assault workers and the location where they work as "shameful" and to be avoided. For example, she describes how two adult daughters accompanied their middle-aged mother to counselling, but advised her to "stay away from this place of shame," in part because "there's a big fear in Indian country that if I was abused, I must be an abuser." Although some northern Ontario communities have services specifically for Francophone and First Nations women, many smaller locales do not. It is important for workers in northern Ontario to understand the unique characteristics and needs of all women, so that they will deliver competent and culturally sensitive services.

COPING STRATEGIES

It may be difficult for some to understand why sexual assault workers remain committed to the work they do given the effects of secondary trauma, coupled in these cases with the added stresses of working and living in northern Ontario. In fact, the participants in this study reported several coping mechanisms that they employ in order to deal with the secondary trauma they experience, and these are similar to coping strategies identified elsewhere in the literature (Briere, 1996; Kahill, 1998). Workers in this study list a range of coping strategies: they avoid reading about and/or watching violent incidents in the media; avoid disclosing their occupation; seek opportunities to job-share; aim to develop positive relationships with men; utilize nature and spirituality to ground themselves; seek support from other women; establish opportunities to discuss and process experiences at work with other women; engage in social action; and recognize their universal affiliation with all women. In light of the findings of this research, we will now consider further the two key issues of "community" and "social support."

One way to cope with a lack of community support and community challenge is to seek support from a group of like-minded people who share the vision, knowledge, and the understanding required to carry on with the struggle against violence and oppression. Support from others was of particular significance to the participants of this study, and has been identified as crucial for women in dealing with job-related stress (Greenglass, 1993; Schauben et al., 1995). All the women in this study identified the importance of belonging to a close supportive network of women. This network provided a place for mutual understanding, emotional support, feedback, acceptance, and re-energizing. The following comments illustrate the importance of this support particularly in their respective workplaces—support that affirms the importance of the work, the effects of the work, and the need to work together to create change.

> It's like a family. We realize we really matter to each other. And we're all doing the same work, we all believe in the same things right. [Some] may do it differently. And when we see somebody getting run down or going through a rough time, it matters to us. For me it becomes a place where I can get support. It's just not about giving. Now I also get a place where something is given back to me, through a hug or someone comes over and offers me tea. Somebody gives me a session. All of it makes a big difference. We have to work together if we are going to make any changes in this world. You can't do it alone. Anglophone and Francophone. While we're together we seem to be able to support one another and work with one another, and I find it's a lot more enriching.

The research participants also identified an affinity with their clients. Many participants shared the perspective that all women experience oppression and violence on a continuum *because we are women*. The viewpoint that women's personal experiences of oppression can be ameliorated only through political change and action appears to be important in helping these participants to cope effectively with secondary trauma. As one woman argues:

> You have to understand the politics of what we are, what we want to do. There's more to it. It's not about being a social worker and helping the poor little woman who doesn't have as much. And if you're going into this kind of work as a career, I'd say get a job. Go paint a house, find another career. There's a political reason why we have a problem in society, a problem with the way things are structured. And that's the reason to do the work that you do.

Along these lines, some of the participants described the work that they do as their *life's work*. They reported growing in vision and strength when they made lifelong commitments to feminist ideas and action. As one worker notes, "The next day we wake up, we are still women, and so as a woman to feel I guess any sort of wholeness, in a weird way I have to do this work. So in a way, that's my spirituality. As a woman I have to give back to other women. And that keeps me grounded." The importance of being part of a women's community or group becomes especially significant when we consider the isolation experienced by northern Ontario women. All of the participants interviewed in this study were able to become part of a supportive community. A serious concern is that many northern Ontario women working and living in small, isolated communities are not as fortunate, and it is these women whom we must consider in the planning and funding of services for northern Ontario.

CONCLUSION

Information gained through interviews with participants in this study points to a number of recommendations. For example, all staff who work with survivors of abuse need increased training opportunities, time for supervision, and means of networking with workers in other agencies across Ontario. Northern workers should be provided with some way of participating in educational forums similar to what is available to workers in the rest of Ontario. Ideas to fulfil this need could include travel and accommodation provisions to attend conferences in the south, funding for conferences in the north on a regular basis, and funding for technological resources that would enable links with others such as internet access and video-conferencing. Given the geographical isolation of many northern Ontario communities, the time and energy expended in travelling to isolated communities must also be considered. All centres should have travel expenses paid, record the time it takes to travel, and have that time recognized in the allocation of staffing hours.

Although opportunities to process or work through emotional reactions with colleagues serve as an important coping mechanism for most workers, time limitations and under-staffing in relation to client demands often limit these opportunities. These factors, coupled with the demands on workers and agencies to be self-sufficient, begs an increase in staff resources. Two centres that participated in this study reported over a one-year waiting list for individual counselling services. Also, while workers in many locations are reaching out to their communities in order to provide both the awareness and the information that is needed to prevent violence against women, resources in languages other than English are required, and are often difficult to obtain in the north.

The findings of this study demonstrate that there are issues associated with the work of sexual assault counselling that are unique to the northern Ontario context, which in turn can compound the effects of secondary trauma. These include the lack of community awareness and support for sexual assault work, insufficient anonymity, issues related to privacy and confidentiality, the isolation of the communities, and the unique cultural characteristics of northern Ontario communities. While the difficulties this kind of work involves are increasingly being recognized, policy-makers, educators, and funding bodies would benefit from a better understanding of the factors associated with doing this work and living in northern Ontario.

NOTE

1. Funding for this study was received from the Ontario Ministry of Northern Development and Mines. A synopsis of this paper was presented previously at the Joint Conference of the Australian Association of Social Work, International Federation of Social Work, Asia & Pacific Association for Social Work Education and the Australian Association for Social Work and Welfare Education—"Promoting Inclusion, Redressing Exclusion: The Social Work Challenge, 1999." This chapter is reprinted with permission from the authors and from *Canadian Social Work*, 2003, 5(1), pp. 43–58. It has been edited for this collection.

REFERENCES

Beauregard, M. (1996). A study of violence and isolation experiences of northern women. In M. Kechnie and M. Reitsma-Street, *Changing lives: Women in northern Ontario*, pp. 232–238. Toronto: Dundurn.

Beckerman, A. & Burrell, L. (1994). A rock and a hard place: Trying to provide culturally-sensitive field experiences in rural, homogeneous communities. *Journal of Multicultural Social Work*, 3(1), 91–99.

Beitchman, J., Zucker, K., Hood, J. E., da Costa, G. A., Akman, D., & Cassavia, E. (1992). A review of the long-term effects of child sexual abuse. *Child Abuse and Neglect*, 16, 101–118.

Briere, J. (1996). *Therapy for adults molested as children: Beyond survival*. New York: Springer.

Cahill, C., Llewelyn, S. P., & Pearson, C. (1991). Treatment of sexual abuse that occurred in childhood: A review. *British Journal of Clinical Psychology*, 30, 117–130.

Chenoweth, L. & Stehlik, D. (2001). Building resilient communities: Social work practice and rural Queensland. *Australian Social Work*, 54(2), 47–54.

Delaney, R., Brownlee, K., Sellick, M., & Tranter, D. (1997). Ethical problems facing northern social workers. *The Social Worker*, 65(3), 55–65.

Greenglass, E. (1993). Social support and coping of employed women. In B. Long & S. Kahn, *Women, Work and Coping*, pp. 154–169. Montreal: McGill Queen's University Press.

Gumpert, J. & Saltman, J. E. (1998). Social group work practice in rural areas: The practitioners speak. *Social Work with Groups*, 21(3), 19–34.

Kahill, S. (1998). Interventions for burnout in the helping professions. *Canadian Journal of Counselling Review*, 22(3), 310–342.

Kauppi, C. & Reitsma-Street, M. (1996). Women and poverty in northern Ontario. In M. Kechni & M. Reitsma-Street, *Changing lives: Women in northern Ontario*, pp. 213–223. Toronto: Dundurn.

Manion, I. G., McIntyre, J., Firestone, P., Ligezinska, M., Ensom, R., & Wells, G. (1996). Secondary traumatization of parents following the disclosure of extra-familial child sexual abuse: Initial effects. *Child Abuse and Neglect*, 20(11), 1095–1109.

Mayer, A. G. K. (2001). Rural social work: The perceptions and experiences of five remote practitioners. *Australian Social Work*, 54(1), 91–102.

McCann, L. & Pearlman, L. (1990). Vicarious traumatization: A framework for understanding the psychological effects of working with victims. *Journal of Traumatic Stress*, 3(1), 131–149.

Mikulincer, M., Florian, V., & Solomon, Z. (1995). Marital intimacy, family support, and secondary traumatization: A study of wives of veterans with combat stress reaction. *Anxiety, Stress, and Coping*, 8, 203–213.

Regehr, C. & Cadell, C. S. (1999). Secondary trauma in sexual assault crisis work: Implications for therapists and therapy. *Canadian Social Work*, 1(1), 56–63.

Schauben, L. & Frazier, P. (1995). Vicarious trauma: The effects on female counsellors of working with sexual violence survivors. *Psychology of Women Quarterly*, 19(1), 49–64.

Struthers, M. (1994). At a crossroads in the work to end the violence: A rural perspective. *Canadian Woman Studies*, 14(4), 15–18.

Taback, R. & Triegaardt, J. D. (1992). Educating social workers to practice in rural South Africa: Dilemmas and challenges—A case study. *Maatskaplike Werk/Social Work*, 28(4), 91–94.

Tice, K. W. (1990). A case study of battered women's shelters in Appalachia. *Affilia*, 5(3), 83–100.

Valentich, M. (1996). Feminist theory and social work practice. In F. Turner (ed.), *Social Work Treatment*, 4th edn, pp. 282–318. New York: Free Press.

Wolf, N. (1993). *Fire with fire: The new power and how it will change the 21st century*. Toronto: Random House.

Chapter Two

GEOGRAPHIC CONTEXT AND NORTHERN CHILD WELFARE PRACTICE

Glen Schmidt

In 1986, a fourteen year-old girl was flown out of a northern Manitoba community after several months of most horrific sexual abuse. She was systematically and regularly gang raped by a group of youths who seemed to carry on their activities with impunity. The girl had returned to this community and her biological family after living away for more than a decade. In virtually all respects she was a stranger to the community and the isolated environment in which she was placed.

The reasons for this tragedy were numerous and included confusion around jurisdiction, lack of information, misinformation, poor case practice, and political imperatives that made the best interests of the child a secondary consideration. The case was unusual, though by no means unique. At the very least, this human tragedy highlighted some of the more extreme elements that create particular challenges for social workers who deliver child welfare services in remote, northern communities.

CHILD WELFARE AND CHILD PROTECTION

Child welfare is a broad concept and includes a whole range of administrative and policy decisions that affect the health and well-being of children in a variety of ways through various jurisdictions. Child protection work, meaning direct, legally sanctioned intervention designed to rescue children from situations of physical danger or peril, is one aspect of child welfare policy.

The generalist education of undergraduate social workers emphasizes the broader view of child welfare, which includes progressive social administration, prevention programs, and holistic approaches to the overall welfare of children. In and of itself this makes good sense, but it does have implications in terms of preparedness for the reality of daily practice. Operative models in contemporary child welfare practice continue to be predominantly residual and statutory, relying on investigation methods and casework delivery. Graduating social workers who are steeped in critical analysis and social administration approaches bring a useful perspective to the work of child protection in northern and remote communities. However, they are generally unprepared for the reality of the micro-practice that confronts them when they venture out into the field. This aspect of education has been neglected and it may help to explain at least part of the high turnover among child protection social workers in isolated communities.

Protection work is difficult and challenging at the best of times. Regretably, educational institutions tend to add to this difficulty through the application of critical theory. Critical theory is an essential component of the education process, but it must also be accompanied by practice knowledge that is context-based. Statutory services that deal with involuntary clients are generally constructed as anti-progressive representations of social control. Student graduates steeped in critical analysis find themselves being asked to do the very things that they may have learned to criticize and even despise during their formal education as a social worker. It is important that critical models of practice recognize these realities and prepare students so that when they begin to work, they do not immediately slip into guilt, despondency, and despair.

One way of achieving this is to examine social work from a position that starts from the practice perspective. In the case of northern and remote child protection this is especially important given the predominance of urban-based theoretical models. By examining contextual elements of northern and remote practice we can better understand and appreciate the requirements of social work approaches in northern communities. These approaches do not involve a neatly packaged paradigm, but rather, a sense of preparedness and knowledge that are rooted in the practice experience itself. It is an experience in which the environment exerts a powerful role.

Social workers who practise in child protection need to be exposed to the environmental reality beginning with the formal education process. Support for child protection social workers, and the implementation of an effective child welfare delivery system, require close integration between educational institutions, employing authorities, and northern communities.

SOCIAL WORK IN THE NORTH

The most striking feature about the north is the immensity of the landscape. Whether one is driving through the mountains of northern British Columbia, flying over the muskeg of Manitoba and Ontario, or walking along the barren shores of Hudson Bay, the sense of space is awe-inspiring. This concept of space governs settlement, communication, and transportation patterns, which in turn have a profound influence on northern social work practice. Usher (1987) has described two different views of the north that represent the cultural and economic context of northern and remote practice. Northern social workers are generally faced with these different worldviews. First Nations people and communities have an historic place and claim to the north. At the same time, the north is also characterized by single industry towns dependent upon the global uncertainty of resource commodities. On the surface they may appear to be different, but for social workers engaged in child protection work around issues of child abuse and neglect, there are many similarities that influence the context of practice. A number of authors have written articles and papers related to the challenges of rural and remote practice.[1] Much of the material paints a somewhat discouraging and negative picture of northern and remote social work. Isolation, lack of supervision, dual relationships, high visibility, practice beyond competence, resource shortages, and role conflict are just some of the characteristics that emerge from the literature. It is important that these realities are honestly described as social work students who contemplate a career in the north must have a realistic appreciation of the challenges. Those who are unfamiliar with the reality of northern practice are unlikely to stay.

These elements or characteristics are a function of northern space and geography. If we begin to cast about for a description of northern social work practice, we might say that it is a form of social work practice that has the environment at its core. The geography of the north greatly influences how and where people live, which in turn creates the structures and constraints of northern social work practice. A number of elements, including visibility, accessibility, professional ethics, and public scrutiny, require special attention in relationship to working with child abuse and neglect in northern communities. All of these elements are integrated and overlap, but for the purposes of discussing issues and practice challenges related to child abuse in a northern context, it is useful to examine them separately.

Visibility

Living and working in small communities exposes the social worker to other community members in a way that is seldom encountered in urban practice. Fenby (1978) has referred to this as "living in a fish bowl." This is an appropriate image as personal space and privacy are difficult, if not impossible, to attain. The social worker's lifestyle is on public display and the characteristics associated with the worker's lifestyle are often used by the community to evaluate his/her competence, ability, and trustworthiness. The worker may face verbal attacks and questions regarding personal credibility and suitability if there are issues in the worker's personal or family life that are visibly problematic. This reality has serious implications for practice, especially for workers engaged in statutory child welfare practice. It extends beyond the worker and also affects the worker's immediate family.

> A colleague, who worked in a northern community of under 1000 people, experienced difficulty with the behaviour of her adolescent child. The adolescent's behaviour included alcohol abuse, inattention to school work, and breaking of curfews. In an urban practice setting the worker would certainly have experienced the anxiety that any loving parent goes through when their child engages in behaviour that is risky and harmful. However, the visibility of the worker and the community's knowledge of the behaviour of the worker's child resulted in immediate consequences. Community members who were experiencing troubles of their own regarding their children's behaviour hesitated to see the worker or stopped using the service altogether. The worker also experienced some difficulty in her relationship with the school. The school was a primary source of referral for cases of child abuse, neglect, and behaviourial problems. As the only school in this small isolated community it was extremely important that the social worker have a close relationship with school personnel. This relationship was adversely influenced owing to the school-related issues and problems experienced by the worker's child. Both the school and the worker attempted to set suitable boundaries around this issue, but it was not always an easy task.

The issue raised by high visibility in child protection work has to do with congruence between what the social worker represents and who the social worker is as a human being. Community members often expect certain behaviour and standards from the social worker. While these expectations may be unfair and in some ways unrealistic, they are a reality for social work practitioners located in northern and remote communities. The standards and the expected behaviour sometimes create an existential crisis of values for social workers.

> I recall working with a young woman, a lone parent, whose children I apprehended as a result of abuse and neglect. The young woman had a serious problem with alcohol misuse, which affected her ability to provide good care for her children. As one aspect of my work with her, I supported and assisted her entry into a treatment facility for people who had difficulty with alcohol misuse. While in treatment she progressed very well. She came to a better understanding of the destructive role that alcohol played in her life and she

gained a greater sense of self-awareness. One evening I was invited over to a friend's place for supper and I decided to buy a bottle of wine to take as a courtesy. While waiting in line, with my bottle in hand, at the town's only liquor outlet, I heard someone call my name. I turned to see who it was and saw the young woman also standing in line with a bottle in her hand. It was one of those very awkward moments, probably much more awkward for me than the young woman. Many thoughts raced through my mind. How would this encounter affect my capacity to work with the woman around her substance misuse problem? What kind of model do I present when I am seen using the same substance that gives grief to so many? Would her children be coming into care again? Should I be doing this work if my lifestyle choices adversely affect the welfare of my clients? I also thought that this same experience, this same encounter, would be unlikely to happen if I worked in a larger urban centre. As it was, my visibility in a small, relatively isolated community created an existential crisis of questioning my lifestyle values and my role as a social worker in an isolated northern town.

This encounter gave new meaning to the term congruence. Congruence in northern social work practice means total honesty, an honesty that moves beyond the artificial constructs of case management, support, advocacy, and casework. Workers cannot be expected to be saints, but an important part of northern practice involves openness and a willingness to be "up front" about personal values and lifestyle choices. The personal is professional in northern social work practice, and workers must be prepared to be called to account for aspects of life that would not even be a consideration in an urban practice environment. Conflict between the professional role and the personal role has to be resolved if a social worker intends to remain in a community as a healthy, contributing member.

This same issue of visibility also has an effect on the people who are recipients of social work services. Child apprehensions, allegations, and investigations of neglect or abuse are highly public in small isolated communities, despite the worker's best intention to conduct investigations in a discreet manner and keep the information confidential. In a larger urban centre the discovery of child maltreatment in a family and the subsequent protective measures are often not the topic of community discussion. However, in small northern communities the actions of protection social workers are highly visible and often lead to embarrassment and humiliation for the family members involved with the child protection system. In single-industry towns, as well as isolated First Nations communities, the actions of child protection services may adversely affect a person's employment circumstances, social relationships, and community status.

Trute et al. (1994) suggest that some rural communities may minimize child sexual abuse and that a reduced community sanction may have the effect of a reduced impact on the lives of people suspected or convicted of child abuse in such communities. They write from the context of rural, southern Manitoba. This may well be the case in that particular environment, but it is also not uncommon for people, especially those from isolated single-industry towns, to relocate following a disclosure of abuse and intervention by social workers.

> A ten-month-old child was referred to me as there was a suspicion of child abuse. The child had a spiral fracture of the arm, a large hand-shaped bruise on the left side of the head and bruising of the testicles and penis. The child was apprehended and placed in a foster home while the police conducted their investigation. The mother's common-law partner was under suspicion, but the allegation could not be substantiated. During the course of the investigation he left the community to return to his province of birth.

The man's decision to leave the community was not unusual or uncommon. The workforce in many northern single-industry towns is fairly mobile and may not have a particular attachment to the community (Himmelfarb, 1982; Kuz, 1984). Rather than struggle with a label of "child abuser," many offenders are inclined to move in order to escape the social marginalization that may result from an accusation of child abuse.

In small, isolated, northern communities the visibility of families and individuals deals a blow to the community itself. Issues of trust, friendship, and an individual's capacity to participate in the community are all affected. Abusers may face exclusion. Some First Nations communities have recognized the significance of these outcomes and engage in creative community healing processes, which include the abused, the abuser, and also the community members who share in the fallout from the abuse. Non-First Nations people and communities often ostracize the abuser or engage in a futile attempt to avoid having to deal with the issue. Avoiding the issue is often ineffective and the abuser, as well as the abused, suffer. Social workers have to be aware of this and prepared to deal with the broader community consequences of the abuse.

Accessibility

While the literature on northern social work practice addresses the element of visibility, it does not devote a lot of attention to the question of accessibility. The concept of accessibility is often subsumed within that of visibility; however, there are important qualitative differences between these two concepts. The visibility of social workers in northern communities guarantees a lack of anonymity, but it also means that people are able to gain ready access to the social worker. This presents workers with challenges that are unique to northern and remote practice. Workers are accessible in ways that further erode privacy, a sense of personal security, and ideas of personal space.

As a new B.S.W. graduate I went to work as a child protection social worker in a northern community. Before I moved into town, my supervisor advised me not to list my phone number as it would guarantee some privacy and, in the event that I would have to deal with violent people, it would make it more difficult for them to find me. At the end of my first week of work I received an abuse referral involving an adolescent boy. He had come to school with a black eye and he advised the guidance counsellor that one of his parents had punched him in the face during the course of an argument. I met with the youth and then his parents in order to assess risk. After completing the assessment I provided some information and counselling for the family around adolescent development, communication, teen management, and non-violent ways of addressing issues of accountability and discipline. We held several meetings over the course of the next week and these went very well. All parties were cooperative and willing to look at different ways of dealing with their conflicts. Friday at midnight I was getting ready to go to bed when there was a loud knock on the door of my basement apartment. When I went to the door, I was greeted by the guardians of the adolescent boy who informed me that he had not kept his agreed upon curfew and they wanted to know what I had to suggest. The unexpected visit caught me by surprise, partly because I thought things were going well for this family, but mostly because I couldn't figure out how they knew where to find me. I had been in town for only two weeks and I lived in an apartment that was somewhat secluded. Nonetheless, this family was able to locate me without difficulty and they were more than ready to discuss the current state of affairs at midnight on a Friday. So much for unlisted telephone numbers.

This situation did not pose any particular personal risk or threat to my safety. It was simply an invasion of personal space and a disruption at a time when I hoped for privacy. However, in some cases worker security or the security of the worker's family can be compromised. For example, when my children were young there were occasions when I would try to avoid being seen with them in the mall because I was afraid that I might compromise their safety if they were noticed by a particularly violent individual who was angry with me. This type of accessibility issue rarely becomes a consideration in large urban centres, but it is a factor for workers in small isolated communities. The person who is physically violent toward children or the person who sexually assaults children is not someone who lives 10 kilometres away in another neighbourhood of a large urban centre. They are a member of the same community living within easy walking distance of your home. This reality creates stress for the social worker and also for members of the social worker's family.

One colleague who lived and worked in a small northern community of fewer than 1000 people left because his partner grew tired of the constant intrusions on their personal space. He was the only social worker in the isolated community, which meant that he could be called to respond to reports of child abuse or neglect at all hours and on all days. The nature of the work created strain in his relationship and the only immediate solution for preserving the relationship was to move.

When accessibility is coupled with fear of violence or reprisal, social workers find themselves under tremendous stress. For workers with children, these fears are multiplied several times over. Fear of violence can often be diffused through good communication and mediation. However, the nature of child abuse work is such that some people experience a tremendous sense of anger and a desire for revenge. The social worker may be seen as an outsider and representative of an unfair or unjust system that is persecuting the abuser (Collier, 1993). In situations of this nature it becomes important for social workers to develop clear safety plans, not only for themselves, but also for members of their families.

It is important to recognize that accessibility is not just an issue for social workers. Reporting the abuse of children and disclosing sensitive information related to personal abuse is extremely difficult in any location. However, in a large urban centre, abused children and reporters of abuse can reasonably expect to avoid contact with the alleged abuser. This is virtually impossible in small isolated communities. In one small northern community where I provided itinerant service, an alleged abuser went door-to-door inquiring as to who might have made the report. In many small communities police service is itinerant and it may be several hours before police can fly in or even several days if the weather is bad. This vulnerability can serve as a deterrent to potential reporters. With increased emphasis on placing apprehended children with relatives, or at least in their home community, additional fears and concerns are raised for victims of abuse. Removal of a child from a violent and harmful situation may lead to new fears and anxieties related to contact and potential contact with the alleged offender.

Professional Ethics

Professional ethics and problems with dual relationships have been discussed fairly extensively as they relate to northern and remote social work practice (Brownlee et al., 1995; Delaney et al., 1995; Brownlee, 1996; Delaney et al., 1997). The issues generally revolve around dual relationships, that is, relationships between social workers and clients that involve some type of association outside of the helping relationship. The most blatant form of dual relationship is one of a sexual nature, but dual relationships can also include business relationships and friendships. Dual relationships involving friendships are virtually unavoidable in small northern towns due to the likelihood that neighbours and friends may become clients of the agency. This is always a complicated matter, but it is especially problematic when dealing with issues of abuse directed toward children. Investigations of child abuse often involve people that northern practitioners know within a different context. They may be co-workers with your partner, members of your church, or a team-mate on your slow-pitch baseball team. On one level, this is positive because the worker knows the person as a community member. The social worker appreciates the fact that there are other dimensions to this person apart from the allegation of child abuse.

In urban practice, it is easier to ignore the alleged abuser's humanity. As child welfare and child abuse have become increasingly investigative and adversarial in approach, workers have a tendency to pay less attention to the full dimension of the human being behind the act of abuse. There is a focus on protecting the child and establishing the facts needed to make a decision about protection. There is close cooperation with police who concentrate on gathering information that may lead to a decision recommending criminal charges against the alleged abuser. Dual relationships add a different and difficult dimension to the work. For some social workers it is an aspect that they cannot accept and they leave the community; other social workers leave the profession completely.

Part of the difficulty stems from the expectations related to professional practice. Peterson (1992) comments on boundary violations and the misuse of power. The discussion is useful and relevant to social workers in all locations; however, some of the examples and the standards are clearly difficult to achieve in small, isolated northern communities. Social work students are indoctrinated with these standards and this in turn leads to role conflict for social workers engaged in northern and remote social work practice.

The issue of confidentiality also becomes very problematic. As social workers we are bound to keep privileged information confidential. However, the reality is that cases of child abuse quickly become part of community knowledge, despite the best intentions of the worker. Workers are frequently placed in double-bind situations in information that enters the public discourse may not be altogether accurate. Workers are aware of the inaccuracies, yet are unable to comment for risk of breaking confidentiality. Pressure is increased when workers are approached at public functions and asked about what happened, what is true, and what is false. Despite the fact that social workers do not disclose confidential information, it does seem to get out in a small community, often through a caregiver or a child who explains to family or friends why the social worker paid a visit. Once confidential information becomes part of the public discourse both the worker and the agency face additional issues around trust. Workers and agency employees may be suspected of disclosing privileged information.

As a profession, social work creates unrealistic expectations for practitioners engaged in northern and remote practice. The reality of living and working in the same small community creates a powerful issue of role conflict between the personal and the professional.

Public Scrutiny

In small isolated communities social workers face the added dilemma of having their practice decisions carefully scrutinized by community officials and members. The public's view of case practice is influenced by gossip, speculation, and media reports. Workers are unable to respond to public perceptions owing to the confidential nature of the work. This often places workers in extremely difficult and stressful situations.

In 1995, British Columbia Judge Thomas Gove released an extensive report that examined the 1992 death of Matthew Vaudreuil, a five-and-a-half year old child who was murdered by his mother. This report was the culmination of a lengthy inquiry process (Gove, 1995). Social workers were required to appear before the inquiry and their information became part of the public media record. Callahan and Callahan (1997) documented the media vilification of social workers. However, there is a story beyond this general commentary on the construction of public perception that relates to the consequences for the workers who practised in northern communities.

One worker related a story, where, following a media report on her testimony to the inquiry, she was approached by a community member in the local grocery store. This person began to shout and threaten the worker, forcing her to abandon her grocery cart and flee the store.

Workers employed in an urban environment also face public scrutiny, but they have relative anonymity and do not face the issue of personal recognition. This creates an additional level of challenge and stress for social workers who practise in northern and remote communities.

Some workers face the burden of knowing that their practice decisions may also result in a threat to job security. The governing structure within the community itself may judge workers in a way that they would not face in a larger centre.

> Child protection workers employed by Chief and Council in a small isolated First Nations community investigated a report of sexual abuse involving a

close relative of the Chief. The workers were dismissed from their positions, ostensibly for other reasons. However, the workers were convinced that their dismissal had to do with political opposition to their abuse investigation.

Work in the area of child abuse is difficult in that workers constantly have to deal with decisions that are life and death in nature. This situation is made even more challenging by virtue of the fact that the worker's decisions are known to the community and the community may quickly move to judge the social worker's practice.

DEVELOPING A SUPPORTIVE PRACTICE ENVIRONMENT FOR NORTHERN CHILD WELFARE

Social work is often divided between policy and practice, and educational theory and work application. Northern child welfare practice requires an integrated approach that breaks down the divisions and effectively links the university, the employing agency, and the community. There also has to be a shift in values that leads to a climate where support for social workers is regarded as a legitimate priority. Divisions between university social work programs and employing agencies, as well as divisions between agencies and communities, foster a non-supportive environment for social workers. Without clear legitimization for the child protection role, social workers will continue to "cycle" through northern communities, reinforcing the idea of social worker as an outsider or external agent.

In the educational setting of the university it is critical that students who intend to work in the north have exposure to the reality of northern practice. This can occur in two ways. First, students need exposure to practice material that is not only theoretical, but also based in the context of northern experience. Furthermore, faculty instructors may have to revisit the critical negativity that often surrounds the delivery of child welfare content. Students require an understanding of the social control functions inherent to this area of social work practice; however, it is counter-productive to create a guilt complex. The statutory protection of children needs to be seen as a legitimate social work practice.

Second, students require exposure to a northern practicum experience. Ideally, the practicum experience can provide a direct link to an employing agency. For example, students in their final field placement at the University of Northern British Columbia have an opportunity to undertake this experience with the Ministry for Children and Families (MCF), a large government organization that provides child welfare services in the province of British Columbia. During the course of the placement students are exposed to northern child welfare practice and they can begin the process of formal MCF training. In turn, MCF gives hiring priority to these students. The overall effect is to create a smooth transition between university studies, the final field practicum experience, and employment as a social worker in the area of northern child welfare.

It is also important for employing agencies to develop collaborative links with communities. Barter (1996) defines collaboration "as a process and a commitment to work together, pool resources, mutually problem-solve, jointly act on decisions, and to share responsibility and authority" (p. 71). Many agencies have been able to develop effective collaboration related to program delivery and linkage to existing agency supports. However, there is a need to expand the collaborative approach to include the hiring of social workers. Community participation in the hiring process accomplishes a number of things. It turns back a portion of power to the community and creates community investment in the human capital of the social worker. The social worker is not imposed on the community. Instead, the community invests its time and trust in the new recruit. This becomes a basis for community support and sanction of the child welfare worker's activities. It also promotes a greater sense of autonomy for the community and can be seen as a step in what Arges and Delaney (1996) refer to as the community liberation process.

Communities are vitally important in the creation of an environment in which social workers feel supported and valued. Without this sense of support, social workers are extremely vulnerable to the negative effects of high visibility, accessibility, ethical dilemmas, and public scrutiny. Community support is most effective when there is a partnership between the community and employing agency. This supports the development of horizontal ties and a greater sense of localism (Martinez-Brawley, 1990; Brownlee et al., 1997). A reciprocal model of social work practice can develop in that the individual social worker benefits from the community support and the community has a stronger sense of connection to child welfare social work. This stronger connection has the potential to create a greater understanding of the social worker's role within the area of child protection.

CONCLUSION

The relative isolation and small size of northern communities result in close daily contact between social workers and their clients. This closeness, which derives from the northern context of geography and space, creates strain in social relationships, not just for the worker and the clients, but also for the broader community. Social workers must be prepared to have their actions scrutinized and they need to come to terms with perceived community pressure relative to visibility, accessibility, professional ethics, and lifestyle issues. The personal self and the professional self are difficult to separate within the northern context. Social workers preparing for child welfare practice in northern communities must enter the work environment with a full awareness of the reality of work in a small, isolated community. Education and preparation of social workers for northern child welfare practice need to reflect a clear sense of context that is derived from practice based experience in geographically remote parts of the country. Closer integration between educational institutions, employing agencies, and communities can provide a more supportive environment for child welfare workers in northern communities.

NOTE

1. Delaney et al. (1995); Fenby (1978); Ingebrigtson (1992); Zapf (1985, 1989, 1993).

REFERENCES

Arges, S. & Delaney, R. (1996). Challenging the southern metaphor: From oppression to empowerment. In R. Delaney, K. Brownlee, & M. K. Zapf (eds.), *Issues in northern social work practice*, pp. 1–22. Thunder Bay: Centre for Northern Studies, Lakehead University.

Barter, K. (1996). Collaboration: A framework for northern social work practice. In R. Delaney, K. Brownlee, & M. K. Zapf (eds.), *Issues in northern social work practice*, pp. 70–94. Thunder Bay: Centre for Northern Studies, Lakehead University.

Brownlee, K. (1996). The ethics of non-sexual dual relationships: A dilemma for the rural mental health professional. *Community Mental Health Journal*, 32(5), 497–503.

Brownlee, K. & Taylor, S. (1995). CASW Code of Ethics and non-sexual dual relationships: The need for clarification. *The Social Worker*, 63(3), 133–136.

Brownlee, K., Graham, J., & Dimond, P. (1997). Strategies for community assessment. In K. Brownlee, R. Delaney, & J. Graham (eds.), *Strategies for northern social work practice*, pp. 113–128. Thunder Bay: Centre for Northern Studies, Lakehead University.

Callahan, M. & Callahan, K. (1997). Victims and villains: Scandals, the press and policy making in child welfare. In J. Pulkingham & G. Ternowetsky (eds.), *Child and family policies: Struggles, strategies and options*, pp. 40–57. Halifax: Fernwood.

Collier, K. (1993). *Social work with rural peoples*, 2nd edn. Vancouver: New Star.

Delaney, R. & Brownlee, K. (1995). Ethical considerations for northern social work practice. In R. Delaney & K. Brownlee (eds.), *Northern social work practice*, pp. 35–57. Thunder Bay: Centre for Northern Studies, Lakehead University.

Delaney, R., Brownlee, K., Sellick, M., & Tranter, D. (1997). Ethical problems facing northern social workers. *The Social Worker*, 65(3), 55–65.

Fenby, B. (1978). Social work in rural settings. *Social Work*, 23(2), 162–163.

Gove, T. (1995). Report of the Gove inquiry into child protection in British Columbia. Vancouver: B.C. Government Publications.

Himelfarb, A. (1982). The social characteristics of one-industry towns in Canada. In R. Bowles (ed.), *Little communities and big industries*, pp. 16–43. Toronto: Butterworths.

Ingebrigtson, K. (1992). Rural and remote social work settings: Characteristics and implications for practice. In M. Tobin & C. Walmsley (eds.), *Northern perspectives: Practice and education in social work*, pp. 7–15. Winnipeg: Manitoba Association of Social Workers and the University of Manitoba Faculty of Social Work.

Kuz, T. (1984). How long do they stay in a single resource community? A study of Thompson, Manitoba. University of Winnipeg: Institute of Urban Studies.

Martinez-Brawley, E. (1990). *Perspectives on the small community: Humanistic views for practitioners.* Silver Spring: NASW Press.

Peterson, M. (1992). *At personal risk: Boundary violations in professional–client relationships.* New York: W. W. Norton.

Trute, B., Adkins, E., & MacDonald, G. (1994). *Coordinating child sexual abuse services in rural communities.* Toronto: University of Toronto Press.

Usher, P. J. (1987). The north: One land, two ways of life. In L. McCann (ed.), *Heartland and hinterland*, 2nd edn. pp. 483–529. Toronto: Prentice-Hall.

Zapf, M. K. (1985). Home is where the target group is: Role conflicts facing an urban-trained social worker in a remote northern Canadian community. In W. Whitaker (ed.), *Social work in rural areas: A celebration of rural people, place, and struggle*, pp. 187–203. Orno: University of Maine.

Zapf, M. K. (1989). Adjustment experiences of social workers in remote and northern communities: A study of culture shock. Unpublished doctoral dissertation, University of Toronto.

Zapf, M. K. (1993). Remote practice and culture shock: Workers moving to isolated northern regions. *Social Work*, 38(6), 694–704.

Chapter Three

INTRA-FAMILIAL ADOLESCENT SEXUAL OFFENDERS IN RURAL AND ISOLATED AREAS

Chantal Morrison-Lambert

The sexual abuse of children by family members has been gaining increased attention and concern over the past twenty years. Much of the focus has been placed on father–daughter incest; however, there is now heightened awareness that sibling incest may be far more prevalent (Adler et al., 1995). Although research is beginning to develop on adolescent sex offenders in general, sibling incest is a phenomenon that remains poorly understood and infrequently researched. Much of the literature on family sexual abuse disregards the seriousness of sibling incest, and sexual relations among siblings is perceived as relatively harmless and as a normal part of sex play (Adler et al., 1995). As a result, sibling incest offenders have been neglected in both research and clinical literatures. It is beginning to be recognized that this is a significant problem that needs professional attention, and information about sibling incest is beginning to develop (Canavan et al., 1992).

Sibling sexual abuse is a serious problem. Sexual abuse committed by adolescents has emotional, physical, and financial consequences, not only for the families involved, but for communities at large. Although literature in the area of sibling incest is beginning to grow, much still needs to be addressed. This chapter has two objectives. The first is to review the relevant literature on intra-familial male adolescent sexual offenders in order to gain an accurate and comprehensive understanding of this population. The second is to review issues related to sibling sexual abuse in rural or isolated areas.

The research seldom separates intra-familial offenders from extra-familial offenders. Therefore, much of the information relates to male adolescent sex offenders in general, not just sibling incest offenders in particular. Rural and isolated areas conceivably introduce different issues and problems when dealing with intra-familial adolescent sex offenders. This is an important issue, as research regarding sibling incest in rural areas is extremely scarce. Rural offenders may be included in research studies, but they are not often distinguished as such. Thus, until research in this area evolves, this chapter takes the position that while the characteristics, assessment, and treatment of rural sibling incest offenders may at once resemble incest elsewhere, it also remains unique. Focusing on the unique issues that sibling incest offenders experience in rural or isolated contexts may reveal areas for further exploration and research.

SEXUAL OFFENCES

Sibling incest may be defined as sexual interaction between children who have one or more parents in common. Adolescent sex offenders are youths between twelve and eighteen years of age as outlined by the Young Offender's Act. Sexual offending includes a range of behaviours and is committed against those who have not given consent or are unable to give consent. Non-physical behaviours such as voyeurism and exhibitionism are considered sexual offences, along with physical offences such as fondling, oral copulation, and digital, penile, or object penetration of the anus or vagina (Scavo et al., 1989; Charles et al., 1997).

Sexual abuse and sexual assaults are prevalent in our society. One study reported that one in four females and one in six males will be abused before they are adults (Kahn et al., 1988). Although it was widely believed that the offenders were usually adult males, there is now recognition that adolescent males commit a significant percentage of these crimes (Charles et al., 1997; Coleman, 1997). Research states that many adult offenders report that their sexual offending behaviour began in adolescence. Studies show that 50 to 80 per cent of adult sex offenders admitted to committing their first offences between the ages of eight and eighteen.[1]

It is argued that offenders' behaviour start off with relatively minor offenses, but without intervention, the acts escalate and become more intrusive (O'Brien, 1991). The earlier the offending occurs, the more entrenched the behaviour becomes, leading to further serious sexual assaults in adulthood. O'Brien (1991) suggests that incestuous adolescent offenders progress to more serious forms of sexual abuse more rapidly than other adolescent sex offenders due to longer durations of contact and the general availability of siblings. The youth is likely to have more opportunity to offend when the victim resides in the same home. He will know when it is "safe" to offend without getting caught, and may be in the position of authority, such as babysitting for the sibling.

In one study where sibling abusers were compared to non-familial sexual assaulters, sibling sexual abusers had offended for longer periods of time, executed more sexual offenses, and participated in more intrusive sexual acts, such as vaginal penetration (O'Brien, 1991). A study of sibling incest victims revealed that the abuse was disclosed only after multiple incidents (De Jong, 1989). O'Brien (1991) found that 53 per cent of sibling sexual offenders had more than one victim, and 46 per cent were more likely to commit penile penetration while only 26 per cent of extra-familial offenders committed penile penetration. Smith et al. (1987) found that 72 per cent of their cases involved either fondling or oral/genital contact, and in 28 per cent of the cases, intercourse was involved.

"Intra-familial sexual abuse of children is rarely a one-time event. Incest generally progresses over time, advancing through predictable stages of increasingly intimate and intrusive activity" (Orten et al., 1988, p. 611). Orten et al. (1988) argue that the offender's behaviour is often compulsive and repetitive. The offender's denial and minimization of the abuse, and the lack of empathy for the sibling victim, maintain the pattern of abuse. Additionally, sibling incest victims may gradually become involved as co-conspirators by the offender and will share in the responsibility, blame, and punishment if the abuse is disclosed. This makes it more difficult for the victim to resist more sexually intrusive demands of the offender (O'Brien, 1991).

PREVALENCE AND REPORTING OF SIBLING INCEST

It is estimated that between 30 to 50 per cent of child sexual abuse is committed by adolescents.[2] It is believed that brother and sister incest is the most common type of incest. Sibling incest has been estimated to be about five times more common than parent–child incest (Adler et al., 1995). A study of college students revealed that 15 per cent of females and 10 per cent of males have had a sexual experience with a sibling. This finding signifies that 13 per cent of the population have had sexual experiences with a sibling (Finkelhor, 1984). Because of the failure to recognize sibling incest as a problem, information on the prevalence of sexual abuse by siblings is difficult to ascertain (Wiehe, 1990). Sexual behaviour among siblings is frequently overlooked and is often regarded as mere sex play—that is, exploratory, mutually consenting, mutually enjoyable, and benign in its effects on later psychological, social, or sexual development (O'Brien, 1991).

Sibling incest is believed to be the most under-reported type of sexual abuse (Carter et al., 1998). It is estimated that 65 per cent of sexually abused children do not report their victimization to anyone. When reporting does occur, many of the complaints are never prosecuted (Bourke et al., 1996). Early disclosure is uncommon because of the family secrecy involved. The secrecy surrounding sibling sexual abuse adds to the trauma (O'Brien, 1991; DiGiorgio-Miller, 1998). Fear of blame, retribution, and punishment also hinders the decision to disclose. The victims in sibling incest often view the abuse as their fault and suffer major guilt, and therefore they do not tell anyone about the abuse. The victims may have been threatened and, therefore, are afraid to come forward with the incident. Often, the victim is not old enough to know that the act is sexual abuse (Wiehe, 1990). "Since the victim is a sibling, the consequences of disclosure-retribution by the offender, disbelief and/or punishment by the parents, removal from the home of either or both the victim and offender and family distribution may be relatively more immediate or sailent" (O'Brien, 1991, p. 79). Offenders hold extreme cognitive distortions used to deny, minimize, or rationalize their offences. It is very rare for offenders to come forward on their own and admit their offences, or to seek help for their behaviour unless they are "caught" (Aljazireh, 1993).

Sexual abuse is often under-reported by parents. They may want to protect the offender, or may fear the embarrassment of being found out. The parents may have a vested interest in not reporting the adolescent's behaviour. For example, there may be adult and child incest in the family.

Parents may also minimize the offence because they do not want outside involvement in their personal affairs. Parents may not realize the extent of the abuse and may consider it innocent. Further, parents may not be able to appreciate the seriousness of the abuse because generational boundaries are not violated. They may not realize the extent of the abuse and may consider it innocent child's play (Charles et al., 1997; Scavo et al., 1989). There is interference with the family's homeostasis and the parents may deny or minimize the abuse to restore family stability.

> If the family is allowed to prevail in these attempts, the dynamics that fostered the abuse will remain, the victim and the offender will go untreated, and ultimately the sibling incest may resume—if not between the current offender and victim, then perhaps between the offender and other siblings or children of the next generation (O'Brien, 1991, p. 89).

There may also be insufficient awareness among both professionals and society in not recognizing that sibling incest as a problem. The offences are often dismissed as normal male behaviour, normal sexual curiosity, or as being situational. Many professionals believe that these offences are not very serious and occur infrequently. Behaviours that are considered illegal if committed by adults are often condoned by adolescents because of their age.[3]

Characteristics of Sibling Sexual Abusers

Much research has been focused on identifying characteristics that are unique to adolescent sex offenders in hopes of finding etiological theories as to why these adolescents offend. This, in turn, would help professionals deal more effectively with this population (Jacobs et al., 1997). Multiple factors are thought to play a role in the development of sexually offending behaviour (Becker et al., 1997).

Siblings as Victims

There are several proposed assumptions as to why adolescents offend within their family. They may be showing rage and revenge on the victimized sibling, or may be seeking power and control. These youth may use sibling relationships as a source of support and comfort if living with abusive and rejecting parents. With the onset of puberty, this relationship with siblings may be at risk of becoming sexualized. They may also be trying to "get back" at their parents for the abuse they have endured (Pierce et al., 1987; Courtois, 1988).

Others have gone further by attempting to classify intra-familial sex offenders as being distinct from one another. Some researchers believe that sibling incest can be differentiated into two categories. Power-oriented incest usually involves deliberate physical or mental abuse and is sadistic, exploitative, and coercive. The second is nurturance-oriented incest. This type may contain elements of erotic pleasure, love, loyalty and compassion, and mutuality. The incest may represent an escape from troubled and disturbed family relationships. However, appropriate individual development or healthy family interactions may not develop. An incestuous relationship may have elements of both orientations (Kahn et al., 1988).

Similarly, Courtois (1988) proposes that three main variations of sibling incest exist. The first type is when a brother uses a younger sister for sexual experimentation. The second type concerns a "misfit" brother who substitutes his sister for female peers to gain affection. Lastly, a much older brother, who may have been a victim of sexual abuse, uses force or coercion on a younger sibling (Courtois, 1988).

Personal Qualities

Studies show that offences are committed by adolescents of all ethnic, racial, and religious groups, and middle- to lower-class adolescents seem to be highly represented (Aljazireh, 1993; Stops et al., 1991). It is also thought that the majority of offenders are male. Adolescents who molest children are seen as introverted, passive, immature, and dependent, and are thought to molest young children because they fear age-appropriate male–female relationships (Charles et al., 1997; Carpenter et al., 1995). Offenders may have poor impulse control, high levels of anxiety, and low self-esteem. They are also found to have a high incidence of emotional disturbances such as compulsive behaviours, depression, and other mental health problems. They may have difficulty making friends, have poor social skills, and are often isolated. Offenders may feel inadequate as males, fear rejection, and hold anger toward women. They tend to have poor academic performances or learning difficulties. They tend to have a history of non-sexual offences and may display a broad range of anti-social behaviours. They often lack proper sex education and usually experience deviant sexual fantasies that contribute to their sexually deviant behaviour.[4]

Family Environment

The family environment has been regarded as an important factor in the development of deviant sexual behaviour. Family dynamics may motivate a youth acting out sexually against a sibling. The following provides a broad overview of some common elements found in the families of incestual siblings. Sibling incest offenders frequently come from families that are unstable, enmeshed, chaotic, disorganized, and described as "severely disturbed." These families often experience role reversals and blurred generational, interpersonal, and sexual boundaries. They tend to have little positive communication, are emotionally distant, and are characterized as being rigid in response to change.[5] The abusing behaviour may be linked to the offender's perception of his status in the family. For example, the youth may have a privileged position in the family or may possess poor boundaries because of neglectful parents. Remarriage can bring about new relationships in the family that could result in the youth losing status and acting out against a sibling (DiGiorgio-Miller, 1998).

The parents may have a sexual pathology or a psychological impairment, and the child may have observed sexual pathology between the parents. Poor parental sexual boundaries and a history of victimization are also factors. For example, Smith et al. (1987) found that 72 per cent of the fathers or mothers in sibling incest families had been sexually abused as children. Substance abuse by parents is also considered a factor. Offending youth have often witnessed violence, or been victims of violence, and may be acting out family problems and their own victimization through learned incestuous behaviour. If the parents model any type of violence within the home, the youth may learn that violence or abuse within families is acceptable (Worling, 1995). The separation of parents, parental rejection, or parental loss is also believed to play a role in intra-familial offending. Poor supervision, such as leaving younger siblings in the care of an older brother, may be an indirect contribution to incestuous behaviour. Parents may also encourage the adolescent to sexually abuse a sibling. It is also believed that sibling incest occurs more often in large families.[6]

Abuse Histories

Many offenders have histories of physical, sexual, and emotional abuse. Studies show that between 23 per cent and 63 per cent of offenders were sexually abused,[7] and between 25 to 75 per cent were physically abused,[8] while Pierce et al. (1987) found that 70 per cent had experienced parental neglect. Offenders often have difficulty disclosing their abuse histories and may deny that they have been victimized (Scavo et al., 1989). They may not disclose their victimization until they feel secure enough to do so, and it is likely that many do not disclose it at all. Although abuse is considered a risk factor, it is not known to what extent a history of abuse contributes in becoming a sexual offender (Lakey, 1994).

ASSESSMENT

It is important to have an understanding of the offender to properly assess and treat the youth (Scavo et al., 1989; Stops et al., 1991). Assessment of adolescent sex offenders involves a data-gathering process similar to any other assessment (Saunders et al., 1988). Each sibling incest case is unique and should be treated as such (Hargett, 1998). A complete assessment will aid in understanding the offender's treatment needs. Often it is not the sexual offence that is the sole problem for the youth. Records that should be reviewed include the victim's statement, juvenile court records, school records, mental health records, and self-reports from parents and significant others. It is also important to identify possible risk factors, including, individual, familial, social, psychological, and environmental variables that may contribute to the adolescent's sexually destructive behaviour.[9]

It is helpful to assess the general psycho-social functioning of the youth. The adolescent's use of drugs or alcohol should also be examined, along with assessing if illicit drugs were involved in the offence and whether the youth has any non-sexual offences. Additionally, any vulnerabilities and/or disabilities should be appraised. In order for treatment to be successful it should be tailored to fit the youth's intellectual functioning. It is helpful to assess the youth's knowledge about sexuality and sex. The youth's peer relationships, recreational activities, impulse control, and social skills should also be examined along with his pornography use and exposure to sexual practices (Bourke et al., 1996; Cashwell et al., 1996).

It is important to determine the nature of the offence. Issues that should be explored include the following: the age difference between the victim and the offender; the progression and frequency of the behaviour; and the nature of fantasies that accompany the incidents; and the assaults themselves.[10]

The extent of persuasion, enticement, threat, or coercion used should also be explored; however, the youth's estimation of violence may be inaccurate (Bourke et al., 1996).

A family history is useful and should address issues such as alcoholism, violence, neglect, psychiatric disturbances, etc. The openness, cohesion, and emotional expressiveness of the family should be evaluated. The family's dysfunction, strengths, and quality of relationships should be considered. Boundaries need to be determined and the sexual atmosphere of the home should be established (Hargett, 1998). It is very important that the victim's safety is ensured, which may result in the offender being removed from the home.

Treatment of Sibling Incest Offenders

Available treatment programs for sibling incest offenders are somewhat unique as there is no agreed-upon treatment approach that has been determined best practice (Jacobs et al., 1997). Because so little is known about adolescent sex offenders, and particularly such special population offenders as sibling incest offenders, there is no one ideal intervention approach that is believed to be most effective with individual offenders. With increased awareness of the varied characteristics and needs of offenders, there is heightened appreciation that a "one size fits all" approach does not work (Charles et al., 1997). Treating adolescents is conducted in a variety of ways, for example, through lectures, discussions, exercises, videos, role-playing, written assignments, journals, etc. (Lakey, 1994). Treatment ranges from highly structured residential or secure programs to less structured out-patient or community ventures (Scavo et al., 1989) and may consist of individual, family, or group approaches.

The main goal of treatment is to prevent re-offending (Lakey, 1994). Despite the differences in many treatment programs, several core issues have been identified as being critical for treatment. These include: uncovering thinking errors and deviant arousal patterns, working through minimization and denial, learning the sexual offence cycle, relapse prevention, sex, sexuality, life skills education, victim impact/empathy, and family therapy and preparation for contact of the sibling victim (Mathews, 1997; Kahn et al., 1988; Hackett et al., 1998). Other areas of treatment can include: covert sensitization, imaginal desensitization, verbal satiation, laboratory satiation (Bourke et al., 1996), and drug therapies (Stevenson et al., 1990). Treatment resources should reflect the needs of the offender and should also acknowledge diverse cultural and geographical characteristics.

SIBLING INCEST IN RURAL OR ISOLATED AREAS

Literature in the area of sibling incest committed in rural areas is very limited. Although studies may include youth from rural areas, these studies do not usually isolate issues related to sibling sexual offenders. Clearly, offences are committed in rural and isolated areas. One study found that 31 per cent of sibling incest offenders were from rural areas (O'Brien, 1991). Sibling incest in rural and isolated areas is an important area to address because there are distinct issues and problems faced by intra-familial adolescent sex offenders and those working with this population in rural or isolated areas.

Rural Values

People from rural areas are believed to be conservative in their values and traditional in their lifestyles (York et al., 1989; Rounds, 1988). Sexual issues are seen as the responsibility of the family or the church rather than the government or private funding sources (Shapiro, 1989). Rural communities may distrust government and place a greater confidence on informal social control such as gossiping and shaming (Farley et al., 1982). Rural people may rely on social networks to provide social support, compared to urban people who rely more on formal agencies. However, these social networks are not value-free and can stigmatize as well as protect (Badger et al., 1997). If the community finds out about the sexual offending, the offender may be completely scorned. The youth may lose his friends, fear retaliation from neighbours, and become completely isolated. Families may also face this response from the community, illustrated by the following case example from a small community. Fifteen-year-old Paul sexually abused his six-year-old brother. His parents have been supportive and want to help Paul get treatment. They are very careful not to leave Paul unsupervised. They also feel guilty that Paul was sexually abused as a child by an uncle, and that they did not try to get Paul any help. Paul's mother told a friend what happened in hope of getting support. This friend told several others, and now the whole community knows about the abuse. Paul has been taken out of school because the other kids are calling him "gay" and "a pervert." The parents are also being targeted by unkind remarks by neighbours who cannot understand why they would keep "that little pervert" in their home. Their home has been vandalized, and no one will talk to them. They have become completely ostracized by the community. They would like to move, but do not have the resources to do so.

Rural communities are, however, more likely to take care of their own, whereas larger communities may more readily segregate individuals who abuse others (Farley et al., 1982). Rural communities may rally behind a family where sibling incest occurs to keep others "out of their business." They may aid the family in keeping the secret to minimize outside involvement. For example, a police officer called to investigate sexual abuse may choose to do nothing if his/her own family is involved. Further, rural courts may view the offender's actions in context of the community's values.

Communities will vary in their response to the offender. As well, if the offence occurs in a "respected" family compared to a "disliked" family, the amount of secrecy, support, ignoring, or banishing may be quite different. Although taking care of their own is seen as a strength in rural areas, when it comes to sibling incest, this could be dangerous. Youths who commit sexual offences do not need people to disregard the issue—they need help. This is illustrated by the following case:

> Sixteen-year-old Jim sexually abused his twelve-year-old sister and her friend Lisa. Jim comes from one of the town's most prominent families, and his uncle is the Chief of Police. Jim has the potential to be a great athlete and makes good grades. He is the "star" of the community. Jim's sister denied that the abuse occurred, but Lisa told her mother what had happened. Lisa's family comes from "the wrong side of town." The investigators involved decided it was a "boys will be boys" type of incident, that both children were engaging in innocent sex play, and that Lisa is a "known" troublemaker and was only trying to get attention. Jim did not get into any trouble, but Lisa is now an outcast in the community, with the other kids calling her names like "liar" and "tramp." Jim is still abusing his sister, but this is being ignored.

LACK OF RESOURCES

Mathews (1997) explains that under-funding burdens many rural communities' attempts to provide social service treatment particularly to adolescent sex offenders and their families. Further, when treatment is provided, many small communities do not have the financial or human capacity to assess the effectiveness of their work with clients. Equipment such as videotapes, manuals, and other training material are not as available. Aside from social services, rural areas also lack services relating to law enforcement (Farley et al., 1982).

Traditionally, existing services in rural areas are aimed at victims rather than offenders. Advocates of victim services may worry that by providing services to the offenders, services for victims may suffer. Unfortunately, this may be true in rural areas because of lack of funding and competition for programs even though, with more programs for offenders, there may be a decrease in the number of future victims. The offenders usually have few treatment options available in their environment. A lack of services for both victims and offenders can conceivably contribute to this confounding problem. With a lack of services, it is likely that this problem may continue unaddressed and largely unrecognized.

Difficulties Faced by Practitioners in Rural Areas

The practitioner who attempts to work with the adolescent offender may also face stigmatization by the community. The community may see the worker as siding with the offender, and therefore lose confidence in the worker's abilities or loyalties. Workers could combat this problem by clearly defining their roles to the community. Workers should actively establish their role within the community and educate the residents on the premise that social work is a valuable resource for every member of the community (Farley et al., 1982). Workers may inform the community of what their work entails, and should function as a respected member of the community. They should treat all members of the community with dignity and respect and should safeguard confidentiality.

If there is a lack of funding to hire qualified workers with specialized training to run programs for sex offenders, which is often the reality in rural areas, workers may be faced with the dilemma of practising beyond their competence (Delaney et al., 1995; Farley et al., 1982). Workers in rural areas often need to be generalists in order to meet the needs of the community (York et al., 1989); however, this could lead to several problems. Working with sex offenders requires certain expertise and specialization. If there is a resource deficit, rural workers may find themselves doing work with sibling incest offenders for which they have not been adequately trained or prepared. They may find themselves being pushed into working with the sibling incest offender, but because of their lack of expertise in the area, they would normally refer the youth to a more qualified worker if the resources were available (Delaney et al., 1995).

Further, the worker will likely need to work with the family, the victim, and the offender, which could cause a conflict of interest (Badger et al., 1997). McElroy et al. (1991) discuss a variety of difficulties that are relevant to working with incest families. The worker would have to decide which members of the family will be seen together, and is expected to be sensitive to the needs of each member of the family. The worker may have difficulty balancing the use of clinical skills with personal authority in working with these families. S/he may also struggle with confronting the offender and trying to form a close therapeutic relationship. It may be difficult to determine who the client is. Is it the victim who is struggling with abuse issues? Is it the offender who obviously needs treatment?

Obviously each family member has different therapeutic needs, and this may be a difficult and overwhelming balancing act, as the best interests of several family members may be in conflict (Delaney et al., 1995). For example, it may be best for the offending youth and the parents for the youth to return home, yet this may be very difficult for the victim. The safety and well-being of the victim, however, should always take priority over the needs and wants of the offender or the family.

The worker may lack the opportunity to consult with other professionals who are more skilled in this area, and also the necessary support systems. Burnout is a very real possibility, especially with lack of training and supportive supervision (Mathews, 1997). To counter these difficulties, Mathews (1997) suggests that workers have access to journals, professional books, training, peer support, and other resources. This will help counter burnout, especially for the rural worker. Situations such as the following can lead to considerable stress and the risk of burnout.

Jane had graduated a year before with her degree in social work. She is now working at her first job, and has come across a difficult case. The parents of an eleven-year-old boy referred him to her because he was sexually acting out against his younger sisters. Jane does not have any experience working with sexually intrusive behaviour and cannot find any information on it in her community. Because the boy is under twelve, she cannot refer him to the court system. There is a crisis centre for women and children who are victims of sexual abuse, but they refuse to help her because they work only with victims, not offenders. Her agency cannot afford to supply extra resources for her to work with a child who is sexually inappropriate because "that type of thing doesn't happen much here." She is very concerned about the boy, even though the other workers dismiss his behaviour as "child's play." She is finding it difficult to work with him and knows she does not have the full expertise. However, she has decided that it is better to work with him, rather than not giving him any help at all.

Treatment for sibling incest offenders, when it is available in rural or isolated areas, may still present a disadvantage compared with urban counterparts. For example, group treatment is seen as possibly the most effective mode of treatment for adolescent sex offenders. It is highly unlikely that there is, at any given time, a sufficient number of identified offenders to constitute a group in a rural or isolated area. This leaves the worker having to rely on individual and family work. If the family does not want to be involved in the treatment, it is doubtful that individual therapy alone will be effective. Further, treatment for offenders is often court-mandated. Given the lack of availability of treatment programs in rural areas it is not likely to be mandated by the judge. The youth may serve a custody term, but not get the treatment he and his family so desperately need.

DIFFICULTIES FACED BY OFFENDERS IN RURAL AREAS

In order to receive treatment, young offenders living in rural communities are often pulled from their families, leaving them with few supports. They may need to "dropout" of their schools to attend treatment. If they do not attend treatment, they risk breaching probation and a possible custody term.

> John is a fifteen-year-old boy who sexually offended against his eight-year-old sister. The abuse had been occurring for about six months. It ended when his sister told her teacher, who contacted the authorities to investigate. He lived in a small community two hours away from a larger, urban centre. John's father is a truck driver, and is away from home often. His mother also works, and left John in charge of his sister's care until she came home from work. John's parents were outraged about the abuse, and do not want anything to do with him. People in the community found out about the abuse. John's friends were not allowed to talk to him, and he feels that everyone he knows has turned their back on him. He was put in foster care in the city, and is now attending treatment. John's treatment will be over soon and he has no idea where he will live. His family and his community have turned their backs on him, and he feels all alone in the world.

DIFFICULTIES FACED BY FAMILIES IN RURAL AREAS

When youth offend against siblings, the family may keep this a secret for fear of having him removed from the home or community. As well, the family may move from the community to obtain treatment for their children or because of the fear of shame. Parents are usually reluctant to experience long-term separation from their children (Hargett, 1998). Conversely, they may turn against the offending child and want nothing to do with him. There may be less anonymity as they may have personal relationships with the professionals in the community and may believe that their secret will not be kept from the rest of the community. The probability that the details of such a sensitive matter will be known by the community members makes it that much more difficult for the family to seek help (Farley et al., 1982). If the community finds out about the abuse, the family may become isolated from other community members. Confidentiality in rural areas becomes an extremely important issue for families as people in rural areas tend to "know" their neighbour's business. Confidentiality is not any more important in rural areas; it is just harder to attain.

> Ken had received treatment for his sexual offence against his sister in another community. His parents told people that Ken was away for summer camp. Now Ken is back home, and is attending family treatment at a small, local agency. Although they were embarrassed that they needed to attend counselling, they told their friends that they were just having a difficult time with Ken. After about a month of therapy, the family walked in and found that

there was a different secretary at the desk. Ken's mother and this [new] secretary had not gotten along in the past. When she noticed the secretary, she told her family that they had to leave. She is now devastated that this woman she despises knows about their "family secret." She refuses to go back because she believes that everyone will find out what happened.

Future Directions for Combatting Sibling Incest in Rural and Isolated Areas

Clearly, there are distinct issues and difficulties faced by those encountering sibling incest in rural and isolated areas. In order to combat these problems, we need to look at the areas that are in dire need of improvement. It is important that we improve research efforts in order to include offenders from rural and isolated areas. A financial commitment must be given and education and prevention are strongly indicated. Treatment strategies are also lacking and procedures need to be put into place in order to really aid those faced by the problem of sibling incest in rural areas.

RESEARCH

Because this field is relatively new, there has not been enough time to conduct long-term research to support the development of standardized intake, assessment, and treatment programs. Further, research has not expanded to include the unique aspects of adolescent offending committed in rural and isolated areas. As we attempt to improve research efforts in general, we need to include offenders from rural and isolated areas—not just offenders from urban centres—in our research. This will help ensure an adequate knowledge base for all offenders, regardless of their geographical location.

Clearly, information regarding areas such as offender characteristics, assessment, and treatment has progressed to a great extent. Unfortunately, we do not know if rural offenders fit neatly into any of these categories. For example, we might, at this time, assume that offenders possess the same personal characteristics despite their geographical location. However, since research has shown that rural families tend to be more traditional and multi-generational, patterns of abuse tend to be far-reaching. It is realistic that rural and urban families may differ greatly, and indeed the offenders may as well. Areas for future research regarding sibling incest offenders and rural and isolated areas could focus on the unique characteristics of offenders, the family environment, effectiveness of treatment, and both descriptive and quantitative studies on unique rural prevention strategies or treatment programs.

EDUCATION AND PREVENTION

Education may greatly reduce the vulnerability and abuse of many children. Sex education is clearly important and should be targeted toward children, youth, parents, professional, and communities at large. Further, Becker (1994) argues that community members, including teachers, police, child protection workers, and juvenile judges need to be educated on age-appropriate and inappropriate behaviour. Communities are in need of information as to how to respond to sexually abusive youths. Communities need to be informed about acceptable sexual behaviours and professionals need to be knowledgeable and trained to deal with destructive sexual behaviour (Becker et al., 1997; Charles et al., 1997). Additionally, small communities may lack useful information about the problem of sexual offending, and the consequence of this may be community secrecy or non-recognition of the problem.

Prevention programs are an important educational tool that may help prevent the sexual abuse of many children. Programs for children should begin early, as children are often victimized at an early age. Clearly, we cannot always rely on proper sex education and abuse prevention to be taught in homes, since we know that many children are sexually abused by members of their family. However, parents need information regarding sex education so they can properly educate their children. Even parents who provide their child with proper information may not think to educate the child on what to do if a family member, especially a sibling, tries to sexually abuse them.

Coleman (1997) argues that treatment for offenders must " ... pick up the pieces left by the failure to provide responsible and complete sex education" (p. 4), resulting in children being denied validation or correction for what they have learned. Rural communities may be even more cautious in teaching sex education in schools as sexual issues are seen as the responsibility of the family or the church. "Rural communities have other pressing needs that demand attention, enabling them to deny the compelling nature of the problems young people face in the areas of sexual learning" (Shapiro, 1989, p. 143).

Education is also needed on a societal level. Additions to the educational curriculum that address sexuality, sexism, and homophobia in general can be integrated into the ongoing material addressing human sexuality. We must also recognize the influence of gender roles that often set males up to be offenders and females to be victims (Coleman, 1997). Children are bombarded with inaccurate information about sex and sexuality and are exposed to sexual information through television, music, advertising, friends, games, etc. They are often given the message that violence and sex are a normal part of a relationship.

Professional training is a problem across the country. Most of the training occurs through brief workshops at large conferences, making it too expensive or too far away for workers who need the training most, particularly those working in the north or in rural and isolated areas. Continuous training is needed at beginning, intermediate, and advanced levels, and should not be isolated events (Mathews, 1997).

Social workers could set up programs in schools that teach sex education and enlist community teachers to provide this information. Workers could also advertise at the heart of communities by placing informational brochures, for example, in laundromats, local gathering places, family health clinics, schools, the library, agencies, and community bulletin boards. Announcements or advertisements could also be made through the local paper or radio station, at religious services, Parent–Teacher Association meetings, or community meetings. Community leaders could be encouraged to spread the word informally. Workers could run programs and workshops to educate the community on appropriate sexual behaviour, and what to do when sexual behaviour is a concern. Resources such as the Internet could be kept current with research and used as a tool to maintain contact with service providers who deal with sexual offenders on a daily basis. Social workers in small communities should be well-versed in all aspects of sexual violence. It is important that they start where the client is, employ community leaders, develop resource systems, and focus on family involvement (Shapiro, 1989). This way, they will be able to help the community and all those impacted to deal with this confounding problem.

TREATMENT

Specialized services must be available in communities, including specialized group homes, therapeutic foster care, residential treatment centres, and community-based treatment for offenders and their families. A continuum of care is needed in smaller communities (Bremer, 1998; Charles et al., 1997). Mathews (1997) suggests that we need to forge close working alliances with the child abuse field and other fields that work to reduce and eliminate sexual violence. Larger areas can assist smaller communities in offering vital services for these offenders so fewer lives will be disrupted (Becker, 1994). This is also likely to support the treatment process of the youth who must travel to obtain treatment.

Sexual offenders have very complex needs. For treatment to be successful, multi-disciplinary and multi-agency collaboration is crucial. For example, this may involve prosecutors, corrections, probation, police, child protection, and mental health agencies (Morrison et al., 1994).

> No single professional or agency has the skills or resources to meet all offender's needs. Working with others helps ensure practitioners have the

professional and personal support they need and enables the development of group work, family therapy and individual approaches, all of which are needed for comprehensive treatment (Morrison et al., 1994, p. 101).

The criminal and juvenile justice systems have an established role in identifying, processing, and treating adolescents in need of help. Therefore it would be beneficial for these systems to take a primary responsibility for the treatment of adolescent sex offenders, since they provide a ready framework for continuity of care. Further, since sibling incest is a criminal offence, the criminal justice system is routinely involved (Solin, 1986). It is important to point out, however, that even if the youth has not been charged, ideally some form of support or treatment should be offered to the victim, the offender, and the family. We need to recognize that some behaviours are responsive to treatment and we have a responsibility to protect families and the community from future sexual offences (Stevenson et al., 1990). Likewise, child welfare agencies can play a vital role functioning as service co-ordinators, selecting necessary services and linking families with appropriate service providers (Solin, 1986).

Rural communities could focus on co-ordinating, strengthening, and expanding existing community resources and networks. Unfortunately, "structural barriers to health and social services in rural areas are longstanding and likely will not be overcome without major economic changes" (Rounds, 1988, p. 259). Likewise, as the number of offenders may be relatively small in rural areas, it may not be realistic to develop separate agencies to provide services to this group. At best, existing agencies and services should join together to provide services to this population (Rounds, 1988). Rural workers could educate those in urban centres of the unique circumstances that they face.

Rural workers could develop alliances with experts in larger centres. The youth and possibly the family could be connected to these resources. If existing networks are unable or unwilling to provide care, social workers could build a network with those people who are willing to be supportive. For example, neighbours or protective services, social workers, doctors, ministers, and others could support the family or the youth with the transition back into the family. The team may play such roles as supervising the family, or running programs or groups. Social workers should utilize these natural helpers as they will be beneficial in developing child sexual abuse programs, providing sex education, and even supporting the adolescent offender and his family.

The utilization of natural helpers in rural communities has been appreciated as a critical resource to rural people.

> In communities grappling with such limitations as poor transportation, social isolation, a dearth of social agencies, and a suspicion of outside service

providers, it is important also to acknowledge the existing strengths: concern for one's neighbours, ability to mobilize human resources, awareness of interlocking social networks, and the desire to work toward stability in family life (Shapiro, 1989, p. 144).

Natural helpers are often aware of what resources exist, know how to involve crucial community members, gain members interest in a cause, and know what they can expect from community members.

CONCLUSION

Adolescent sibling incest is a very complex phenomenon. Although this is a relatively new field, and knowledge has developed significantly, we still have a long way to go. Sexual abuse against children is often seen as one of the most heinous crimes that can be committed. These offences cause public outrage and fear. Finding the most effective assessment and treatment strategies are extremely important. To do this, we must examine the literature to find out what has been done, and then forge ahead and learn more. The discussion in this chapter provided insight into the areas of the literature deemed relevant for an increasingly accurate and thorough picture of intra-familial male adolescent sex offenders. It is essential that both professionals and the public are educated in this area. We need to sharpen our identification of the causes of sexually destructive behaviour, prevent that behaviour from occurring, and enrich our treatment modalities for offenders to prevent the future assault of victims (Becker et al., 1987). "Only when we are willing to openly and effectively deal with abusive behaviour will we begin to appropriately address the levels of victimization that are occurring in our communities" (Charles et al., 1997, p. 22).

We must also acknowledge the uniqueness of rural and isolated regions and should understand how these areas may differ from urban areas in the context of sibling sexual abuse. These regions have special problems and difficulties not faced by urban centres. "People who have problems in rural areas are not always well heard and because they are not always well heard, they are not always well served" (Farley et al., 1982, p. 14).

Although this chapter addresses the problems and issues rural communities face in dealing with intra-familial adolescent sex offenders, much more attention and research needs to be devoted to this problem. In order to really help the victims of sexual assault, we must be willing and able to help the offenders who commit these crimes. This is truly the best gift we can give as professionals. By helping the offenders, we help all of society.

NOTES

1. Scavo et al. (1989); Becker et al. (1997); Carpenter et al. (1995).
2. Charles et al. (1997); Coleman (1997); Kempton et al. (1991).
3. Bourke et al. (1996); Coleman (1997); Hackett et al. (1998).
4. Charles et al. (1997); Becker et al. (1997); Scavo et al. (1989); Saunders et al. (1988); Oliver, Nagayama et al. (1993).
5. Becker et al. (1997); Bischof et al. (1995); Blaske et al. (1989).
6. Becker (1994); Aljazireh (1993); Stops et al. (1991).
7. Becker et al. (1987); O'Brien (1991); Pierce et al. (1987); Smith et al. (1987).
8. Aljazireh (1993); Becker et al. (1997), O'Brien (1991); Pierce et al. (1987).
9. Stops et al. (1991); Becker et al. (1997); Hargett (1998).
10. Becker et al. (1997); Bourke et al. (1996); Saunders et al. (1988).

REFERENCES

Adler, N. & Schutz, J. (1995). Sibling incest offenders. *Child Abuse and Neglect*, 19(7), 811–819.

Aljazireh, L. (1993). Historical, environmental, and behavioural correlates of sexual offending by male adolescents: A critical review. *Behavioral Sciences and the Law*, 11, 423–440.

Badger, L. W., Ackerson, B., Buttel, F., & Rand, E. (1997). The case for integration of social work psychosocial services into rural primary care practice. *Health in Social Work*, 22(1), 20–29.

Becker, J. V. (1994). Offenders: Characteristics and treatment. *Sexual Abuse of Children*, 4(2), 176–197.

Becker, J. V., Cunningham-Rathner, J., & Kaplan, M. S. (1987). Adolescent sex offenders: Demographics, criminal and sexual histories, and recommendations for reducing future offences. *Journal of Interpersonal Violence*, 1(4), 431–445.

Becker, J. V., & Hunter, J. A. (1997). Understanding and treating child and adolescent offenders. *Advances in Clinical Child Psychology*, 19, 177–197.

Bischof, G. P., Stith, S. M., & Whitney, M. L. (1995). Family environments of adolescent sex offenders and other juvenile delinquents. *Adolescence*, 30(117), 157–169.

Blaske, D. M., Borduin, C. M., Henggeler, S. W., & Mann, B. J. (1989). Individual, family and peer characteristics of adolescent sex offender and assaultive offenders. *Developmental Psychology*, 25(5), 846–855.

Bourke, M. L. & Donohue, B. (1996). Assessment and treatment of juvenile sex offenders: An empirical review. *Journal of Child Sexual Abuse*, 5(1), 47–70.

Bremer, J. F. (1998). Challenges in the assessment and treatment of sexually abusive adolescents. *The Irish Journal of Psychology*, 19, 82–92.

Canavan, M. M., Meyer, W. J., & Higgs, D. C. (1992). The female experience of sibling incest. *Journal of Marital and Family Therapy*, 18(2), 129–142.

Carpenter, D. R., Peed, S. F., & Eastman, B. (1995). Personality characteristics of adolescent sexual offenders: A pilot study. *Sexual Abuse: A Journal of Research and Treatment*, 7(3), 195–203.

Carter, G. S. & van Dalen, A. (1998). Sibling incest: Time limited group as an assessment and treatment planning tool. *Journal of Adolescent and Group Therapy*, 8(2), 45–54.

Cashwell, C. S. & Caruso, M. E. (1996). Adolescent sex offenders: Identification and intervention strategies. *Journal of Mental Health Counseling*, 21, 336–348.

Charles, G. & McDonald, M. (1997). Adolescent sexual offenders. *Journal of Child and Youth Care*, 11(1), 15–25.

Coleman, H. (1997). Gaps and silences: The culture and adolescent sex offenders. *Journal of Child and Youth Care*, 11(1), 1–13.

Courtois, C. A. (1988). *Healing the incest wound: Adult survivors in therapy*. New York: Norton.

De Jong, A. R. (1989). Sexual interactions among siblings and cousins: Experimentation or exploitation? *Child Abuse and Neglect*, 13, 271–279.

Delaney, R. & Brownlee, K. (1995). *Northern social work practice*. Thunder Bay: Centre for Northern Studies, Lakehead University.

DiGiorgio-Miller, J. (1998). Sibling incest: Treatment of the family and the offender. *Child Welfare*, 3, 335–346.

Farley, W. O., Griffiths, K. A., Skidmore, R. A., & Thackeray, M. G. (1982). *Rural social work practice*. New York: Free Press.

Finkelhor, D. (1984). *Child sexual abuse: New theory and research*. New York: Free Press.

Hackett, S., Print, B., & Dey, C. (1998). *Brother nature? Therapeutic intervention with young men who sexually abuse their siblings*. New York: John Wiley.

Hargett, H. (1998). Reconciling the victim and perpetrator in sibling incest. *Sexual Addiction and Compulsivity*, 5, 93–106.

Jacobs, W. L., Kennedy, W. A., & Meyer, J. B. (1997). Juvenile delinquents: A between-group comparison study of sexual and nonsexual offenders. *Sexual Abuse: A Journal of Research and Treatment*, 9(3), 201–217.

Kahn, T. J. & Lafond, M. A. (1988). Treatment of the adolescent sexual offender. *Child and Adolescent Social Work*, 5(2), 135–149.

Kempton, T. & Forehand, R. (1991). Juvenile sex offenders: Similar to, or different from, other incarcerated delinquent offenders? *Behavioural Residential Therapy*, 30(5), 533–536.

Lakey, J. F. (1994). The profile and treatment of male adolescent sex offenders. *Adolescence*, 29(116), 755–761.

McElroy, L. P. & McElroy, R. A. (1991). Countertransference issues on the treatment of incest families. *Psychotherapy*, 28, 48–54.

Mathews, F. (1997). The adolescent sex offender field in Canada: Old problems, current issues, and emerging controversies. *Journal of Child and Youth Care*, 11(1), 55–62.

Morrison, T., Erooga, M., & Beckett, R. C. (1994). *Sexual offending against children: Assessment and treatment of male abusers*. London: Routledge.

O'Brien, M. (1991). *Taking sibling incest seriously*. Newbury Park: Sage.

Oliver, L. L., Nagayama Hall, G. C., & Neuhaus, S. N. (1993). A comparison of the personality and background characteristics of adolescent sex offenders and other adolescent offenders. *Criminal Justice and Behavior*, 20(4), 359–370.

Orten, J. D. & Rich, L. L. (1988). A model for assessment of incestuous families. *Social Casework*, 69(10), 611–619.

Pierce, L. H. & Pierce, R. L. (1987). Incestuous victimization by juvenile sex offenders. *Journal of Family Violence*, 2(4), 341–364.

Rounds, K. A. (1988). Aids in rural areas: Challenge to providing care. *Social Work*, 33(3), 257–261.

Saunders, E. B. & Awad, G. A. (1988). Assessment, management, and treatment planning for male adolescent sexual offenders. *American Journal of Orthopsychiatry*, 58(4), 571–579.

Scavo, R. & Buchanan, B. D. (1989). Group therapy for male adolescent sex offenders: A model for residential treatment. *Residential Treatment for Children and Youth*, 7(2), 59–75.

Shapiro, C. H. (1989). *Networking with rural adolescents and their parents to promote communication about sexual issues*. New York: Haworth.

Smith, H. & Israel, E. (1987). Sibling incest: A study of the dynamics of 25 cases. *Child Abuse and Neglect*, 11, 101–108.

Solin, C. A. (1986). Displacement of affect in families following incest disclosure. *American Journal of Orthopsychiatry*, 56(4), 570–576.

Stevenson, H. C. & Wimberly, R. (1990). Assessment of treatment impact of sexually aggressive youth. *Journal of Offender Counseling, Services and Rehabilitation*, 15(2), 55–61.

Stops, M. & Mays, L. L. (1991). Treating adolescent sex offenders in a multi-cultural community Setting. *Journal of Offender Rehabilitation*, 17, 87–103.

Weihe, V. R. (1990). *Sibling abuse*. Toronto: Lexington.

Worling, J. R. (1995). Adolescent sibling-incest offenders: Differences in family and individual functioning when compared to adolescent non-sibling sex offenders. *Child Abuse and Neglect*, 19(5), 633–643.

York, R. O., Denton, R. T., & Moran, J. R. (1989). Rural and urban social work practice: Is there a difference? *Social Casework*, 70, 201–209.

Chapter Four

SEXUAL ABUSE IN RURAL, REMOTE, AND SMALL COMMUNITIES

Michelle Aukema

> The farm was miles away from anywhere significant, and I was there alone with my grandparents. I can remember one day sitting under the big kitchen table in the farmhouse, pushing around a tiny toy tractor and wagon aimlessly. I felt an overwhelming sense of despair and hopelessness. I had tried to tell the Sunday school teacher what my grandfather was doing to me, but I couldn't make her understand. I tried so hard, but I couldn't make her understand. And even though I was only four years old, I was old enough to understand that she was not going to help me, that I was all alone, that no one was going to come and rescue me.

This young woman's recollection of her experiences of sexual abuse demonstrates common themes about incest in small, isolated, or rural communities. While many of the basic issues surrounding familial incest—shame, guilt, hopelessness—are same in both urban and remote situations, isolated geographical circumstances raise unique issues.

DEFINING SEXUAL ABUSE

Sexual abuse can be defined as "any contact or interaction (visual, verbal, or psychological) between a child/adolescent and an adult when the child/adolescent is being used for the sexual stimulation of the perpetrator or any other person" (Allendar, 1995, p. 48). This definition allows for sexual abuse to include all forms of inappropriate sexual contact (genital, oral and anal intercourse, clothed and unclothed sexual touching of body parts, sexual kissing), as well as interactions such as sexual nicknames, seductive innuendo, exposure to pornography, intentional exposure to adult sexual acts and nudity, and intrusive interest in the child's sexual activity (Allendar, 1995). Sexual abuse can have devastating consequences on a child or adolescent, leading to multiple problems such as depression, low self-esteem, and suicidal ideation or behaviour. Also, the abused child may display behaviours such as self-injury, graphic play, eating disorders, withdrawal, running away, and changes in school performance may be observed. Further, the effects of childhood sexual abuse have long-lasting repercussions that may reach into adulthood if neglected (Heitritter et al., 1989). When sexual abuse occurs within families, it is viewed as more traumatic than sexual abuse by a stranger, as the family is seen by the child as both safe haven and security. When this image is shattered by the very people who are supposed to provide safety for the child, the effects are devastating (Allendar, 1995). If sexual abuse is defined as "any contact or interaction (visual, verbal, or psychological) between a child/adolescent and an adult when the child/adolescent is being used for the sexual stimulation of the perpetrator or any other person" (Allendar, 1995, p. 48), the incidence of sexual abuse has been found to be high. It has been estimated that approximately one in three females and one in six males will be sexually abused before the age of eighteen (Allendar, 1995; Heitritter et al., 1989). Approximately one in every ten American families are involved in some form of incestuous abuse, but fewer than 2 per cent of sexual abuse cases are reported to formal authorities (Heitritter et al., 1989). There appears to be no difference in the incidence of sexual abuse in rural as opposed to urban settings.

ISSUES PERTAINING TO SEXUAL ABUSE IN ISOLATED SETTINGS

Confidentiality and Disclosure

In small communities, confidentiality in social work practice becomes a problematic issue. It is more difficult to maintain the anonymity of a client when it is likely that the entire community will not only know one another, but will also know each other's backgrounds, personalities, and daily habits. Since the professional helper will be easily identified in these small settings, those who are seen speaking with the social worker or entering the social worker's office will also be easily identified. The social worker, as a member of the community, may also hold preconceived ideas about individuals who become clients.[1] For example, Sara, who was abused as a small child on her grandfather's farm, says that many family members as well as a professional counsellor first assumed that her abuser was an uncle on the other side of the family. This uncle was widely known to be a paedophile, as opposed to her grandfather, who was the actual abuser.

Disclosure of sexual abuse is difficult in urban settings where the abuser may not be well known. Coming forward involves risks of being disbelieved and possible rejection from peers and family. When disclosure occurs in a large urban setting, the victim has a wider choice of people to whom he or she may disclose—anonymous crisis lines, police or professional helpers, or specialized sexual abuse trauma centres. Since it is unlikely that these helpers would know the perpetrator or the victim personally, they would not have a preconceived opinion of either person, therefore increasing the likelihood that the victim would be supported and believed. However, in small communities, disclosure becomes problematic as the perpetrator will likely be known and in some cases even respected in the community. The child has a very realistic fear that he or she may not be believed due to this fact, which proves true in many cases. When Sara tried to disclose the abuse, this barrier of her abuser's good public reputation blocked her:

> I did try to tell, once. I tried to tell a Sunday school teacher at the small church my grandparents attended. It was the only time I was able to get away from him. I was crying uncontrollably, but the Sunday school teacher did nothing to help. My grandfather was widely respected within the community; he was an elder in the church. Everyone loved him, everyone thought he was the greatest. It would have been unthinkable that this highly respected man could be doing that to his small granddaughter. Even now, as an adult, I have to be so careful about who I tell in that community. My grandmother doesn't know, she worshipped Grandpa and would never believe me. It would destroy her and our family if she ever found out. People talk, and it's a small community … if the wrong person found out, this story would spread like wildfire and become the latest gossip over Sunday lunch—and I would never be believed.

SERVICE DELIVERY

In remote settings, service delivery becomes difficult. Sara recalls that:

> Even if I had been able to tell my grandmother, the farm was far out of town. She wasn't allowed to drive very often. My grandfather had put the telephone in the kitchen, which was a very high-traffic area. How were we supposed to get to where help was? And even if we had, the small town we lived by didn't have anything that would provide useful service—it still doesn't.

Accessing appropriate services suddenly becomes a major obstacle when living in a small or remote community. Services become scarcer as the community becomes smaller, since the majority of funding and the best of staff and resources are given to larger urban centres. Those that are available may be inaccessible due to distances and problems with transportation. Typically, services are located in the nearby towns or larger urban centres, forcing rural clients to travel to where help is located. Poor or non-existent roads, shared family vehicles, and no available public transit present barriers to reaching help. Emergency infrastructures such as police or ambulance may be available, but it may take these workers a significant length of time to reach the victim. Telephone help may be unavailable or problematic—not all houses may be equipped with telephone lines, and shared party lines with neighbouring houses are common in rural and remote areas, thus threatening confidentiality. Also, for child victims of familial sexual abuse, the child is most often dependent on the abuser for help. The abuser may control the family car or telephone. When this is the case, help is almost impossible to obtain.[3]

New services in remote areas may be looked upon suspiciously. Anne, who was a victim of incest in a small town, notes that "the Children's Aid Society was seen as an evil place. It was the place that came and took away children if their parents were bad." When disclosing sexual abuse, children need to know that they will be believed, and that they will be secure afterwards. It is of particular importance to note that children understand that if they tell, they may be taken away and never see their parents again. Children, no matter how bad the situation is with their parents, almost always want to remain in contact with their parents; they still love their parents and their home. Education must take place within the community to change the image of child welfare services to assure children and their families that if help is sought, every effort will be taken to help reunite the family in a healthy and healing manner.

COMMUNITY ATTITUDES AND COMMUNITY AWARENESS

It has been noted that many isolated areas tend to be more conservative and religious in their beliefs (Delaney et al., 1995). York observes that "historically, religion has been a major influence on the culture and values of American society and continues to play a vital role in the lives of the population, especially the rural population" (York, 1989, p.16). Churches are often central to northern and rural communities, and are frequently divided along ethnic and social lines (Delaney et al., 1995). Denial of problems can be strong, and is usually religiously based (Ray et al., 1990; York, 1989). The church typically defines family roles and the duties that accompany these roles, and stresses that whatever outcomes occur are the will of God (York, 1989). Sara recalls:

> One sermon is burned into my memory. It was when I was an adult, and had just begun to deal with the abuse. The sermon was about how we were as children to obey our fathers and mothers and grandparents, for this is good in the sight of the Lord. I was so blinded by anger and hurt—I don't think God thought it was good when my grandfather made me honour him with sexual favours! But as a little girl, this confused me. I was taught to obey, and I believed God thought I was a bad little girl if he was allowing this to happen.

Children are taught that their place in the family is to honour and obey their parents or those people acting in a parental role (Allendar, 1995). They are taught that what happens to them is God's will for their lives (York, 1989).

These two basic instructions create massive confusion for victims of sexual abuse, who know on an instinctual level that the abuse is wrong, but on an intellectual level they are led to believe that they must submit to it and accept it (Allendar, 1995).

Attitudes in these small locales tend to be conservative, and those who deviate from the established normative behaviours tend to be ostracized by the community. Given the small stage on which daily life is played out, an individual's actions tend to be highly public and noticeable.[4] Differences and deviations become community gossip (MacDonald, 1990). Anne felt the sting of these community attitudes. The small town in which she grew up was dominated by a particular church, which was extremely patriarchal in nature.

> I grew up in this small religious denomination in this small community. My parents could not afford tuition money to the denomination school, so the others paid for us—we were "welfare cases." I was the "low man on the totem pole" because we did not pay the school tuition and my dad was not on the church board. The kids would pick up these attitudes about me and my family from hearing them at home from their parents, and then they would say them to me. I do not know if I could have disclosed about the sexual abuse—I had no one to turn to. My friends' parents ignored me, and the teachers looked down on me.

There were rigid family and gender role expectations that played out in Anne's home. Males were given preferential treatment and women, in accordance to church teachings, were to be submissive. Also, denial had a strong force. When she told her mother about the abuse she was subjected to by an older brother, her mother did little to protect her:

> When I did tell her about the abuse, she said that it was what boys did. I could no longer sleep in my own bed or play with my dolls upstairs when the abuser was in the house. I felt like it was my fault and that I was responsible to see

that it did not happen again. My parents could not believe he was guilty. Years later, my father told me to just forget it and my mother remained adamant that all the victims that came forward were liars. There was no way out. I never even told my parents, or anyone else for that matter, about two other men that abused me. What was the use? It was my fault anyway.

Lack of community awareness contributes to the denial of sexual abuse in some small communities. When the population is unsure of how to react to the situation, it becomes easier to ignore the problem or to treat it as an individual, family dilemma, as opposed to a community issue. In a study conducted by Ray et al. (1990), it was discovered that less than 25 per cent of agencies in rural areas that worked with victims of sexual abuse partnered with the local child clubs, churches, or community centres. It has been emphasized that community education must be focused on in order to provide effective help to rural victims of abuse (Ray et al., 1990). Anne points out the lack of awareness and privatization of individual problems that occurred in her town:

> In terms of community awareness, there was nothing. You did not talk about anything like that. I remember once, when my sister was ten, she left the house in her pyjamas because Mom was committing suicide by turning on the gas oven. The neighbours called the police, and the police returned my sister to the house even though you could still smell the gas, no questions asked.

Sara cites similar experiences surrounding community awareness and denial:

> No one ever told us about sexual abuse, and what to do if it happened. The people who were in a position to help—like that Sunday school teacher—did not have a clue as to what to do. It was a lot easier to ignore the problem. I remember in seventh grade there was a teacher who liked to touch the girls; he made us all uncomfortable. One of the girls told her mother about him, because her mother was on the school board. The mother told us all to just forget about it, there was nothing that could be done. Now if that happened with thirteen girls all reporting the same story, how could I alone have possibly accused my grandfather?

Education to the public about the devastating effects of sexual abuse and how to help victims is a necessity in order to bring this problem out into the open. People need to know that sexual abuse exists and that it can and should be addressed. Knowledge empowers, and it is more difficult to ignore this problem if community members are armed with information on how to deal with sexual abuse (Brownlee et al., 1997).

Insider/Outsider

MacDonald (1990) notes that there are two distinct populations in a small, rural, or remote community. The first consists of people who are insiders: that is, they were born into the community or are long-term residents of the area. They are aware of the history, values, norms, morals, and the social and behavioural expectations of their particular community. The second group is made up of people who are termed "outsiders." They are people who are "born and raised outside of the area and whose family names have no historical consequence to people in the area. They are seen as temporary residents" (MacDonald, 1990, p. 16). Often included in this group are professional helpers, like social workers, who enter into the community in order to provide services to the residents. These temporary residents do not have knowledge of the expected behaviours and unwritten social rules that make up the fabric of the community, and often break them. As a result, the outsiders are frequently viewed with suspicion and are not trusted by the insider group. Handled cautiously, insiders are hesitant to approach them (Delaney et al., 1996; MacDonald, 1990). Independence is valued, leading to many people preferring to keep their problems and issues away from the help of outside professionals (Hartung Hagen et al., 1992). Asking for help becomes difficult (MacDonald, 1990). Anne notes that her struggle with the insider versus outsider phenomenon prevented her from seeking help:

> I never talked to my guidance counsellor at school, because outsiders were evil. Looking back on things, I can see that I was indirectly asked by my teachers if something was wrong, but I grew up thinking that I was normal, and that everyone else who is not the same culture as you was evil.... I had no one to go to. I did visit with one of the neighbours—she talked to me and listened to me, but she was an outsider, so I could not tell her about the abuse.

Hope for the Future

The issues identified above hinder the delivery of help to victims of incest in rural and remote communities. However, these issues are gaining awareness, and glimmers of hope are beginning to shine that these obstacles will be overcome. Survivors such as Anne and Sara are beginning to come forward and share not only their stories, but also their solutions:

> What could have been done back then to make things different? I wish that someone had come along side of me, identified with me—a trusted adult, a trusted friend. Teachers should be made aware of sexual abuse and what to do

about it. It should be a required part of medical school education and teachers' college education. You need to find the trusted authority figures, and make them aware. They must be members of the community—in Native communities, for example, they need to be Native teachers—they cannot be outsiders. You must keep the language and the culture, build bridges, and educate the people in the community who are trusted and work with the children. —Anne

Educate the people who are working with the children that sexual abuse does happen within families, even in families you would least suspect. These people who work with the children must be taught how to identify signs and symptoms of sexual abuse, and what to do if they suspect incest or if a child discloses it. As well, it is important to go into the schools and teach the children what sexual abuse is and that it is WRONG. Children must be given reassurance that if it is happening to them it is not their fault, and that they need to tell until someone listens.—Sara

As identified above, community education is crucial to reaching victims of incest in small, rural, and remote settings. This education should include:

- Educating the public: this would involve working with the church groups, community centres, and other interest clubs and groups. Information should be provided about incest and sexual abuse, how to identify it, and what can be done to help the child and the family. As well, members of the public can be recruited to work together on ways to increase services to victims of incest and their families.
- Educating adults who work with the children: this would include teachers, child caregivers, Sunday school teachers, recreational workers, and any others who come into direct contact with children. Specific training must be provided on how to identify signs and symptoms of sexual abuse, how to deal with a disclosure, what to do if abuse is suspected.[5]
- Educating children: children themselves need to be taught that sexual abuse is never their fault and that it is always wrong. They need to be taught how to identify sexual abuse that is occurring to them, and they need to be told how they can access help. This can be done by providing context sensitive education within the local schools.

It is important that the education and teaching materials provided be context sensitive and appropriate to the community. For example, a common approach to teaching children about sexual abuse involves educating them about touching private areas of the body, where private areas are defined as those parts of the body covered by a bathing suit. However, in areas such as Alaska children may not relate to the concept of a bathing suit if swimming is not a common practice. Alternative steps for defining private areas, such as with the use of dolls, may make more sense. If the resources and teaching methods used are not appropriate to the needs and culture of the community, confusion and misinformation may result.

It is also crucial to improve service delivery. Efforts should be made to establish transportation for clients to attend needed services. Government can be lobbied for funding to provide transportation services, or a volunteer driver pool can be established in which members of the community volunteer their time and vehicles to transport clients to services. Small satellite offices in rural areas can be set up, providing easier access to the rural clients than the main service office located in a larger centre can provide.

For those homes with phone and Internet access, help and information can be obtained through these mediums (Kelly et al., 1996). Victims of abuse should be educated on how to access websites that may provide useful information. Also, it should be emphasized that toll-free crisis lines such as the Kid's Help Phone can be accessed for no charge from the pay phones located in the small communities.

CONCLUSION

Familial sexual abuse is a devastating and tragic event, and presents great difficulties for the social worker. In small, rural, and remote communities, sexual abuse becomes even more difficult to confront due to problems with confidentiality, service delivery, community attitudes and awareness, and the insider/outsider phenomenon. However, through increasing public education and awareness and improving on the service provision, there is hope that victims of incest will be able to access the help they need.

NOTES

1. Delaney et al. (1996); Delaney et al. (1995); Trute et al. (1994); Hartung et al. (1992); Ray et al. (1990).
2. In this chapter and throughout the book, names have been changed to protect confidentiality.
3. Delaney et al. (1995); Trute, et al. (1994); Hartung Hagen et al. (1992); Ray et al. (1990).
4. Delaney et al. (1995); Trute et al. (1994); Ray et al. (1990).
5. For further information on the signs and symptoms of sexual abuse, as well as information on how to respond to disclosure of abuse, please refer to Heitritter et al. (1989). *Helping victims of sexual abuse.* Minneapolis: Bethany House Publishers.

REFERENCES

Allender, D. B. (1995). *The wounded heart.* Colorado Springs: Navpress.

Brownlee, K., Delaney, R., & Graham, J. R. (1997). *Strategies for northern social work practice.* Thunder Bay: Centre for Northern Studies, Lakehead University.

Delaney, R. & Brownlee, K. (1995). *Northern social work practice.* Thunder Bay: Centre for Northern Studies, Lakehead University.

Delaney, R., Brownlee, K., & Zapf, K. M. (1996). *Issues in northern social work practice.* Thunder Bay: Centre for Northern Studies, Lakehead University.

Hartung Hagen, B. & McKinley, K. (1992). Using family crisis groups to treat rural child sexual abuse. *Human Services and the Rural Environment,* 16(1), 15–19.

Heitritter, L. & Vought, J. (1989). *Helping victims of sexual abuse.* Minneapolis: Bethany House.

Kelly, M. J. & Lauderdale, M. L. (1996). The internet: Opportunities for rural, outreach, exchange and resource development. *Human Services in the Rural Environment,* 19(4), 4–9.

MacDonald, F. F. (1990). A case study of insider–outsider dynamics in rural community development. *Human Services in the Rural Environment,* 14(1), 15–20.

Ray, J. & Murty, S. A. (1990). Rural child sexual abuse prevention and treatment. *Human Services in the Rural Environment,* 13(4), 24–29.

Trute, B., Adkins, E., & MacDonald, G. (1994). *Coordinating child sexual abuse services in rural communities.* Toronto: University of Toronto Press.

York, G. Y. (1989). Strategies for managing religious-based denial of rural clients. *Human Services in the Rural Environment,* 13(2), 16–22.

Chapter Five

THE EFFECTS OF A TIME-LIMITED GROUP WITH PRE-ADOLESCENT GIRLS WHO HAVE BEEN SEXUALLY ABUSED

Susan van Yzendoorn and Keith Brownlee

This chapter examines sexual abuse treatment groups, in particular the extent to which attending a group will result in increased self-esteem and positive changes in the behaviour of the girls. A particular feature of the group under study is its location in a northern-based agency. One characteristic of smaller northern towns is that the lower population density results in fewer clients of a similar kind and age group, who at a given point in time are suitable for group participation. In one response to this, a wider range of ages was included in the group. The question that emerged was whether the group would continue to have value for the participants.

Sexual abuse of children has been acknowledged as a widespread problem of alarming proportions (Finkelhor, 1986b). Considerable research has emerged on the effects of sexual abuse upon children,[1] and much work has been done on developing appropriate treatment programs (Health and Welfare Canada, 1989). Treatment approaches have included family, group, and individual therapy, with many authors arguing that group work is particularly effective with this client group,[2] perhaps even the treatment of choice (Steward et al., 1986). Recent work has supported this position, suggesting that individual therapy is not sufficient and that group work may be needed in addition to individual work (DeLuca et al., 1992). However, relatively little attention has been directed to the effects of treatment (Thomlison, 1988). As with other therapeutic approaches, few empirical studies have been conducted on the effects of group treatment (De Luca et al., 1992). This chapter contributes to the research literature on the effects of group work with child victims of sexual abuse and, specifically, the effects of a group in a northern-based agency where age ranges of the participants were extended to accommodate additional participants.

As stated in previous chapters, abuse has been identified with a wide range of negative behaviour changes,[3] including: increased anxiety,[4] withdrawal,[5] somatic complaints,[6] school problems,[7] delinquency/acting out and behaviour disorders.[8] There is also considerable evidence that lowered self-esteem is an important effect of sexual abuse.[9] Further, low self-esteem, combined with feelings of being damaged, sometimes undermines the victim's self-confidence (Sgroi, 1982).

The value of group work is largely regarded as arising from its effect on increasing personal empowerment. It can also be useful in reducing isolation, pain, and guilt by allowing children to share their experiences with others who have been similarly traumatized (Blick & Porter, 1982; Lubell & Soong, 1982) and through helping others in the group (Bhatti et al., 1989). With group participation, victims begin to realize that others in the group are worthwhile, decent individuals who, like themselves, have been emotionally and physically coerced into a non-consenting relationship by adults (Thomlison, 1988). Further, group work facilitates a major aspect of recovery from sexual abuse, in particular resolving feelings of difference or stigmatization that can be worked through with peers who have experienced similar circumstances and concerns (Berliner et al., 1984). For such children, it is often a revelation to learn that their outward appearance does not reveal their history of sexual abuse; this hidden fear is often alleviated when they meet peers who have also experienced abuse. Halliday (1985) notes that "talking to someone who has been in the same situation makes the victims more at ease and less afraid of judgement" (p. 54). This helps children to develop increased self-esteem and a general acceptance of themselves (Bagley et al., 1990).

The available research on group work has attested to its effectiveness. Burke et al. (1987) reported that short-term group intervention resulted in the resolution of anxiety and depression in sexually abused girls (cited by Thomlison, 1988). Brief cognitive behavioural group treatment for sexually abused children has been found to be effective in reducing internalizing adjustment problems (Hoier et al., 1987). Group treatment has been reported as leading to improved emotional functioning, as well as an overall improved situation of victims (Thomlison, 1988).

DESIGN

This research was conducted within the normal mandate of a children's mental health agency in northwestern Ontario. The specific criteria for inclusion of participants in the group was set by therapeutic need and not research requirements, and for this reason a control group was not available for comparison. Consent to participate in the study was obtained from both the parents of the children and the children themselves. Since group therapy was part of the services ordinarily provided to the participating clients, this study is primarily an evaluation of the therapeutic effects of the group. This was done by obtaining measures of self-esteem and behaviour both before and after the sexual abuse treatment group took place.

To assess outcome, the Piers-Harris Self-Concept Scale (Piers, 1984) and the Achenbach Child Behaviour Checklist were used as measures of self-esteem and behaviour. The Piers-Harris Self-Concept Scale has been described as useful for clinical application with children aged nine to twelve because of its high reliability and validity (Hughes, 1984). This scale provides a measure of six aspects of the child's self-esteem including: behaviour; intellectual and school status; physical appearance and attributes; anxiety; popularity; and happiness and satisfaction. The Child Behaviour Checklist (CBCL) was developed as a descriptive rating instrument to assess both adaptive competencies and behaviour problems (Achenbach, 1991). It is appropriate for children from the ages of four to eighteen years (Keyser et al., 1983) and can be filled out by most parents or caregivers who have at least fifth grade reading skills (Achenbach, 1991). The CBCL provides a measure of withdrawal, somatic complaints, anxiety/depression, social problems, thought problems, attention problems, delinquent behaviour, aggressive behaviour, and other problems. A total Behaviour Problem Score can be calculated as can two broad factor scores described as externalizing and internalizing behaviours. The Child Behaviour Checklist has been reported as reliable (Achenbach et al., 1978) and valid (Achenbach, 1991).

Participants

The participants for this study were five (N = 5) sexually abused girls who ranged in age from nine to thirteen years old (mean age = eleven). This age range is not necessarily ideal for a group of this sort, but is probably typical given the difficulties that occur in smaller agencies with fewer clients of similar age for participation at the time the group is held. The study participants had received some form of individual counselling to deal with the effects of sexual abuse prior to participating in the group. Information regarding the type and length of abuse was not made available to the researcher.

Criteria

The agency determined the criteria for participation in the group. The decision for inclusion was not based upon the research but on the clinical needs of the client. To be eligible for this group the agency determined that the child must be a female between nine and thirteen years of age; have a diagnosis of sexual abuse that has been acknowledged with an investigation either completed or near completion; be referred by the social worker after individual therapy has been completed; be identified by a social worker, teacher, or parent as appropriate for group intervention; agree to participate in the group; be willing and able to interact with others; not be disruptive, acting out or overly aggressive; not be developmentally delayed such that she would not be able to join in activities. The rationale for the criteria was based on the assumption that groups are most effective when there is a common purpose and group needs are similar (Zastrow, 1993).

The Group

The group was comprised of six two-hour sessions over a period of six weeks. Two qualified social workers acted as facilitators for the group. During the first session, participants were introduced to the objectives of the group and were asked to contribute to the development of rules for conducting the group. Time was also taken for the girls to get to know one another and the group leaders. It was decided that the purpose of the group was to introduce respect for boundaries, to offer an opportunity for exercising a sense of power and control, and to establish a safe environment for addressing issues related to sexual abuse. The participation of the girls in establishing clear rules for behaviour in the group and rules for how to respond to transgressions was considered an important first step in developing boundaries.

In the second session, the girls discussed the definition of sexual abuse. The girls were presented with descriptions of situations that could represent sexual abuse and were encouraged to discuss whether they thought the situation represented abuse and why. Examples such as the following were used: If your brother walks into your room without knocking and sees you undressed, is that sexual abuse? If your babysitter kisses you on the lips when he tucks you into bed, is that sexual abuse? The girls also had an opportunity to watch and discuss a video about experiences after sexual abuse called "Good things can still happen." The girls were encouraged to draw upon their own experiences and feelings in discussing their views. They also had a chance to develop a folder and keep a journal of thoughts and experiences important to them. Session three was devoted to recounting their own experiences and eventually to consider sharing one positive and one negative thing about what had happened to them.

During session four of the girls were encouraged to write a letter to the offender or to journal or draw experiences related to the abuse. As an example, the girls were encouraged to draw their family before and after the abuse and to draw pictures of what they would like to see happen to the abuser. At the end of the exercise, the girls discussed with the group their feelings of having done the exercise. Finally, the girls engaged in fun exercises to achieve a more positive closure.

Session five was devoted to a discussion of self-esteem and ways that they can take pride in themselves. Exercises were included to direct the girls' attention to positive qualities about themselves such as naming qualities about friends they liked, and then considering qualities about themselves they liked. The girls then discussed why it is easy to notice positive qualities in others and so difficult to recognize these in themselves.

Session six was devoted to a consideration of personal safety. The girls were encouraged to develop their own personal safety kit and to highlight unsafe situations for themselves. Handouts on personal safety were also included and discussed. Finally, closure included a review of what had been learned and a small celebration party.

Results

Two broad questions were explored in this study: Would participation in a time-limited sexual abuse group for girls contribute to improved self-esteem? And would it be associated with a change in the behaviour of the girls?

Results from the Piers-Harris Children's Self-Concept Scale

All of the five group members completed the Piers-Harris Children's Self-Concept Scales before and after the group, whereas only four girls completed the Child Behaviour Checklists after the group. The Piers-Harris Children's Self-Concept Scale was examined in terms of the total score yielded by this measure as well as by the separate six factors scores of the scale. For total scores and factor scores an increase in the score would be associated with a positive change.

Table 1 summarizes the results, displaying the accumulated scores of the five participants pre-test, post-test from the total score, the six factors, and the differences between them.

Table 1 shows that the girls reported an increase in self-concept at the end of the group when compared to their ratings at the beginning of the group. Two of the factor scales, Anxiety and Popularity, showed a particularly marked positive change at the end of the group. The Happiness and Satisfaction factors, while not as marked, also reflected a strong positive change. These scores indicate that on the Piers-Harris Scale, the girls reported positive changes in the post-test scores of self-esteem, especially related to anxiety, popularity, and happiness and satisfaction. An issue related to positive change on the Piers-Harris scale is the initial level of self-concept reflected by the girls. The normal range for scores on the Piers-Harris scale is between 40 and 50 points; scores above 50 reflect high self-esteem and below 40 reflect low self-esteem (Piers, 1984). Individual total scores on the Piers-Harris scale for each subject is shown in Table 2. It can be seen from

Table 1

PRE-TEST/POST-TEST COMPARISON OF THE PIERS-HARRIS SELF-CONCEPT SCALE

Piers-Harris Self-Concept Scale

Factors	Pre-test	Post-test	Difference
Behaviour	254	283	29
Intellectual and school status	273	309	36
Physical appearance	229	277	48
Anxiety	200	261	61
Popularity	208	240	32
Happiness/satisfaction	211	274	63
Total Behaviour Problem Score	**245**	**304**	**59**

Table 2 that two of the girls began the group with high self-esteem, two began within the low average range of self-esteem, and only one revealed a low level of self-esteem at the outset. It is interesting to note that the greatest gain in self-esteem was recorded by the participant who began with the lowest level of self-esteem at the beginning of the groups. Two other participants moved from an above-normal range at pre-test, with T-scores of 60 and 62, to post-test scores of 67 and 70. These children rated themselves as having higher than normal levels of self-esteem before the group intervention and even higher levels after the group. These results suggest that the group was helpful in raising overall self-esteem despite the level of self-esteem at the outset.

The individual factors, naturally, showed a similar pattern of improvement. In some cases the change could be described as clinically significant, such as the factor of "anxiety" where some of the girls began with scores in the lower range and had moved to the normal to above-normal range after the group. This pattern of moving from the below-normal range to at least a normal range held for the factors Popularity, and Happiness and Satisfaction. In only one instance was a negative change reflected. A decrease of 10 points for the factor of Intellectual and School Status was recorded for one participant, whereas all other participants showed an increase. Although this was a sizeable decrease, the change was from above the normal zone to within the normal zone.

Table 2

TOTAL SCORES OF PIERS-HARRIS SELF-CONCEPT SCALE FOR EACH PARTICIPANT

Subject	Pre-test total scores	Post-test total scores	Difference
1	42	45	3
2	39	68	29
3	62	70	8
4	43	54	11
5	60	67	7

Results for the Child Behaviour Checklist

The Child Behaviour Checklist was examined in terms of total scores yielded by this measure as well as eight separate factors and two broad factor scores given as internalizing and externalizing behaviour problems. On the Child Behaviour Checklist a lower score would reflect a positive change. Table 3 summarizes the results, displaying the accumulated scores of the four participants' pre-test and post-test scores (one post-test was missing) from the total score and factors.

The results are discussed in terms of two levels of analysis. The first level of analysis is the size or amount of the change and the second is the clinical significance of the change based on the standardization or the normal range associated with the Child Behaviour Checklist.

As can be seen in Table 3, none of the changes in the individual factors or total scores after the treatment were found to be very marked. The small differences in scores would probably be typical of the normal variation in ratings on any two separate instances of a parent completing the Child Behaviour Checklist. It is interesting to note that the ratings reflect mostly a decrease in behaviour at the post-test period; only three out of the twelve factors emerged with an increased score. The increased scores, which would reflect greater problems in those areas, were also very small. These results would suggest that taken as a group, the parents did not notice any immediate differences in the behaviour of the girls; however, if there were any noticeable differences, they tended to be in a positive direction.

Table 3

CHILD BEHAVIOUR CHECKLIST TOTAL SCORES AND FACTORS

Variables	Pre-test	Post-test	Differences
Withdrawn	269	271	+2
Somatic complaints	266	251	−15
Anxious and depressed	280	256	−24
Social problems	275	282	+7
Thought problems	242	241	−1
Attention problems	262	259	−3
Delinquent behaviour	228	214	−14
Aggressive behaviour	243	234	−9
Internalizing behaviours	284	265	−19
Externalizing behaviours	243	237	−6
Total Behaviour Problem Score	**271**	**264**	

On the Child Behaviour Checklist, scores greater than the 95th percentile were regarded as clinically significant. This level applied to all the factors of the scale and the total behaviour problems scale. The latter scale provides a summary of general changes in behaviours and is naturally sensitive to changes on the factor scores.

Table 4 shows that three of the participants were rated as showing significant levels of behaviour problems on the total behaviour problems scale at the pre-test stage. Three of the four girls also revealed significant elevations on a number of the factors including the general factors of internalizing and externalizing behaviours. The participants had already been involved with individual therapy. As the significant elevations were at the pre-test stage, it suggests that the girls continued to experience behavioural problems even though they had received individual therapy. It would also suggest that a referral to a group was appropriate and likely to have positive benefits for the girls.

At the post-test stage one of the girls was rated by her parent as revealing increased levels of behaviour problems. The other three girls reflected decreases

Table 4

RAW DATA FOR THE TOTAL SCORES FOR THE CHILD BEHAVIOUR CHECKLIST

Subject	Pre-test total scores	Post-test total scores	Differences
1	70*	62	−8
2	55	65	+10
3	78*	76*	−2
4	68*	61	−7

* Clinically significant elevations

in behaviour problems, with some scales moving from significant to non-significant behaviour problems. However, overall the variations were small and with no clear pattern of changes in scores.

DISCUSSION

The hypothesis that participation in the treatment group would be associated with improved self-esteem was supported by the girls' self-reported changes; however, the hypothesis that participation in the group would be associated with improved behaviour was not supported by the parents' ratings of the girls' behaviour.

At post-test, all of the children attained higher total scores on the PHSCS indicating an increase in self-esteem after attending the sexual abuse group. The overall changes in self-esteem as measured by the Piers-Harris Children's Self-Concept Scale were positive despite the level of self-esteem at the start. The results of the total self-esteem scores showed that only one of the five participants had a pre-test total score below the normal range. All other participants were either in the normal range or above the normal range in the pre-test, indicating that they did not have a low self-esteem prior to the sexual abuse group. With respect to the more specific factors of the Piers-Harris scale, positive changes after the group were also noted for Anxiety and Popularity. Thus, the girls had a more positive view of themselves with a greater sense of popularity and less anxiety at the end of the group. These changes appear to show meaningful clinical changes suggesting that the sexual abuse group had a positive effect on the self-concept of the girls. These findings support the study by Burke et al. (1987 cited in Thomlison, 1988), which suggests that a short-term group intervention can lead to a reduction of anxiety.

For the Child Behaviour Checklist, none of the differences in scores of the individual variables or total scores were found to be meaningful. Some decreases in total scores emerged, but they were not sufficiently extensive to appear to be more than random scoring variations on the scale. This would suggest that no noticeable change in the behaviour of the children took place, according to the parents of the participants. While there was an increase in self-esteem, the absence of meaningful behaviour change may be accounted for by the lack of sufficient time for the behaviour to develop, or for it to have been sufficiently noticed by the parents. However, the relatively high levels of self-esteem reported by the girls may suggest that an increase in an already adequate self-esteem may make little difference to behaviour.

The results of this study do not compare favourably with other research findings given that the results showed that only one of the four participants had pre-test self-esteem scores lower than the clinical significant range. Previous studies have found the self-esteem of sexually abused girls to be low.[10] One possible explanation for this difference is that all of the participants in the present study had received individual counselling prior to participating in the group treatment. The issue of self-esteem may have been a focus for some of the girls in their individual treatment and this may have led to higher scores being reflected. Results from previous research on changes to self-esteem following participation in a sexual abuse group have proven to be inconclusive. In one study, self-esteem was reported to increase (Deluca et al., 1991) while in another study, little overall change in self-esteem was reported after the sexual abuse group (Hiebert-Murphy et al., 1992). The present study provides some support for the conclusion that attending the sexual abuse group leads to an increase in self-esteem. This finding must be seen as tentative given the limited sample size and wider age composition of the present group.

The results for the Child Behaviour Checklist indicate that the parents did not report a significant change in the behaviour of the children after the sexual abuse group. This finding is in contrast to results indicating that group treatment leads to a decrease in problem behaviours reported by parents (Deluca et al., 1991). Such findings raise questions about the extent to which parental reports of child behaviour can be used as an important measure to assess therapeutic change for girls (Hiebert-Murphy et al., 1992). Although parents' reports are potentially useful, they are not completely reliable (Hiebert-Murphy et al., 1992). An additional problem with collecting parent report data from a population such as this one is the possibility of unstable home environments, which would make it difficult for a caregiver to fill out parent rating scales (Hiebert-Murphy et al., 1992). It is also difficult to maintain parent motivation to complete the measure (Hiebert-Murphy et al., 1992). In this study, one of the parents did not complete the post-test and one of the parents returned the post-test late. One other limitation to the parent reports is that they may be difficult to understand (Hiebert-Murphy et al., 1992). Parents who spend a great deal of time with their children may be able to determine if a change in behaviour has taken place, whereas parents who are not able to spend much time with their children may not be able to do the same. In this particular study there was no way of knowing the amount of time that the parent spent with the child, and therefore no way of assessing the parents' ability to rate their child's behaviour.

One of the major limitations of the present study was the very small number of participants. This limitation severely restricts the generalizability of the study. Further, the role of individual counselling upon the girls and their ability to participate in the group treatment would be unknown, as well as its effects on the behaviour and self-esteem of the girls. Another limitation was the lack of a control group. The one group pre-test, post-test design poses some difficulties in evaluating the study. Two potential difficulties found in this type of design are maturation and history (Singleton et al., 1993). The longer the period is between pre-test and post-test, the greater likelihood that either of these threats will confound the results. In this study the time factor played an important role in two ways. There were only six weeks between the pre-test and the post-test, which may not have been enough time for parents to notice any change in their child's behaviour. They may have rated their child's behaviour on how they had been previously and not necessarily specifically noticed changes that have occurred within the last six weeks.

CONCLUSION

While a great deal of research has been done on the effects of sexual abuse, there is a gap in the area of empirical research on the effectiveness of different types of treatment. In this study, the effects of group treatment upon the levels of self-esteem and behaviour of sexually abused girls were investigated. The authors report findings from a one-group, pre-test/post-test design using a convenience sample to investigate the effects of group treatment upon sexually abused girls between the age of nine and thirteen years. The results of this chapter conclude that participants noted an increase in their self-esteem, but that no behavioural changes were noted. The implications of these findings for practitioners in smaller northern towns are important. The chapter points to the potential value of group treatment even when a wider spread of ages is necessary. The problems that present themselves for the practitioner in a smaller town should not be minimized. Often, there simply are not enough participants for a treatment group. It should also be noted that the issue of suitability for a group is important as it is frequently the experience of remote practitioners to include unsuitable participants in order to increase the group's size. These results, while limited, do add some support for the position that in a smaller community where participants are fewer and age matching is less feasible, there is still value to be gained by running groups for sexually abused girls.

NOTES

1. Alter-Reid et al. (1986); Beitchman et al. (1990); Finkelhor (1986a); McEvoy (1990); McGuire et al. (1991); Sgroi (1982).
2. Berliner et al. (1984); Carozza et al. (1982); Giarretto (1982).
3. Browne et al. (1986); Sauzier et al. (1990).
4. Adams-Tucker (1984); MacVicar (1979); Peters (1976).
5. Adams-Tucker (1982); Peters (1976).
6. Lewis et al. (1969); Peters (1976).
7. Lewis et al. (1969); MacVicar (1979).
8. Adams-Tucker (1982); Lewis et al. (1969); MacVicar (1979).
9. Bhatti et al. (1989); Briere (1984); Herman (1982); McEvoy (1990); Smelser (1989); Sgroi (1982); Tong et al. (1987).
10. Peters (1976); Mannarino et al. (1986); McEvoy (1990); Sgroi (1982); Tong et al. (1987).

REFERENCES

Achenbach, T. M. (1991). *Manual for the child behaviour Checklist/4-18 and 1991 profile.* Burlington: University of Vermont Department of Psychiatry.

Achenbach, T. M. & Edelbrock, C. S. (1978). The classification of child psychopathology: A review and analysis of empirical efforts. *Psychological Bulletin,* 85, 1275–1301.

Adams-Tucker, C. (1982). Proximate effects of sexual abuse in childhood: A report on 28 children. *American Journal of Psychiatry,* 139, 1252–1256.

Adams-Tucker, C. (1984). The unmet psychiatric needs of sexually abused youth: Referrals from a child protection agency and clinical evaluations. *Journal of the American Academy of Child Psychiatry,* 23, 659–667.

Alter-Reid, K., Gibbs, N., Lachenmeyer, J., Massoth, M., & Sigal, M. (1986). Sexual abuse of children: A review of the empirical findings. *Clinical Psychology Review,* 6, 249–266.

Bagley, C. & King K. (1990). *Child abuse: The search for healing.* London: Tavistock/Rouledge.

Beitchman, J., Hood, J., Zucker, K., DaCosta, G., & Akman, G. (1990). *The short and long term effects of child sexual abuse on the child*. National clearing house on family violence. Ottawa: Health and Welfare.

Berliner, L. & Ernst, E. (1984). Group work with preadolescent sexual assault victims. In I. R. Stuart & J. G. Green (eds.), *Victims of sexual aggression: Treatment of children women and men*, pp. 105–124. New York: Van Nostrand Reinhold.

Bhatti, B., Derezotes, D., Seung-Ock, K., & Spect, H. (1989). The association between child maltreatment and self-esteem. In A. Mecca, N. J. Smelser, & J. Vasconcellos (eds), *The social importance of self-esteem*. Berkeley: University of California Press.

Blick, L. C. & Porter, F. S. (1982). Group therapy with female adolescent incest victims. In S. M. Sgroi (ed.), *Handbook of clinical intervention in child sexual abuse*, pp. 1147–1175. Lexington: Lexington Books.

Briere, J. (1984). The long-term effects of childhood sexual abuse: Defining a post-sexual-abuse syndrome. Paper presented at the third National Conference on Sexual Victimization of children, Washington, D.C.

Browne, A. & Finkelor, D. (1986). Impacts of child sexual abuse: A review of research. *Psychological Bulletin*, 99(1), 66–77.

Burke, M. M., Townsley, R., Messner, S., & Jackson, J. (1987). Short-term group therapy for sexually abused girls. Unpublished manuscript. Department of Psychology, University of Georgia, Athens, GA. Cited by Thomlison, R. J. (1988). *A review of child sexual abuse treatment outcome research*. Ottawa: National Clearing House on Family Violence.

Carozza, P. M. & Heirsteiner, C. L. (1982). Young female incest victims in treatment: Stages of growth seen with a group art therapy model. *Clinical Social Work Journal*, 10, 165–175.

DeLuca, R., Hazen, A. & Cutler, J. (1991). Effects of group therapy for preadolescent female victims of intrafamiliar sexual abuse. Unpublished manuscript, Department of Psychology, University of Manitoba, Winnipeg, Manitoba, Canada.

DeLuca, R., Hiebert-Murphy, D., & Runtz, M. (1992). Group treatment for sexually abused girls: Evaluating outcome. *Families in Society*, 73, 205–213.

Finkelhor, D. (1986a). *Sourcebook on child sexual abuse*. Newbury Park: Sage.

Finkelhor, D. (1986b). How widespread is child sexual abuse? In D. C. Haden (ed.), *Out of harm's way: Readings on child sexual abuse, its prevention and treatment*. Phoenix: Oryx Press.

Giarretto, H. (1982). A comprehensive sexual abuse treatment program. *Child Abuse and Neglect*, 6, 263–278.

Halliday, L. (1985). *The silent scream: The sexual abuse of children*. Toronto: University of Toronto Press.

Health and Welfare Canada. (1989). *Family violence: A review of theoretical and clinical literature*. Ottawa: Health and Welfare Canada.

Herman, J. (1982). *Father–daughter incest*. Cambridge: Harvard University Press.

Hiebert-Murphy, D., Delcua, R., & Runtz, M. (1992). Group treatment for sexually abused girls: Evaluating outcome. *Families in Society*, 73, 203–213.

Hoier, T. S., Smith, G., Shawchuck, C., & Freeman, T. (1987). Behavioral group treatment of sexually abused children: A pilot study. Paper presented at the meeting of the Association for the Advancement of Behaviour Therapy, Boston, MA.

Hughes, H. (1984). Measures of self-concept and self-esteem for children ages 3–12 years: A review and recommendations. *Clinical Psychology Review*, 4, 657–692.

Keyser, D. J. & Sweetland, R. C. (eds.). (1983). *Tests: A comprehensive reference for assessments in psychology, education and business*, 3rd edn. New York: Library of Congress in Publication Data.

Lewis, M. & Sarrel, P. M. (1969). Some psychological aspects of seduction, incest, and rape in childhood. *Journal of the American Academy of Child Psychiatry*, 8, 606–619.

Lubell, D. & Soong, W. (1982). Group therapy with sexually abused adolescents. *Canadian Journal of Psychiatry*, 27, 311–315.

MacVicar, K. (1979). Psychotherapeutic issues in the treatment of sexually abused girls. *Journal of the American Academy of Child Psychiatry*, 19, 342–353.

Mannarino, A. & Cohen, J. (1986). A clinical-demographic of sexually abused children. *Child Abuse & Neglect*, 10, 17–23.

McEvoy, M. (1990). *Let the healing begin: Breaking the cycle of child sexual abuse in our communities*. Merritt: Nicola Valley Institute of Technology.

McGuire, T. L. & Grant, F. E. (1991). *Understanding child sexual abuse*. Toronto: Butterworths Canada.

Peters, J. J. (1976). Children who were victims of sexual assault and the psychology of offenders. *American Journal of Psychotherapy*, 30, 398–421.

Piers, E. V. (1984). *Piers-Harris children's self-concept scale: Revised manual 1984*. Los Angeles: Western Psychological Services.

Sauzier, M., Salt, P., & Calhoun, R. (1990). The effects of sexual abuse. In B. Gomes-Schwartz, J.M. Horowitz, & A. P. Cardarelli (eds.), *Child sexual abuse: The initial effects*, pp. 75–108. Newbury Park: Sage.

Sgroi, S. M. (1982). *Handbook of clinical intervention in child sexual abuse*. Lexington: Lexington Books.

Singleton, R. A., Straits, B. C., & Miller-Straits, M. (1993). *Approaches to social science research*, 2nd edn. New York: Oxford University Press.

Smelser, N. (1989). Self-esteem and social problems: An introduction. In A. M. Mecca, N. J. Smelser, & J. Vasconcellos (eds.), *The social importance of self-esteem*, pp. 1–23. Los Angeles: University of California Press.

Steward, M. S., Farquahar, L. C., Dicharry, D. C., Glick D. R., & Martin, P. W. (1986). Group therapy: A treatment choice for young victims of child sexual abuse. *International Journal of Group Psychotherapy*, 36, 261–277.

Thomlison, R. J. (1988). *A review of child sexual abuse treatment outcome research*. Ottawa: National Clearing House on Family Violence.

Tong, L., Oates, K., & McDowell, M. (1987). Personality development following sexual abuse. *Child Abuse & Neglect*, 11, 371–383.

Zastrow, C. (1993). *Social work with groups*, 3rd edn. Chicago: Nelson-Hall.

Chapter Six

CONNECTING VIOLENCE AND CHEMICAL DEPENDENCY WITH FEMALE ADDICTS

Teresa Legowski

This chapter discusses pertinent statistical information, theories, and models that connect substance abuse and trauma, as well as the implications for treatment in a northern context. Trauma takes many forms. For women, trauma generally takes the form of physical and sexual abuse, domestic violence, and sexual assault. There is often a high occurrence of violent and abusive incidents over the span of a woman's life. Her ability to overcome the severely debilitating effects of this trauma depends for the most part on the woman's stage of developmental and chronological age when the trauma occurred, as well as her coping skills, mental health, personal resilience, and support network. The research in this field indicates that there is a statistically significant association between trauma and substance abuse in women. The level of violence in the lives of women with chemical dependency is extremely disturbing This chapter suggests that dual treatment for trauma and substance abuse should potentially be the norm, rather than the exception, in the treatment of women suffering from trauma.

LITERATURE REVIEW

An Australian survey by Swift et al. (1996) indicates that 83 per cent of the women in substance abuse treatment were experiencing ongoing domestic violence that had lasted an average of thirty-six months. Thirty-five per cent had been sexually assaulted, while 38 per cent had been physically assaulted as adults. Teets (1997) reported that 73 per cent of women studied in a treatment centre over a two-year period indicated that they had been raped. Gil-Rivas et al. (1997) state that from their sample of women in twenty-six California treatment centres, approximately 50 per cent (compared to 33 per cent in the general population) reported physical and sexual abuse.

In a qualitative study of a perinatal program for individuals addicted to crack cocaine, 75 per cent of the women (n = 19) reported that they were victims of trauma (Pursley-Crotteau et al., 1996). The authors described these circumstance as "captivity," which created "the potential for coercive control" (p. 357). They stated the women in their sample used cocaine to medicate themselves from the pain of their past and current traumatic lifestyle.

Reports on violent incidents in Stevens et al.'s (1995) description of the Amity program in Arizona (n = 61 women), indicated 95 per cent of them had been raped and assaulted as adults. As children, their first assault occurred at the mean age of thirteen years for 90 per cent of the women. These women's first incident of alcohol use occurred at a mean age of 13.7 years. At the mean age of fourteen years, 95 per cent of these women reported experiencing their first rape. Their first drug use occurred at the mean age of 14.3 years. The authors go on to state "it is apparent that even at the initiation phase of alcohol and other drug use, violence and drug use go hand in hand" (p. 55). It seems that in this particular sample, the violence preceded drug and alcohol use, and could have been fundamental to continued substance abuse. Boyd (1993) supports this connection by stating that sexual trauma and sexual abuse may be etiological to substance abuse in women.

A poignant, qualitative study by Woodhouse (1992) concluded that the most "glaring" theme in the lives of women with addiction was violence and abuse. The study found that about half of the women had been raped and sexually abused prior to becoming substance abusers, using the substance to medicate the emotional pain. Woodhouse (1992) points out that "isolation, dependency and male dominance issues [are] all conditions associated with violence [and] are the most striking aspects of the lives of these women" (p. 273).

The use of drugs and alcohol to numb emotional pain is also reiterated by Hagan et al. (1994) in their discussion of impediments to effective treatment for women. They state that substance abuse is often a normal reaction to bizarre and horrendous situations. In their clinical sample of opioid-dependent women in Philadelphia, 75 per cent reported that they had been sexually abused before the age of sixteen. The authors also surmise that the experiences of sexual and physical abuse likely lead to their drug abuse.

A rare sample from a study using an Aboriginal tribe from the American southwest revealed that of the women seeking substance abuse treatment, 65 per cent reported childhood sexual abuse, compared to 26 per cent of the men (Robin et al., 1997). In a study of violence in the lives of homeless mothers (n = 84), North et al. (1996) found that 91 per cent met the criteria for a drug use disorder. Lifetime victimization (both as a child and an adult) was experienced by 83.8 per cent of the women; 60.3 per cent had experienced either physical or sexual abuse during childhood; and 51 per cent experienced abuse by partners as adults. These women were also perpetrators of violence. Some reported participating in murders, stabbing partners and others, and shooting family members. Almost half (47.6 per cent) reported child neglect. North et al. (1996) speculated that these women abuse substances to relieve the misery of their lives. They strongly advocate that treatment initiate the long-term provision of a safe environment for the women and their children, as well as the usual features of an integrated and comprehensive program for women.

An extensive survey of 1099 women in the United States concluded that a history of childhood sexual abuse was most strongly related to illicit drug use. The survey revealed that 34.9 per cent of women who had experienced this trauma used drugs illicitly compared to 13.5 per cent of the general population of women (Wilsnack et al., 1997). The authors state that "cross sectional analyses of this large and representative non-clinical sample reveal strong associations between childhood sexual abuse history and women's alcohol and illicit drug use" (p. 269). Childhood sexual abuse was also significantly associated with at least one episode of clinically significant depression.

Likely the range of statistical information represented in these articles stems from the researcher's definitions of physical and sexual abuse, rape, and violence. Additionally, culturally diverse populations of women were located in a variety of geographical locations, most of them in clinical settings. Finally, the timing and wording of the questions posed to the research participants may also have led to differing results. These variables could also have contributed to the differences in results.

Sexual abuse increases the potential of substance abuse in a woman's lifetime by three to four times (El-Guebaly, 1995). El-Guebaly also reported that 60 per cent of women who drank reported more aggressive sexual attention from male drinking companions. Thus it seems that "society sanctions violence against people deemed to be unacceptable" (Addiction Research Foundation, 1996, p. 32).

Some authors do propose that addiction is likely related to post-traumatic stress disorder and that survivors of abuse are likely to be at risk for developing a chemical dependency (Evans et al., 1995). Wilsnack et al. (1997) theorize that immediate and delayed responses to trauma cause alcohol and drug abuse. Immediate responses include anxiety, helplessness, and a decreased ability to learn effective coping skills. Delayed responses involve mood and anxiety problems, dissociation, and emotional detachment. Drug and alcohol use may be attempts on the woman's part to cope with overwhelming negative states, temporarily blocking memories and feelings, and as an attempt to facilitate sexual functioning that was disrupted by early trauma.

Wilsnack et al. (1997) and Evans et al. (1995) discuss other theories to explain the effects of childhood sexual abuse. They argue that childhood sexual abuse leads to chronic dissociation as a coping mechanism, which results in impaired social and cognitive functioning, and problems with behaviour regulation. In turn, this leads to drug and alcohol misuse as an attempt to alter mood and overcome inabilities to function socially.

Another theory relates the adverse home environment to adult dysfunction. Likely the woman is modelling the dysfunctional behaviour learned at home, including alcohol and drug use. Attachment theory states that childhood sexual abuse disrupts the healthy development of attachments. Rather than possessing a positive self-identity, self-regulation, and appropriate social relations, the woman experiences fearfulness, avoidance, rejection, and disturbances in personality, mood, and behaviour. She uses drugs and alcohol in a relational context to facilitate a sense of connection.

One might assume that when trauma issues, homelessness, and substance abuse issues are resolved, the violence in the lives of these women would decrease. However, North et al. (1996) suggest that violence may be endemic to the environment in which the women live and that it may be a trait characteristic among individuals prone to substance abuse. Woodhouse (1992) states that these methods of coping increase vulnerability and dependence on men in violent, "abuse-oriented" subculture, and increase the risks of raising children who will become chemically dependent. In order to shed these beliefs and behaviours, Woodhouse (1992) states that women need gender-specific support and empowerment in all aspects of treatment.

TREATMENT

Harris (1996) and Evans et al. (1995) propose therapeutic modalities to working with sexual abuse trauma and chemical dependency. They strongly support an integration of substance abuse, mental health, and sexual abuse treatment. Evans et al. (1995) stress a co-ordinated approach that focuses on common issues in the disorders in order to "blend" elements of intervention.

Harris (1996) emphasizes cognitive reframing to deal with internal assumptions and beliefs the women may have. For example, a woman who became drunk with friends may view herself as fun-loving. Harris (1996) replaces this category with viewing herself as abusing alcohol, labelling it as self-destructive and as self-hating. Harris (1996) argues that Skill Modules need to be included in treatment for safety and education about physical and sexual abuse, female identity, sexuality, self-soothing, and parenting, conducted in a gender-specific, structured, group therapy format.

Evans et al. (1995) state that an effective recovery program for both childhood sexual abuse and addiction disorders require abstinence, education, sober support, structured time, skills development, working the twelve-step program, and involvement of supportive family members. They describe safety as the cornerstone of their program. Safety includes no substance use whatsoever, no self-harming behaviour, no harming of others, no contact with dangerous people, and no running or moving. Their treatment program also stresses visiting a physician if need be, and observing a medication regime. The authors have had overwhelming support of the twelve-step paradigm of incorporating the twelve-step concepts and slogans into their program. Recognizing that many women have difficulties with this approach, they even hold pre-twelve step group meetings on their premises to help facilitate further attendance at other meetings by their clients.

Evans et al. (1995) do not have the same reservations many other authors have about mixing women and twelve-step programs. However, in their arguments in favour of the twelve-step approach, they only address the issue of powerlessness. In their discussion about the "paradox" of powerlessness, the authors distinguish between things that can and cannot be changed. For example, willpower has both strengths and limitations. By admitting powerlessness over the uncontrollable, one finds freedom by letting go of control. Oppression is not addressed.

Woodhouse (1990) discusses a life history approach to treatment that highlights collaboration with the participants in a group format. Life history discussions help group participants examine the effects of violence on their lives within gender-specific treatment. Sharing life histories with each other points out the similarities to the women, especially the experience of emotional and psychic pain that has been "bottled up for years," resulting in "fear, anger, self-hate and neglect" (p. 13). The life history method facilitates consciousness-raising.

Finnegan et al. (1996) discuss dual treatment for trauma and alcoholism for lesbians and bisexual women. The added trauma for this population is the exposure to heterosexism and homophobia. Their approach is more cautious. They state that it is very difficult for this population to develop a strong sense of self in recovery. As well, depending on the stages of recovery in relation to her risk of relapse and of her development of a sexual identity, the exploration of sexual and physical abuse has a high potential for causing relapse. The clinician must consider the stability of her life and her support network. It may be prudent to wait before delving into past traumatic issues until the client demonstrates more stability, such as being able to hold a job, maintaining a relationship for a reasonable length of time, and having close and supportive friends. The clinician must also evaluate and plan the woman's treatment to coincide with the development stage of her sexual identity. For example, the clinician may have to focus on exploring external and internal homophobia, rather than attempting to get the woman to an all-women's support group.

A third consideration that Finnegan et al. (1996) mention is that of family history. If the woman's family was actively alcoholic, then the woman may require assistance with the most basic tasks of self-care, such as time and money management, personal hygiene, healthy eating and sleeping habits, dealing with urges and cravings, and protecting herself. A fourth consideration is the woman's use of her defences. One may need to work on establishing safety, and developing healthy ways to self-soothe (rather than compulsive behaviours such as overeating and spending), before exploring traumatic issues.

The final consideration put forth by Finnegan et al. (1996) is an assessment of the extent and strength of the woman's support network. If she has no close friends, does not attend support groups, and has no supportive family, then she is clearly not in a safe place to do trauma work. Finnegan et al. (1996) state that the clinician needs to be mindful of re-traumatizing the lesbian and bisexual woman by opening "Pandora's Box" too soon and too quickly.

Wadsworth et al. (1995) also discuss concerns surrounding trauma memories triggering relapse. They admit there are differing views on whether to force discussion about past trauma before relapse, or whether to allow for a significant period of sobriety before dealing with these issues. As with Finnegan et al. (1996), they stress looking at other stabilizing factors, not just the length of sobriety, including mood states, unsatisfactory relationships, social support networks, feelings of "perceived helplessness," and the re-emergence of traumatic memories. Their approach stems from cognitive-behavioural and cathartic frameworks. As with most other authors, they suggest using single gendered group therapy in working with women with childhood sexual abuse, using non-directive techniques (rather than confrontational ones), abstinence from all mood-altering drugs, and making the therapy "client-paced." Wadsworth et al. (1995) conclude that "a relapse may be a signal that the client is preparing to do the emotional work required to heal.... [It] may be indicative of the overwhelming pain experienced by the client in coming to terms with the trauma and not an indication of an unwillingness to abstain from mood altering or harmful behaviour" (p. 405).

The literature discusses comprehensive treatment programming and generally lists the following ancillary components, which are important features in promoting access to treatment: child care, flexible program hours, parenting, dealing with physical and sexual abuse, dealing with emotional issues, a focus on building up self-esteem rather than the traditional confrontational model of "breaking down," living skills, including where possible the use of significant others for support, case management that provides and/or connects women with services of advocacy, housing, psychiatric care, transportation, medical care, income support services, education of the effects of drugs and alcohol on the fetus, and vocational counselling.

By far, the literature uncovers the almost overwhelming nature of the oppression of women with addictions. The research advocates major social change. The optimal approaches to achieve this change seem to be those that are delivered through a non-judgmental, non-pathologizing group format. The literature outlines some of the key considerations in programming for women addicts who have experienced trauma, safety being the most important.

Using the cognitive-behavioural approach provides tools and alternative coping skills to help women change their lifestyles. It focuses on self-image, self-talk, and the role of substances in their lives. It teaches women how to challenge their addictive thinking processes. The literature overwhelmingly supports an integrated approach, which includes cognitive-behavioural therapy (Beck et al., 1993) and involves a group format. Instead of focussing on a single, "correct" intervention, an integrated model moves us toward "... a larger strategy which incorporates a variety of alternative strategies" (Miller et al., 1989, p. 10). This concept is not new and has been termed "informed eclecticism" by Miller et al. (1989). These authors reviewed several models of treatment, including the moral, disease, educational, biomedical, social learning, conditioning, systems, sociocultural, and public health models. Their conclusions are:

1. There is no single superior approach to treatment for all individuals.
2. Different types of individuals respond best to different treatment approaches.
3. It is possible to match individuals to optimal treatments, thereby increasing treatment effectiveness and efficiency (Miller et al., 1989, p. 11).

Gender differences in attitudes, perceptions, and causal factors of addiction lead to the logical conclusion that women require different programming. Since women tend to view substance abuse as influenced by biology, environment, family history, and relationship problems (Kauffman et al., 1997), it would be advisable to use multifaceted and integrated interventions.

The Addiction Research Foundation (1996) advocates an integrated as well as comprehensive program. It promotes a combination of biopsychosocial, cognitive-behavioural, and harm-reduction viewpoints. Advantages of the biopsychosocial approach include the examination of the context in which women find themselves; exploring the context of substance abuse in our society; matching treatment to the client within her present situation. An "integrated" approach seems to be an optimal model to move toward. Such an approach is capable of incorporating useful and appropriate features of different modalities of treatment that best meet the needs of women within one agency.

For women, substance abuse is set in the context of mental health issues, current and past physical and sexual assault, violence, poverty, and oppression. Treating these separately is not advocated by feminist models.[1] However, the expansion necessary for such an integrated approach on the caregivers' and the agencies' parts is dependent on their willingness to broaden their perspectives and attitudes on women's addiction issues, and to alter the organizational structure to support such a change.

Harm reduction respects the woman at whatever stage of change she happens to be. It promotes self-care for the woman. As well, it provides the caregiver with an attitude of empathy and non-judgment. It also promotes a larger framework from which an agency serves the community by supporting a broad and comprehensive mandate that accommodates the delivery of various interventions for people at various stages of change.

From a therapeutic standpoint, the use of a feminist empowerment approach and the stages of change models advocate integration of various therapies in a purposeful manner to establish a feminist approach within a program. Considering the complexity of the context of women's addictions, such an integrated approach is encouraged.

IMPLICATIONS FOR TREATMENT

If a woman is presenting with chemical dependency or substance abuse, then a complete assessment would typically include questions of a trauma history, whether past and/or recent. Additionally, the practitioner needs to address treatment for both the trauma and the substance abuse. Although the woman may be reluctant at first, the practitioner can gently begin making the connections, particularly when the link is made to using drugs and alcohol to numb the emotional and psychic pain of the trauma. A gender-specific group poses a good opportunity for women to develop the sense of safety, to begin disclosing these similar connections to other women while applying the consciousness-raising links to their lives. The literature suggests that single-gendered group therapy is the optimal means with which to work with female addicts, particularly marginalized groups of women.[2]

Another option available is a twelve-step self-help group and twelve-step based program. However, in the last ten years, the twelve-step approach has come under attack due to its perceived predominance for white, middle-aged men. Kasl (1992) argues that the twelve-step model was developed by a white male physician, Bill Wilson. Bill Wilson and his colleagues had what Kasl suggests are typical 1930s' attitudes, including overly inflated egos, the inability to disclose deep feelings to others, and insensitivity to others' emotional pain. By confrontation and shaming, these kinds of male-oriented blocks were overcome. However, some women typically have underdeveloped egos, possess considerable shame and guilt stemming from victimization, and are usually more relationally focused. The confrontational style with them is not likely to be appropriate, as it could be experienced as disrespectful. Kasl (1992) continues to develop a sixteen-step program, which she claims is much more sensitive to women's experiences and needs.

Humphrey et al. (1991) researched 201 self-help group participants in an urban setting and found that women addicts were more likely to attend Alcoholics and Narcotics Anonymous meetings than men. The study quoted that 37.1 per cent of the attendees were women. They also stated that 65.3 per cent were African Americans. "Attenders had significantly worse psychological ..., family/social ... and substance abuse ... problems" (Humphrey et al., 1991, p. 593). The results suggest that self-help groups tend to reflect the socioeconomic and cultural diversity of the communities in which they are located. It also seems to confirm that women tend to attend group counselling more frequently than men. Whether the twelve-step approach was helpful for these women was not discussed.

Another qualitative study suggests that the twelve-step group approach may not necessarily be helpful to women. Saulnier (1996) interviewed a sample of thirteen African American women and found the approach was lacking in the ability to address the activities of this marginalized group of women, since it is based on the notion of powerlessness and individuality, applicable largely to white, middle-aged men. Apparently, research respondents reported that they felt confused, did not feel welcome at twelve-step meetings, and that white people sometimes did not understand what the African American women were saying. The author states that feminist analysis of the twelve-step notion of powerlessness concludes it is a "confinement tactic" meant to degrade and depoliticize women, making their behaviour pathological rather than rooted in the context of larger social, economic, and cultural factors. She states that " ... the twelve-step/addiction philosophy provides a questionable approach for intervention with people who are in need of social justice" (Saulnier, 1996, p. 100). Saulnier found that the women she interviewed had absorbed the highly personal twelve-step language and philosophy. However, their caring for and strong connection to their community and pertinent political issues made them decide to change their community rather than remove themselves from it.

Saulnier (1996) argues that the twelve-step approach does not question inherent male and heterosexual superiority of society, let alone any sexism or heterosexism within the movement. She states that it oversimplifies and stresses individual responsibility to the exclusion of possible collective, political action. Certainly, mutual aid has been a key component to consciousness-raising. Saulnier (1996) concludes that in spite of the twelve-step approach, marginalized women will mingle individual and social transformation, as evidenced by their historical organizing efforts.

Hall (1993) questions whether confrontational interventions really work for marginalized women, since women's experience of addiction is not substantiated by the dominant addiction-treatment culture. Confrontation, therefore, would tend to reflect androcentric standards for these women. The twelve-step format of treatment lacks the structure and the language to adequately address critical consciousness-raising with women addicts, let alone marginalized groups. As well, the literature reveals problems in the areas of inclusion of difference for women in twelve-step programs. A stand-alone twelve-step program may not necessarily be optimal.

However, in combination with other approaches, it might be able to address the broader, contextual issues of violence and oppression in women's lives. An integrated feminist approach, including cognitive-behavioural therapy and the stages of change model, complement each other well, since they emphasize mutuality and the respect of individual needs and perspectives within a supportive organizational structure. If a twelve-step model is unable to fit into such an organizational structure, it is still readily available as a choice to women at the community level.

Single-gendered group therapies have the potential to instil social action on the part of the women who are participating in them through the use of consciousness-raising techniques. Women-only treatment attracts women who may not have considered traditional treatment (Copeland et al., 1992). Studies also found that women in single-gendered groups increased their length of stay in the program. This speaks to the likelihood of a better outcome after completion of treatment.

The advantages of single-gendered groups for women include safety in disclosure surrounding physical and sexual abuse by men, no deference to the tendency of men to dominate both in numbers and in conversation, the ability to relate to other women's commonality of experience, and the facilitation of consciousness-raising without potential interference from insecure males. Affirming Copeland et al.'s (1992) study, Hodgins et al.'s review of research (1997) states that single-gendered groups for women lead to greater engagement and retention in treatment.

Women with addictions come from contextually located experiences and treatment programs need to honour their perceptions, beliefs, and diversity in order to provide effective and respectful services. The structure and attitudes of an organization delivering services can be sources of oppression.[3] Some of the questions a practitioner who is working with female addicts needs to ask are: How does the treatment respect the stage of change the woman is presenting in terms of her addiction and her coping with trauma? Is she ready to change? How is she treated if she is not ready and are staff trained in and applying models of treatment that reflect their support of the woman's stage of change? Adapting consideration of the stages of change into the structure of the program leads to treatment that meets the needs of female addicts with trauma histories, especially if group interaction is provided.

Another therapeutic model that supports single-gendered group work for female addicts is Wald et al.'s (1995) empowerment model. The authors mention sensitivity to the distinctions between urban and rural women in their presentation. They specifically highlight single-gendered group work as being very empowering for female addicts. They use group consciousness-raising strategies developed in the field of popular education, such as webs of causation, group action plans, and problem definition, making the articulation of oppression a central theme. If integrated with cognitive-behavioural therapy to include skill building, the authors suggest that it would serve women addicts very well.

THE NORTHERN CONTEXT

Not only do northern practitioners need to be aware of the limitations of the 12-step approach, they also need to be aware of how the local twelve-step support group is functioning. In most communities, the AA and NA meetings are the only self-help support networks in town. Unfortunately, there are times when people attending these meetings may be still using, which may, in turn, trigger other members to use. At other times, confidentiality may be a serious concern for the female client, since her perpetrator (or the perpetrator's relatives) may be attending meetings. By no means is it advisable to send the client to these meetings under these circumstances. Safety for the traumatized female addict is the most important aspect of her treatment.

Northern practitioners are strongly encouraged to seek out training opportunities that broaden the addictions perspectives they bring to the communities they serve. Specifically, training that promotes an integrated approach such as cognitive-behavioural therapy and the stages of change models would complement the counselling they provide to their female addict clients.

Additionally, a strong understanding of counselling for survivors of physical and sexual abuse is advised. Depending on the services available in the community, the practitioner may have the option of a collaborative arrangement with other service providers who work in the areas of sexual assault, sexual abuse, and domestic violence. Even though the addictions practitioner may not necessarily be delivering trauma counselling, knowledge of these fields, as well as community liaison skills, are highly recommended.

In some communities, there may not be any organized support network available. In this case, addiction practitioners may be in a position to develop a small, confidential support group for their female clients. As an adjunct to counselling, the female client may also consider the following self-help options:

journaling, self-care, supportive family and friends, church, clubs, volunteer activities, workshops, retreats, meditation, visualization, body work, art, pottery, sports, outdoor recreation, exercise, healthy eating, correspondence courses, reading personal development literature, and music lessons. By no means are these the only suggestions. In some communities where counselling may not be available (or only minimally available), these self-help options could be a substitute for counselling for the female client.

Two important aspects of treatment for females who are addicts are both the support and the legitimization of their experiences. The key awareness stems from the recognition that the trauma and the addiction are intertwined in women. Thus, it follows that female addicts will participate in treatment for the long-term. They may initially complete a residential program and not address the trauma. Eventually they may return to this trauma. Continuation of quality treatment on an outpatient basis is the long-term commitment that the northern practitioner makes to the female addict. The optimal quality of treatment is to deal with the addiction and the trauma concurrently, since this supports and validates the woman's experience. There are, however, risks of relapse associated with concurrent treatment, and the practitioner (hopefully with consultation) undoubtedly uses professional judgment to weigh the benefits, assess progress, and determine timing.

CONCLUSION

The literature on trauma suggests there is a significant etiological association between past traumatic events, particularly childhood sexual abuse, ongoing violence, and substance abuse by women. It suggests that promoting safety considerations, along with integrated and comprehensive programming, cognitive-behavioural and group therapy, and abstinence from mood-altering substances, are key considerations for treating women who are and who have experienced trauma.

Some literature on trauma support single-gendered group therapy for female addicts. Through this format, women have the potential to validate their experiences and encounter mutuality and respect. Some cautions and considerations surrounding the timing of trauma work with female addicts are raised. One strategy involves conducting life histories with clients, reflecting the exploration of oppression in their lives. Another approach, the empowerment model, integrates consciousness-raising through the utilization of popular education techniques and group therapy.

Within a non-judgmental, supportive, responsive, and validating treatment environment, women can be helped to gain awareness of their beliefs, feelings, and behaviours and how these are linked to their lifestyles, trauma history, and chemical dependency. This serves to de-pathologize their life circumstances. Thus issues that have the potential for an adverse confrontational effect can be discussed in an environment of support. In a group format, recognition of some of the women's universal experiences gives them the consciousness and the empowerment from which social action can take place.

Feminist treatment needs to be aware of and systematically discuss the oppression of women. In order to help overcome this oppression, feminist treatment programs need to develop community partnerships (Wellisch et al., 1997) and change their own internal structures to support female clients within the context of their experiences.

Oppression appears to be the causal factor in creating and maintaining chemical abuse and dependency among women, as well as a significant factor interfering with services that would help recovery (Goldberg, 1995, p. 790).

The task of social change in this field seems at times both overwhelming and discouraging. However, small and effective approaches using feminist principles do bring positive results into the lives of many women. These effective approaches are the building blocks of social change.

NOTES

1. Alexander (1996); Evans et al. (1995); Finkelstein (1996); Finnegan et al. (1996); Gil-Rivas et al. (1997); Hagan et al. (1994); Harris (1996); Luthar et al. (1995); Markoff et al. (1996); Nelson-Zlupko et al. (1995); North et al. (1996); Pursley-Crotteau et al. (1996); Teets (1997); Wadsworth et al. (1995); Woodhouse (1990, 1992).
2. Copeland et al. (1992); Hodgins et al. (1997); Kauffman et al. (1995); Wald et al. (1995).
3. Corse et al. (1995); Prochaska et al. (1992); Pursley-Crotteau et al. (1996).

REFERENCES

Addiction Research Foundation. (1996). *The hidden majority: A guidebook on alcohol and other drug issues for counsellors who work with women.* Toronto: Addiction Research Foundation.

Alexander, M. (1996). Women with co-occurring addictive and mental disorder: An emerging profile of vulnerability. *American Journal of Orthopsychiatry,* 66(1), 61–70.

Beck, A., Wright, F., Newman, C., & Liese, B. (1993). *Cognitive therapy of substance abuse.* New York: Guilford Press.

Boyd, C. (1993). The antecedents of women's crack cocaine abuse: Family substance abuse, sexual abuse, depression and illicit drug use. *Journal of Substance Abuse Treatment,* 10(5), 433–438.

Copeland, J. & Hall, W. (1992). A comparison of women seeking drug and alcohol treatment in a specialist women's and two traditional mixed-sex treatment services.

British Journal of Addiction, 87(9), 1293–1302.

Corse, S., McHugh, M., & Gordon, S. (1995). Enhancing provider effectiveness in treating pregnant women with addictions. *Journal of Substance Abuse Treatment,* 12(1), 3–12.

El-Guebaly, N. (1995). Alcohol and polysubstance abuse among women. *Canadian Journal of Psychiatry,* 40(2), 73–79.

Evans, K. & Sullivan, J. (1995). *Treating addicted survivors of trauma.* New York: Guilford Press.

Finkelstein, N. (1996). Using the relational model as a context for treating pregnant and parenting chemically dependent women. *Journal of Chemical Dependency Treatment,* 6(2), 23–44.

Finnegan, D. & McNally, E. (1996). Chemically dependent lesbian and bisexual women: Recovery from many traumas. *Journal of Chemical Dependency Treatment,* 6(2), 87–107.

Gil-Rivas, V., Fiorentine, R., Anglin, M., & Taylor, E. (1997). Sexual and physical abuse: Do they compromise drug treatment outcomes? *Journal of Substance Abuse Treatment,* 14(4), 351–358.

Goldberg, M. (1995). Substance abusing women: False stereotypes and real needs. *Social Work,* 40(6), 789–798.

Hagan, T., Finnegan, L., & Nelson-Zlupko, L. (1994). Impediments to comprehensive treatment models for substance dependent women: Treatment and research questions. *Journal of Psychoactive Drugs,* 26(2), 163–171.

Hall, J. (1993). What really worked? A case analysis and discussion of confrontational intervention for substance abuse in marginalized women. *Archives of Psychiatric Nursing,* 7(6), 322–327.

Harris, M. (1996). Treating sexual abuse trauma with dually diagnosed women. *Community Mental Health Journal,* 32(4), 371–385.

Hodgins, D. C., El-Guebaly, N., & Addington, J. (1997). Treatment of substance abusers: Single or mixed gender programs? *Addiction,* 92(7), 805–812.

Humphreys, K., Mavis, B., & Stofflemayr, B. (1991). Factors predicting attendance at self-help groups after substance abuse treatment: Preliminary findings. *Journal of Consulting and Clinical Psychology,* 59(4), 591–593.

Kasl, C. (1992). *Many roads, one journey—Moving beyond the 12 steps.* New York: Harper Perennial.

Kauffman, E., Dore, M., & Nelson-Zlupko, L. (1995). The role of women's therapy groups in treatment of chemical dependence. *American Journal of Orthopsychiatry,* 65(3), 355–363.

Kauffman, S., Sliver, P., & Poulin, J. (1997). Gender differences in attitudes towards alcohol, tobacco and other drugs. *Social Work,* 42(3), 231–241.

Luthar, S. & Walsh, K. (1995). Treatment needs of drug addicted mother: Integrated parenting and psychotherapy interventions. *Journal of Substance Abuse Treatment,* 12(5), 341–348.

Markoff, L. S. & Cawley, P. A. (1996). Retaining your clients and your sanity: Using the relational model of multi-systems case management. *Journal of Chemical Dependency Treatment,* 6(2), 45–65.

Miller, W. R. & Hester, R. K. (1989). Treating alcohol problems: Toward an informed eclecticism. In K. H. Reid and W. R. Miller (eds.), *Handbook of alcoholism treatment approaches*, pp. 3–13. New York: Pergamon Press.

Nelson-Zlupko, L., Kauffman, E., & Dore, M. (1995). Gender differences in drug addiction and treatment: Implications for social work intervention with substance-abusing women. *Social Work*, (40)1, 45–54.

North, C., Thompson, S., & Smith, E. (1996). Violence in the lives of homeless mothers in a substance abuse treatment program: A descriptive study. *Journal of Interpersonal Violence*, 11(2), 234–247.

Prochaska, J. O., DiClemente, C. C., & Norcoss, J. C. (1992). In search of how people change. *American Psychologist*, 47(4), 1102–1114.

Pursley-Crotteau, S. & Stern, P. (1996). Creating a new life: Dimensions of temperance in perinatal cocaine crack users. *Qualitative Health Research*, 6(3), 350–367.

Robin, R., Chester, B., Rasmussen, J., Jaranson, J., & Goldman, D. (1997). Factors influencing utilization of mental health and substance abuse services by American Indian men and women. *Psychiatric Services*, 48(6), 826–832.

Saulnier, C. F. (1996). Images of the twelve-step model, and sex and love addiction in an alcohol intervention group for black women. *Journal of Drug Issues*, 1, 95–123.

Stevens, S. & Arbiter, N. (1995). A therapeutic community for substance abuse in pregnant women and women with children: Process and outcome. *Journal of Psychoactive Drugs*, 27(1), 49–56.

Swift, W., Copeland, J., & Hall, W. (1996). Characteristics of women with alcohol and other drug problems: Findings of an Australian national survey. *Addiction*, 91(8), 1141–1150.

Teets, J. (1997). The incidence and experience of rape among chemically dependent women. *Journal of Psychoactive Drugs*, 29(4), 331–336.

Wadsworth, R., Spampneto, A., & Halbrook, B. (1995). The role of sexual trauma in the treatment of chemically dependent women: Addressing the relapse issue. *Journal of Counselling and Development*, 73(4), 401–406.

Wald, R., Harvey, S. M., & Hibbard, J. (1995). A treatment model for women substance abusers. *The International Journal of the Addictions*, 30(7), 881–888.

Wellisch, J., Perrochet, B., & Anglin, M. (1997). Afterword: Future directions for perinatal alcohol and drug treatment services. *Journal of Psychoactive Drugs*, 29(1), 123–125.

Wilsnack, S., Vogeltanz, N., Klassen, A., & Harris, R. (1997). Childhood sexual abuse and women's substance abuse: National survey findings. *Journal of Studies on Alcohol*, 58(3), 264–271.

Woodhouse, L. (1990). An exploratory study of the use of life history methods to determine treatment needs for female substance abusers. *Response to the Victimization of Women and Children: A Journal of the Centre for Women's Studies*, 13(3), 12–15.

Woodhouse, L. (1992). Women with jagged edges: Voices from a culture of substance abuse. *Qualitative Research*, 2(3), 262–281.

Chapter Seven

CLIENT CONFIDENTIALITY, ANONYMITY, FACILITATOR CREDIBILITY, AND CONTAMINATION IN RURAL FAMILY VIOLENCE SELF-HELP GROUPS

Colleen Ginter

It has been well documented that many women experience partner abuse.[1] One common form of assistance available to battered women is the self-help style group (Romeder, 1990). While there is extensive literature attesting to the effectiveness of self-help groups with other populations,[2] there is little research examining the effectiveness of self-help groups for abused women.[3]

Halpern (1987) describes self-help groups as having "become increasingly recognized as agents for providing significant mental health services. They enable their members to deal with problems such as alcoholism, gambling, obesity, narcotics, drug abuse, and cult affiliation" (p. 47). Self-help support groups can be defined as:

> Voluntary associations of non-professional people whose purpose and therapeutic function is to share common needs or problems and meet together for extended periods of time for the purpose of mutual support and exchange of information about activities and resources that have been found useful in problem solving (Barker, 1991, p. 210).

Freeman et al. (1993) note that such groups can be closed or open; of varying duration and may be led by one or more facilitators, professional or lay; or co-led by a combination of both. Typically, in self-help groups power is centred upon the members rather than a therapist or professional leader, and they function on collaborative rather than hierarchical principles (Marecek et al., 1977). Romeder (1990) adds that a mutual aid in a group includes a common experience shared by group members, free participation, and a willingness on the part of the group members to accept one another as equals (Romeder, 1990). The key therapeutic ingredients of self-help groups have been described as group autonomy, sharing personal resources, and the opportunity to share their personal stories, strengths, and resources in an egalitarian environment (Riordan et al., 1988).

Battering is part of a pattern of coercive tactics, including verbal, psychological, and sexual abuse, that a man uses to intimidate, undermine, and force his female partner to comply with his wishes. The experience can be likened to brainwashing (Woods et al., 1993). The results of living in an abusive relationship, according to writers such as Pence et al. (1987), Hartman (1987), Macleod (1990), and Evans (1992, 1993) are that women become isolated, disempowered, and silenced. There is very limited support systems that would validate the victim's reality, feelings of oppression and inequality, misunderstandings, fears, self-doubt, loss of self-confidence and self-esteem, and questioning of perceptions. Abused women, therefore, need a place to undo and unlearn all the negative changes they have undergone, to learn to share information in an egalitarian environment, to be empowered and supported, while empowering and supporting others. Oppressed women need a vehicle by which they can both break the silence of their abuse and reduce their own isolation.

The philosophical framework of self-help includes a focus on the principle of reciprocity, with women accepted as experts on their own lives. This is in keeping with the belief that with shared information and mutual support, women can empower each other. The self-help tradition is marked by a reduced emphasis on the professional as expert, and a focus on the empowerment of, and sensitivity to, individual and group needs. Thus, Hartman suggests that "the characteristics of the therapeutic self-help model make it a particularly appropriate vehicle for meeting the needs of women in violent relationships" (1987, p. 73). Lawyer (1989) stresses three reasons why the self-help style is especially appropriate for abused women. First, government cutbacks or changes in organizational policies no longer allow funds to pay group facilitators. Second, there is a shortage of women who have been trained as facilitators, especially in isolated towns. Finally, feminists have valued equality, or the sharing of power and skills in groups, rather than the concentration of power of one expert facilitator.

Studies of self-help groups with populations other than abused women support the above observations. A study of a self-help group for parents of children with cancer emphasized that participants found it helpful to share experiences with other parents in similar situations, to learn from and teach each other, and to create a new social network (Chesney et al., 1990). In a study of a self-help group that assisted women in identifying women's issues, Glaser (1976) reported that the women liked being responsible for their own work and making changes in their lives. Deeble et al. (1991) reported on a self-help group for anorexia nervosa and found that the most valued features of the group included social involvement, supportive sharing, and the reduction of social isolation. Biegel et al. (1984), in a study of self-help groups for families of the mentally ill, found that participants valued the social supports achieved through sharing experiences, the interaction with others in a similar situation, and the education and information components.

One study by Hartman (1987) has specifically reported on the use of a self-help group as a therapeutic tool to empower women. Hartman found that the group experience was described as providing hope, empowerment, interdependence, and a mobilization for anger. It was also described as providing knowledge and skills.

RISK GROUP: A SELF-HELP GROUP FOR ABUSED WOMEN

With this in mind, the writer, a social worker, and several female clients of a Thunder Bay agency decided to offer a self-help style group to women experiencing power and control issues (partner abuse) in their relationships. The group was comprised of twelve female members of the Thunder Bay Catholic Family Development Centre RISK group for abused women.

My involvement with the First Step program, a program for abusive men, began several years prior to the organization of the women's group while co-facilitating a group with the men themselves and, to a very limited degree, via telephone with their female partners. Over the course of time it became very apparent that the program in some cases was isolating the women and having the opposite effect of what the program's goals and purposes intended. It became evident that the women needed service as well as the men.

The women of the RISK group elected the group process and format. They decided they wanted their group to be autonomous and egalitarian in nature, but they also wanted to have some professional support. Thus, the group was co-facilitated by a peer from the group and a professional consultant (the writer). The women chose to decide as a whole any changes or additions to the format. The participants decided what the role of the professional was to be. The women established that the nature and function of the group would be guided by these goals:

1. The group is assisted by a professional who works closely with a group leader, who is one of the group members. Group leaders are usually veterans of the group. The professional does not act in authority but as helper to the group leader and to provide education and requested information. The professional also acts as advocate with the agency.
2. The format included: (A). An opening and self-introduction with an

affirmation; (B.) Stories about self-care; (C.) Business; (D.) Check-In and Problem-Solving; and (E.) Education.
3. The structure, organization, and format are determined by the women themselves. The topic of the educational portion of the evening is decided upon by the women and is given by the professional and group members.
4. There is a business portion of the evening as well as a special business meeting, held quarterly. During business we decide upon criteria such as the group's mission statement, its goals, whether we are meeting our goals, the group structure and format, membership criteria, etc.
5. During our "Problem Solving" portion of the group, the women utilize their own personal strengths and supports to brainstorm ideas to help each other solve issues.
6. The group strives to maintain an autonomous and egalitarian structure by inviting the women to openly discuss any issues regarding the group with the rest of the group members.
7. RISK meets once a week, is ongoing, and has an open membership to partners of men in the First Step Program.

HOW WAS THE RISK GROUP HELPFUL?

When the group had been operating for approximately eight months, the women and I decided that it would be advantageous to ask group participants what was helpful and what was not helpful about their group. This was considered, in part, for the purposes of providing the best group experience possible.

Women were asked open-ended questions in a semi-structured interview format, including questions such as:

- What were you looking for when you came to RISK?
- What have you found most helpful about RISK?
- What changes have you experienced?
- What have you found to be least helpful?
- What needs of yours have not been met by the group?
- How were you treated by the other members of RISK?
- How did the other members treat each other?

Finally, the respondents were asked to picture someone else in a similar predicament and to imagine that "she has come to you and asked you about RISK with questions like 'What is it like or what do like about it?' What would you be able to tell her about RISK that might be helpful to her?"

A number of consistent themes emerged regarding why the women came to the group. The majority of the themes regarding initial involvement focused on emotional support and expansion of social support systems. Emotional support was sought through reducing isolation and validation of the problem. Group participants varied in their reasons for needing emotional support. For some of the women, the group provided the first and only opportunity to break the silence of their abuse by sharing their stories. For others, whose previous support systems had wearied of hearing their stories or were not empathetic (often because they lacked knowledge of abuse dynamics) the group was useful in addressing ongoing trauma. Many women reported that they needed to know that they were not alone in experiencing their particular problems. One woman said that initially she just wanted to "find out if there were other people like me, going through what I was going through." One woman said, "I had nobody to talk to and no one who understood." Another woman described her experiences after attending one group session in the following way:

> I felt like a ton of bricks had been taken off my shoulders—like I'm not the only one out there in the world, there are other people that have experienced the same thing. No matter how many of my family members I talk to who support and love me, they just don't understand.

Romeder states that "a conscious or unconscious feeling of isolation or loneliness is an important source of motivation for joining a self-help group" (1984, p. 18). He goes on to say that "some see loneliness as the result of a lack of opportunity to relate to others intimately and to express one's thoughts and emotions freely and without fear of rejection or misunderstanding" (Romeder, 1984, p. 18). This latter quote clearly reflects the reality of most of these abused women, many of whom do not have the opportunity to relate to their partners in an intimate way, and are unable to express themselves without fear of rejection and punishment through verbal and/or physical abuse.

Another way in which women sought emotional support was through sharing their stories and having the experiences believed and verified as abusive. Often this enabled women to address their issues. Many women who have experienced abuse respond either by blaming themselves for the abuse or believing the abuse is imagined; these views are often promoted by the abusing partner. Some women assume that through some defect or behaviour, they provoke the abuse (Evans, 1993). Despite the fact that they are repeatedly told it is their fault by their abusers, many women are able to cling to the knowledge that it is not their fault, but at the same time need this validated by others. Additionally, women reported knowing on an instinctive level that something was terribly wrong, but could not identify the source of their discomfort.

One woman described the pursuit of validation by saying that "I needed to know it wasn't me, that I wasn't at fault." Another woman stated that she came to the group to "validate my own ideas that what I was going through was abuse." Other comments included coming to the group to validate that "I wasn't crazy like my husband says I am, and that there was something terribly wrong."

Education was also a consistent theme that the women gave as a reason for attending the group. The women reported the desire to receive information about how to identify what abuse is, how to cope with it while they were in the relationship, and how to cope with the residual effects once they were out. While education was mentioned less often than reducing isolation and validation, many women indicated that the need to learn was also one of the precipitating factors that led to group membership. One woman commented that she wanted "to learn ways to cope in order to get through what I was living." Most women stated that they were seeking "more knowledge and more information about abuse."

Other less prevalent themes for women's attendance in the group included seeking peace and tranquillity in their lives, and sharing personal experiences to serve as an example of what happens when a woman endures years of abuse and fear.

When asked what they found helpful about RISK, mutual sharing during check-in was overwhelmingly what women said was most helpful of the three group components of check-in, education, and problem solving. Mutual sharing in many ways reduces the isolation that abused women often feel. The women said:

> It gives me a chance to get everything off my chest. Otherwise I don't get a chance to unload. Also, I find it not just helpful when I'm unloading, but when other people are sitting there talking about the things they have been through. I can relate to a lot of it and apply their solutions to my own personal experience.

> I find that the opportunity to voice my problems and to listen to other people's feelings is helpful. I find that everyone is very supportive. It doesn't matter what kind of mood I am when I attend, top of the world or really low, or that I have not been there for awhile, the women make me feel comfortable. I slide right in. When we come into that room, we are connected.

> Hearing other people's stories and having mine heard made me feel like it wasn't just in my head. You validated me here, that my feelings were worth something and valid.

> It gave me a chance to release and vent what I was feeling, to either cry or laugh, or swear if I had to. It also gave me a chance to listen to the other women, to feel supportive with them and they would do the same for me. We had a bond, a really strong bond.

> Listening to other people's problems helped me because a lot of their problems were similar to mine. This helped me solve mine.

> I had to tell somebody my shit! I had to tell people who wanted to listen to me. Other people were getting sick and tired of listening to me. I felt comfortable that I could say anything I wanted to say and not have to worry about being criticized.

The women who rated the three components of check-in, in matter of importance, had this to say:

> Check-in was the unloading part for me because it's not the type of subject you can discuss with people on the outside. It's a safe environment and an acceptable place to talk about it.

> Check-in lets me know I am not going crazy. When the other women check-in, I find it helpful because they are sharing about the same kind of experiences I was having. This validates me and makes me stronger.

Education was rated next in importance of the three meeting components. Two group participants expressed that they found the education segment helpful for the following reasons:

> I knew about physical abuse when I came here, but I didn't have any knowledge about emotional abuse. Learning about getting in touch with my feelings was helpful. As well, when I came here, I thought it was all my fault. The education element taught me "that's my stuff and that's my partner's stuff."

> The most helpful part was the education. It broke down all the different types of abuse. While I was learning I was being validated about what I was thinking, that what I had thought was correct. Learning more about what abuse is has made me stronger and knowledgeable.

> Reading the Verbally Abusive Relationship was good. It made me realize that I wasn't imagining everything and it wasn't me. I wondered a lot if I overreacted or if I didn't do this, or if I didn't do that, if things would be different.

> I learned a lot from the chart with all the different types of verbal abuse. I learned a lot because I didn't know what abuse was.

Additionally, almost all of the women made comments to the effect that they received education about abuse not only during the formal portion of the evening's agenda, but also during other parts of the meeting. Women commented that they received helpful information while listening to other people's stories throughout the evening and while problem-solving, such as:

> I did enjoy the problem-solving worksheet. I got a lot of brainstorming ideas—solutions, answers that you wouldn't find in reading. It was helpful to hear someone else's ideas who had lived through a similar incident and to hear what they did about it.

PERSONAL GROWTH FACILITATED BY RISK

When asked about what other elements the women found helpful about RISK and whether RISK had facilitated any changes in them, many of the women described changes related to an increase in self-esteem and self-confidence. When referring to how the group participants' self-respect and self-confidence were raised, the following themes emerged: Group support, self-care, increase in assertiveness, being validated, egalitarian environment, helping self by helping others, and safe environment

Many women attributed an increase in self-confidence to the ongoing support of RISK. The nature of self-help is that it is ongoing and not a time-limited group and was indicated as being helpful to the women because the group was available to them when they needed it. The women expressed it this way:

> Whenever I must confront my husband about something, I feel as if I have all the women in the group standing behind me. They would support me and say yes, this is abusive. Had I not gone to this group, it would be me standing alone.

Closely connected to increased self-esteem is increased assertiveness. Horley (1988) states that "assertiveness occurs when women take control of their lives and stand up for themselves and their children in a positive but not aggressive way" (p. 93). Many of the women reported that once they felt secure within themselves, they were able to set down physical and emotional boundaries within their relationships.

> It taught me how to stand up for myself in a positive way—not yelling and screaming back—but just to say, "listen, when you do this, it hurts me." I was enabled to talk, to listen, to compromise.

In many instances the women reported that the strengthening of their self-esteem and self-confidence was related to their being validated. The women expressed how helpful it was to have their thoughts and feelings validated by the group in the following ways:

> Maybe that's the word—understanding, because if you talk to people that haven't lived through it, they don't understand. They say: "Just leave, leave!" But it's not that easy to walk out. The women know that there and you feel understood.

> Validation. I wasn't getting it at home. From not combing my hair right or wearing the wrong clothes to coming here where you fit in.

> I don't have to accept it. I am not thinking crazy. I'm not the only one that thinks this is wrong.

> Sometimes you think you are just going insane. You don't trust your own instincts. You stop believing in your inner feelings. But the women helped reinforce me. To me, that was the most important aspect, to have my feelings validated.

> I think what's mostly helpful is that you are validated. Even just talking about your feelings, the way you feel, and have somebody validate them.

Many of the women reported that the egalitarian atmosphere of the group, where everyone helped everybody else on an equal level with respect and encouragement, showed them an alternative way of being treated. This alternative way of being treated was in direct contrast to the way they were being treated in their relationships. Moreover, women found that when other women listened to their helping suggestions, it made them feel good about themselves and their abilities. Offering solutions to other women also provided the opportunity to re-commit these same solutions in their own life. Their comments included the following:

> It felt good helping others. It makes me feel grateful that I was able to help, to understand.

> It was very therapeutic. You say something to somebody and you have to carry that through in your own life. You do! You can't suggest something and go home and do the opposite.

> We are treated with respect and dignity. Anything I say or do, or voice an opinion about, is respected whether or not others agree. I feel listened to. There is no confrontation. Suggestions, yes, but there is not direct confrontation.

It gives me a sense of pride and accomplishment in myself when I can share my experiences or even just sit there and listen. I feel I'm being helpful just by listening or by voicing concerns. It shows me how much I've grown. It also gives me the feeling that I'm not in a constant state of crisis anymore. It shows me my growth to see when I'm helping others.

The women experienced personal affirmation through being treated with respect and developed a sense of increased self-worth when they took pride in their ability to help others. They also felt a significant amount of acceptance and tolerance that they attributed to involvement in a safe and compassionate environment. Their comments contained the following sentiments:

It's very safe, it's comfortable, people are friendly. There is no fear.

Because others have been non-judgmental, I have become less judgmental. We accept each other. It comes down to love. Loving yourself and your neighbour. Accepting yourself and then extending it. When you are living in a fearful environment, loving yourself is a hard thing to do.

It was a safe place to go to talk about what was happening to me. I think the key is that it is safe, safe to talk. I felt accepted—something that I did not have anywhere else.

FACILITATOR EXPERIENCE IN A REMOTE COMMUNITY

Although the participants reported that they felt that the group met their needs, there were some uncomfortable moments for some of the women and for me (the professional helper) as a result of the size of our small remote city. There are many examples cited in the literature about the unique problems of service delivery in rural and remote communities.[4] When looking at the issue of partner abuse in isolated communities, the concept of context may be helpful in arriving at a clearer understanding of the unique situations women in isolated communities face. In an urban setting, women may have greater access to shelters, subsidized housing, retraining programs, legal aid, counselling, and other services. For those who reside a great distance from other people and have no transportation, an open field may be the only avenue of escape (Hymers, 1993). In considering other issues for women in remote communities, the challenge of obtaining confidentiality and anonymity has been experienced by women. Additionally, compromised facilitator credibility and contamination lead to loss of confidence in the professional helper.

Particular to this group facilitator's experience was the one of the participants' questionable confidentiality and anonymity. Several experiences of the women reflect this. Halfway through the group meeting we take a short break. One evening during the break, two of the participants approached me on separate occasions, alarmed about the presence of each other, expressing concerns that they were not feeling like they could freely express themselves for fear of their confidentiality being at risk. This particular situation was attributed to the fact that the first woman revealed to me that she was dating the ex-partner of a third participant, while the second woman revealed that she was dating the ex-partner of the first woman. The women had several concerns. How were they to trust that what they said stayed within the group? What should they do when their new partners started talking about their ex-partners? What should they think when what their new partner's story differed from what the (group participant, his ex-partner) was saying? Prior to this experience, our individual orientation sessions did not always extend the subject of confidentiality and anonymity much beyond the point of expressing that the group participants expressed this as being a necessary part of the group rules. Thereafter, I made it a point to also remind the new members during orientation that we did live in a very small, isolated community and that there existed a strong possibility that she might see someone she knows. I expressed the importance of confidentiality as expressed by the group members, but that this did not guarantee it to be so. There were times when this became too big an issue for women to risk joining the group and others when they realized the risk and were willing to take it anyway.

Another experience that was particularly troubling was one where a participant was in the middle of separation agreement negotiations. An employee of her ex-partner's company started attending the group. This made the woman feel extremely anxious and despite many reminders within the group context about the issue of confidentiality, the woman was not able to feel safe enough. We offered the new group member (the employee) several options to receive support, but none that involved continuation in the group. We did assure her that she would be welcome after a few months when things had stabilized with the other participant. The woman chose not to act upon any of our alternate offers for support, including joining the group at a later date.

Yet another acquaintance met through my participation in a parenting group called the centre one day and I recognized her voice. Upon my invitation to talk about the group and the possible uncomfortable feelings she might have resulting from me being the facilitator, she came in and we talked about the shame and embarrassment she felt about me knowing her secret. We also talked about the possibility of her meeting other women whom she knew and processed how she would handle this. Despite this she did want to try attending the group. In the end she left the group within minutes of her first meeting; I called her thereafter to reassure her that these feelings were normal, and that I would be available to her whenever she wanted. I also gave her the numbers of other agencies where she could receive individual counselling. Often afterwards, I would see her in the grocery store and she would quietly share some of her concerns and ask for suggestions, to which I was glad to respond. Despite the fact that as group facilitators in small communities there are issues about confidentiality that are required to be addressed and are addressed, there are times when alternate arrangements must be made. It is sometimes necessary to come up with more creative ways to offer assistance.

FACILITATOR CREDIBILITY AND CONTAMINATION

In small remote centres, the privacy of professional helpers is greatly reduced. Several experiences I have had as group facilitator in both the First Step Program and the RISK Group reflect this. Wearing the hats of both a parent of a special needs child and a professional helper, I have experienced a number of incidents where I have had contact with my clients while out in the community with my son. By outward appearances my son looks like any normal young individual. Therefore, when he acts inappropriately in social settings, onlookers may believe we are a combination of poor parenting and spoiled child instead of a son and mother with limitations and significant challenges. While I have been in situations where I have had to publicly parent a challenged child while in the presence of clients, I have felt that not only did they question my professionalism in that "if you can't be successful in your own problems, how can you help others?" but I too questioned my effectiveness. These experiences promoted a questioning or undervaluing of my own skills both as a professional helper and as a parent.

Other experiences that reflect the suggestions of Simon (1999) arose out of my living in Thunder Bay for most of my life. There have been many instances and a myriad of ways in which I have been previously connected to my clients in my personal life. Either my siblings or I attended school or worked with some clients. One particular client came "very close to home" in that we had double-dated in high school, and we lived in the same neighbourhood while I facilitated one partner in the First Step Group, then the other in the RISK Group. I often wondered how the client could take me seriously as a helper when he must have retained memories of our youthful experiences together. At the same time, I wondered if I knew too much about the client while I struggled to maintain my objectivity. This theme is referred to as facilitator contamination.

Contamination has been experienced in situations such as couple counselling where the therapist has prior knowledge about one partner that may or not be known by the other partner. The partner in question also may not be aware of either his or her partner's or the therapist's knowledge of the information. This situation, if at all possible, is avoided by the clinician who strives to maintain objectivity.

Mental health practitioners working in small, remote communities are especially challenged to ensure the maintenance of confidentiality and anonymity, and to remind group participants that this may not be entirely possible. Prior knowledge that they may see a neighbour, friend, co-worker, or relative in the group allows them the choice to join the group or seek out alternative treatment opportunities. These issues are especially important to the abused woman whose boundaries have already been compromised.

NOTES

1. Fassel et al. (1987); Faulkner et al. (1993); Freeman et al. (1993); Horley (1988); Jaffe et al. (1982); Macleod (1990); Ontario Native Women's Association (1989); Pappas (1990); Rouette et al. (1993); Schettino-Casale (1984).
2. Biegel et al. (1984); Chesney et al. (1990); Deeble et al. (1991); Glaser (1976).
3. Bowker et al. (1986); Hartman (1987).
4. Brownlee (1992); Delaney et al. (1995); Simon (1999); Zapf (1993).

REFERENCES

Barker, R. L. (1991). *The social work dictionary*, 2nd edn. Washington: National Association of Social Workers.

Biegel, D. E. & Yamatani, H. (1984). Self-help groups for families of the mentally ill. *International Journal of Family Psychiatry*, 8, 151–173.

Bowker, L. & Maurer, L. (1986). The effectiveness of counselling services utilized by battered women. *Women and Therapy*, 5, 65–81.

Brownlee, K. (1992). Constructivist family therapy: A promising method for rural settings. *Human Services in the Rural Environment*, 16(2), 18–23.

Chesney, B. K., Rounds, D., & Cheslder, M. (1990). Support for parents of children with cancer: The value of self-help groups. *Social Work with Groups*, 12, 119–139.

Deeble, E. & Bhat, A. V. (1991). Women attending a self-help group for anorexia nervosa and bulimia: Views on self-help and professional treatment. *British Review of Bulimia and Anorexia Nervosa*, 5, 23–28.

Delaney, R. & Brownlee, K. (eds.). (1995). *Northern social work practice*. Lakehead University, Thunder Bay: Centre for Northern Studies.

Evans, P. (1992). *The verbally abusive relationship*. Holbrook: Bob Adams.

Evans, P. (1993). *Verbal abuse survivors speak out*. Holbrook: Bob Adams.

Fassel, M. L. & Majury, D. (1987). *Against women's interests*. Ottawa: National Action Committee on the Status of Women.

Faulkner, A., Isac, S., Jacob, U., Jenns, J., & Newrick, M. (1993). *Women's experiences in family law proceedings*. Toronto: Mothers on Trial.

Freeman, J. & Larcombe, K. (1993). *Peer-facilitated support groups for abused women*. Self-Help Canada Series, H72-21/1993. Ottawa: Health and Welfare Canada.

Glaser, K. (1976). Women's self-help groups as an alternative to therapy. *Psychotherapy: Theory, Research and Practice*, 13, 77–81.

Halpern, D. (1987). The self-help group: The mental health professional's role. *Group*, 11, 45–50.

Hartman, S. (1987). Therapeutic self-help group: A process of empowerment for women in abusive relationships. In C. Brody (ed.), *Women's therapy groups: Paradigms of feminist treatment*. New York: Springer.

Horley, S. (1988). *Love and pain: A survival handbook for abused women*. London: Bedford Square Press of the National Council for Voluntary Organizations.

Hymers, D. (1993). Abused women in rural and remote communities: Isolated in more ways than one. *Vis-à-Vis*, 11(1).

Jaffe, P. & Burroes, C. A. (1982). *An integrated response to wife assault: A community approach model*. Ottawa: The Solicitor-General of Canada.

Lawyer, L. (1989). *Changing places: From facilitator to mutual support: A guide for women's mutual support groups*. Vancouver: YWCA.

Macleod, L. (1990). *Counselling for change: Evolutionary trends in counselling services for women who are abused and for their children in Canada*. Ottawa: National Clearinghouse on Family Violence.

Marecek, J. & Kravetz, D. (1977). Women and mental health: A review of feminist change efforts. *Psychiatry*, 40, 323–329.

Ontario Native Women's Association. (1989). *A proposal for change to aboriginal family violence*. Thunder Bay: Ontario Native Women's Association.

Pappas, C. (1990). *Mediation in family law: Families with a history of violence*. Thunder Bay: North-Western Ontario Women's Decade Council Violence Sub-Committee and the Ontario Association of Interval and Transition Houses.

Pence, E. & Paymar, M. (1987). *In our best interest: A process for personal and social change*. Duluth: Minnesota Program Development Inc.

Riordan, R. & Beggs, M. (1988). Some critical differences between self-help and therapy groups. *Journal for Specialists in Groupwork*, 13, 24–29.

Romeder, J. M. (1984). *Self-help groups in Canada*. Ottawa: The Ministry of National Health and Welfare.

Romeder, J. M. (1990). *The self-help way*. Ottawa: The Canadian Council on Social Development.

Rouette, J. & Williams, P. (eds.). (1993). *Changing the landscape: Ending violence and achieving equality*. Final Report on the Canadian Panel on Violence against Women. Ottawa: Minister of Supply and Services.

Schettino-Casale, A. (1984). *Battering battered women*. Toronto: Ontario Women's Directorate.

Simon, R. I. (1999). Maintaining treatment boundaries in small communities and rural areas. *Psychiatric Services*, 50, 11.

Woods, G. & Middleman, R. (1993). Groups to empower battered women. *AFFILIA: Journal of Women and Social Work*, 29, 163.

Zapf, M. K. (1993). Remote practice and culture shock: Social workers moving to isolated northern regions. *Social Work*, 38(6), 694–704.

Chapter Eight

BREAKING THE CONNECTION BETWEEN TRADITIONAL MASCULINITY AND VIOLENCE:
Toward a Context and Gender-Sensitive Approach to Counselling Males

David Tranter

Despite decades of feminist critique, our image of the ideal man remains surprisingly unchanged. Most men still measure themselves against a definition of masculinity that emphasizes strength, authority, self-reliance, and aggression. Traditional masculinity continues to be celebrated in the entertainment media and enacted by males in their everyday lives. This might merely be an interesting observation regarding our continued rigidity in respect to culturally prescribed gender roles if it weren't for the fact that traditional masculinity is associated with such a wide variety of social problems. There is much evidence to suggest that men who maintain a traditional gender role orientation experience a variety of problems, including the perpetration of spouse abuse, physical and sexual assault, child sex offences, homicide, sexual harassment, stress-related fatalities, and a whole host of health-related problems.[1] In short, our definition of what it means to be a man has not significantly changed, and this definition is highly problematic for women, children, and men alike.

It must be acknowledged, however, that gender roles have expanded over the last three decades. The boundaries of what makes a man have been both challenged and pushed thanks largely to the combined forces of feminist movements, gay pride movements, and the infusion of other cultures. Still, gender role flexibility tends to be greater where the population is more heterogeneous. Large cities experience significant race, ethnic, and class diversity. However, smaller, non-urban centres—particularly male-dominated, single-industry-based towns—tend to have a more homogenous population mix that maintains a class-based and very traditional orientation to gender roles (Tolson, 1977; Dunk, 1994). Thus, a narrow and dysfunctional form of masculinity is often much more pervasive and entrenched in smaller, single-industry cities and towns.

Therefore, there is a pressing need to challenge and expand the conception of masculinity in rural and northern settings. New ways of being need to be opened up for men, which are not necessarily associated with violence and other anti-social behaviours. Masculinity is at the heart of many of today's most devastating social problems, yet men are frequently not required or helped to change in meaningful ways. For change to occur and endure, men, perhaps more than women, need to make fundamental changes. If violence of all forms is to be successfully challenged, then men need to examine and redefine themselves in ways that are more functional for everyone.

Unfortunately, social workers and other helping professionals have not been very successful when it comes to helping men make changes in their lives. Conventional counselling has done a relatively poor job of encouraging male participation. It often fails to attract men even to attempt counselling and frequently fails to successfully engage the men who do seek help (Robertson et al., 1992). For those men who do participate in counselling, it usually fails to help them make meaningful change both personally and in their relationships (Levant, 1996). Men do not seek counselling to the degree that women do, nor follow through with intervention plans and goals (Cheatham et al., 1987). However, it is not for lack of personal difficulties that men avoid counselling, but rather that the goals and processes of traditional counselling are in sharp contrast to what it has traditionally meant to be a man.

The imperatives of traditional masculine socialization exhort men to avoid all things in which vulnerability, emotional expression, and relegation of control is emphasized. Yet these sorts of goals are precisely what traditional counselling has been about. Many counselling approaches require clients to admit their failings openly, while men are socialized to hide any vulnerability. Many counselling approaches encourage the expression of emotional pain, while men are taught to react to hurt with aggression. Counselling often requires the spontaneous exploration of innermost thoughts, while men are told that independence means never sharing personal thoughts with others. These and many other expectations run counter to traditional masculinity, which encourages men to appear competent at all times, control and hide vulnerable feelings, and deal with emotional difficulties independently and on an intellectual level (O'Neil, 1981). Worse still, traditional forms of counselling often make women the primary focus of change, reinforcing gender stereotypes and perpetuating gender inequality.

Therefore, in order to help men change successfully—particularly in northern and rural centres—context and gender-sensitive ways of understanding and treating men need to be further developed. This chapter examines some of the recent advances in understanding the socialization of males in order to develop counselling approaches that are better attuned to the particular needs of men. I conclude with ten principles that serve as guidelines to working more effectively to helping men change. It is hoped that the problem of violence and other significant social concerns can be better addressed by taking into account the unique needs of men and the pressures of their gender role expectations.

THE PROBLEM OF MASCULINITY

In the prevailing traditional view of masculinity it is believed that there exists an innate, biologically determined gender role to which men inherently conform. The extent to which a male lives up to this imperative is therefore a measure of his psychological well-being. Males who fail to conform are typically seen along increasing lines of deviance. For example, men who show vulnerability or indecision are often seen as feminine and therefore inferior. Men who are gay have transgressed further from their "nature" and are seen as highly deviant, even pathological. Many males go to great lengths to demonstrate their masculine prowess and engage in exaggerated displays of strength and power to establish their gender role conformity. In northern towns, there is probably no better and more obvious example of this display of masculinity than the stereotypical but all too frequent possession of oversized pickups with large snowmobiles in the bed of the truck. This very public display of power, size, and achievement is a transparent attempt to demonstrate successful gender role adherence.

In this traditional positivistic view of masculinity there is only one view of "healthy" masculine identity (Levant, 1996). Here, the more one fulfils his biological destiny, the greater his perceived integrity and mental health. Parents, schools, and other social institutions work toward reinforcing this singular definition of masculinity, understood to be the identity that will ensure personal happiness and fulfilment.

Many authors have described the identity and particular collection of traits to which men are traditionally socialized. In attempting to encapsulate the fundamentals of traditional masculine ideology, David et al. (1976) suggest that there exists four basic components: "no sissy stuff," "the big wheel," "the sturdy oak," and "give 'em hell." These components combine to lead men to avoid all things feminine, strive to be seen as successful, never show vulnerability, and seek risky, even violent activities. O'Neil (1981) suggests that men are socialized to dominate, compete, avoid emotions—especially vulnerable ones—control self and environment, avoid seeking help, and to be homophobic. Subsequent empirical studies have lent strong support to these assertions.[2]

In *It's a Working Man's Town* (1994), Dunk provides many examples of how men in Thunder Bay attempt to live up to a rigid gender role, as well as how they pressure peers to conform in a similar manner. From regular sexist and homophobic responses to ritualized gender-specific social patterns (such as baseball and hunting), many activities serve to preserve a narrow conception of masculinity that is in strong opposition to all things perceived as feminine. A powerful and pervasive belief in a "true male" is revealed, which dominates the intellectual, emotional, and social structure of men's lives.

The difficulties with this conception of masculinity are numerous. At best it is based upon an outmoded understanding one's identity in terms of traditional patriarchal values. Traditional masculine ideals fail to enable men adequately to live up to the new demands placed on them, in which they are increasingly being asked to share their inner emotional world, take on nurturing roles with their children, and avoid violence. At worst, traditional masculinity is associated with a range of anti-social behaviours, including violence, sexism, racism, and homophobia.

THE SOCIAL CONSTRUCTION OF MASCULINITY

Increasingly the view of masculinity as a biological imperative is being challenged by a social constructionist view of gender. Here, masculinity is no longer a normative referent against which all men should be measured. Rather, masculinity is seen as primarily a narrow social construct that is a product of the prevailing cultural norm. The prevailing culture determines how men see themselves and how men are seen in our society. The social constructionist view sees the traditional conception of masculinity as inherently problematic for men and women, and contributing to a range of social difficulties, the most notable of which is the perpetuation of patriarchal oppression. Most importantly, from this perspective masculinity is seen as a changeable identity, with different meanings for different men, as opposed to one ideal to which all men must conform.

The most established and well-researched deconstruction of traditional masculine ideology is found within the gender role strain paradigm originally formulated by Pleck (1981). In this view, traditional masculinity is seen as creating roles that are contradictory, often violated, inevitably leading to negative psychological consequences. Actual or imagined violations of the narrow confines of masculinity lead to over-conformity and strong reactions of inadequacy. Here, optimal development is no longer contingent on a definition of absolute masculinity. Rather it is believed that any narrow prescription of gender role is fundamentally flawed and unattainable.

Since Pleck's original work on male gender role strain, there has been considerable research undertaken to test his hypothesis. It is contended that the negative effects on men of traditional masculine ideology comprise three separate areas of strain. The three types of strain are: discrepancy strain, dysfunction strain, and trauma strain.

DISCREPANCY STRAIN

Discrepancy strain results from failing to live up to an internalized ideal of masculinity. Difficulties arise when men perceive themselves as falling short of the dominant definition of a man. The discrepancy between what a man "should be" and how he perceives himself causes within him psychic distress.

Research in this area has been done using the Gender Role Conflict Scale (O'Neil et al, 1986). In a summary of fifteen years of work using this scale, O'Neil et al. (1995) conclude that gender role conflict is a significant area of difficulty for men: it may pose hazards to their mental health, and may be associated with anxiety and depression. In a recent study of over 1000 participants, Good et al. (1995) found that male gender role conflict was significantly related to psychological distress. Further, the sub-scale of restricted emotionality (e.g., "I have difficulty telling others I care about them") arises as the strongest predictor of distress level.

Other studies have used the Masculine Gender Role Conflict Scale to examine discrepancy strain (Eisler et al., 1987). Here, evidence of gender role strain has been supported whereby gender role conflict is positively related to cardiovascular reactivity (Eisler, 1995). The findings suggest that addressing role stress may be an important consideration in improving cardiovascular health and reducing mortality rates.

DYSFUNCTION STRAIN

Dysfunction strain results from successfully fulfilling the requirements of traditional masculinity. Difficulties arise because many traditional masculine traits are inherently dysfunctional to the individual and others. In this view, traditional masculinity is, by its very nature, problematic, and those men who fulfil their traditional gender role inevitably experience problems. For example, Brooks et al. (1995) argue that traditional masculine ideology is largely responsible for the creation and perpetuation of significant social problems, including violence (e.g., abuse of women), sexual excess (e.g., sexual addiction), socially irresponsible behaviour (e.g., chemical dependence), and relationship dysfunction (e.g., non-nurturing fathering).

TRAUMA STRAIN

This third type of role strain results from the ordeal of male role socialization, which is thought to be inherently traumatic. This exists in more apparent ways in the rigours of the socialization of male athletes (Messner, 1992), veterans

(Brooks, 1990), or gay and bisexual men (Harrison, 1995). But beyond this, some authors contend that socialization under traditional masculinity ideology is inherently traumatic for all men. This theory suggests that the imperative for males to be emotionally independent leads them to experience the traumatizing negation of vulnerable and hurtful emotions, especially in childhood.

For example, Levant (1996) lays out the ordeal of emotional socialization under traditional masculine ideology as follows: males start out more emotionally expressive than girls; mothers work harder to manage their more excitable and emotional male infants; fathers involve themselves actively only after the thirteenth month of their child's life and then along gender stereotyped lines; both parents reinforce a gender-differentiated development of language of emotions whereby their son's vulnerable emotions are discouraged; and then sex-segregated peer groups reinforce traits such as toughness and competition. The result, says Levant, is that men are not only emotionally less developed, but they have suffered a succession of traumatic experiences that inhibit their normal emotional and interpersonal development.

MEN AND EMOTIONS

Closely related to, and derived from, the notion of trauma strain, critical theories related to masculinity emphasize the great difficulty that many men have in understanding and appropriately expressing their emotions in general. Emotional expression has long been considered to be a necessary component of overall health (Goleman, 1995). However, the socialization of males both through trauma and everyday expectation leads men to restrict and devalue much of their emotional experiencing (Levant, 1992). It is suggested that men are systematically socialized to lack essential emotional skills.

Many authors have suggested that men's socialization can lead to a mild form of the clinical syndrome "alexithymia" ("without words for emotions") in which men are more prone to express anger aggressively, more inclined to hide or transform their vulnerable emotions into aggressive ones, are unable to tolerate emotional intimacy, and are more likely to prefer non-relational sexuality (Levant et al., 1995). In a recent study, traditional gender roles were strongly related to the existence of alexithymia in men (Fischer et al., 1997).

FEAR OF INTIMACY

Fear of intimacy is another common characteristic of traditional masculine men (Fischer et al., 1997). Here, men avoid close emotional contact with others and prefer instead to maintain a casual relatedness with friends or emotional detachment from partners. This inability to tolerate emotionally intimate relationships usually leads men to have great difficulty exchanging thoughts and feelings with a romantic partner and connecting with significant others in meaningful ways. Here, men also tend to have restricted social networks usually comprised only of a romantic partner or very few others (Antonucci et al., 1987; Burda et al., 1987). Researchers have also suggested that men further avoid intimacy by shunting their caring emotions through the channel of sexuality (Brooks et al., 1995; Hudson et al., 1991).

EMPATHY

Traditional masculine ideology is also believed to lead to the restricted ability to fully empathize with others. Levant (1996) suggests that traditional men only develop a form of empathy called "action empathy" in which men have the ability to see things from another's point of view and to predict what they will do. However, they do not develop "emotional empathy," which can be defined as taking another person's perspective and being able to know how they feel. Thus, traditional men are fairly effective at predicting the behaviour of others, but are much less skilled at identifying the internal processes that occur within others and knowing how best to respond.

GRIEF AND LOSS

Another important issue related to traditional masculinity relates to how men deal with grief. Traditionally socialized men are thought to be limited in their ability to express and address grief in their lives (Cochran et al., 1996). This is considered to be due to the combined effect of emotional suppression and early childhood loss (trauma strain), which often go unresolved. It is suggested that men suffer from chronically unresolved grief arising from the loss of detachment from their mothers at an early age in order to proceed with masculine identity development. Grief is then compounded by the fact that—having experienced the loss of their mother—they seek out their father, only to find that he is emotionally unavailable. They then experience the second loss of a father who cannot care for their emotional needs.

The "mother wound" and "father wound" are thought to be traumatic, and men may adopt such strategies as shifting their focus to forms of action: "doing," achieving, seeking success, problem-solving, etc., in order to ward off the pain and vulnerability of these losses. Men continue to use these strategies throughout their lives, and continue to fear connection with others as a result of ongoing abandonment issues.

A CONTEXT AND GENDER-SENSITIVE APPROACH TO WORKING WITH MALES

Males in rural and northern contexts, where the pressures to adhere to traditional gender roles are great, have a tremendous potential to experience a range of social and personal difficulties. This fact, combined with the difficulty of assuring anonymity when receiving help in a smaller centre, strongly impairs men's ability to change, or even engage in change-producing processes such as counselling.

What is necessary then is to develop new ways of thinking about and working with men on change that takes into account their social and cultural context. Helping men in rural and northern settings means developing interventions that are better tailored to meet their needs. A social constructionist understanding of masculinity helps to develop guidelines and practices that can increase the likelihood that men will address issues such as violence. The following ten "recommendations" are an attempt to extrapolate practice guidelines that are consistent with a context- and gender-sensitive counselling approach for men.

1. *See gender as a central organizing schema.*

   It is essential to view men within their social/psychological conditioning, in which there is tremendous pressure to conform to a traditional stereotype of masculinity. The social prescription of gender powerfully shapes behaviour, both because of its pervasiveness as well as its insidiousness. Rarely does a male specifically present to counselling wishing to address gender issues. In fact many men initially find specific questions regarding their views of masculinity entirely unrelated to their presenting problem. Nevertheless, for most men the difficulties they present are inextricably linked to their concept of masculinity. Whether this is in couple counselling or individual work, for problems such as sexual abuse or stress management, using gender as an organizing schema helps illuminate the wider context of the problem as well as exposes barriers to overcoming the problem.

2. *Assess the degree of traditional/nontraditional views.*

   In assessing a male client's situation and determining an intervention plan, it is important to attain some measure of the degree of traditional versus nontraditional views held by the client. This is likely done by most practitioners on a less conscious level. However, a more explicit determination of each client's level of traditional masculine orientation will shed light on the relative fixedness of traits such as emotional expressiveness, rigidity, lack of empathy, need for independence and competence, and other traditional traits. Assessment of traditional views can be accomplished through formal measures of masculinity such as the Gender Role Conflict Scale (Eisler et al., 1987). Assessment can also occur less formally through observation and questions such as: "What is your view on the differences between men and women?" or "What, for you, are the defining characteristics of what it means to be a man?" Through an assessment such as this, the practitioner can determine the best treatment approach and modality to best suit the needs of each male. No doubt less traditional males will feel fairly comfortable in conventional counselling, whereas traditional males may need alternative approaches.

3. *Consider other more appropriate treatment modalities.*

Rather than trying to change men to fit counselling, it is preferable to change the counselling to fit men. Studies have indicated that more traditional men are much less inclined to seek counselling, but more inclined to attend courses, workshops, seminars, and the like (Robertson et al., 1992). Men may feel less threatened by services that, in their view, will bolster their competence and mastery.

Also, traditional men are socialized to be action-oriented rather than process-oriented (Levant, 1996). In this manner, therapies that emphasize the development of skills rather than self-reflection tend to be better suited to men. For example, psychoeducational courses are often well suited to men, especially if men are informed of the skills that they will learn at the outset. Another recommendation is to prepare men for treatment rather than simply assuming that they will conform to the role that is expected of them. They can view videos or read descriptions of the counselling to enable them to learn the required roles that they are to play. Otherwise, the male may not participate or even understand the purpose of the process.

4. *Recognize signs of discomfort and address them directly*

As previously indicated, men have been socialized to avoid such things as discussions of weakness or expressions of vulnerable emotions. This leads to strong feelings of discomfort and predictable responses. Common responses include: providing vague answers (e.g., "I don't know"), becoming impatient or aggressive, and avoiding the issue through storytelling or topic-changing. It is important to be aware of any response that indicates discomfort. It is important to address the discomfort in a way that will not cause the man to become defensive. Comments such as "I know this is hard to articulate, but let's go over it again," or "Let's take our time so we can really understand this," can be helpful ways of staying on track without alienating the man.

5. *Don't go too deep too soon.*

A common phenomenon in couple counselling is when the counsellor and female client talk readily about relationship issues and the male sits quietly left far behind in the discussion. It is therefore important to go slowly with emotional or relational content with men. Some authors have pointed out that counselling that proceeds too quickly and exposes too much emotion can alienate men from the process, exposing too much of their shame and pain (Cochran et al., 1996).

Another useful consideration in this regard is that traditional men tend to respond more quickly to discussions of existential concerns rather than interpersonal issues. This is thought to be consistent with men's need to be concerned with larger issues rather than more personal and seemingly trivial ones (Cochran et al., 1996). For example, a discussion of stress and anger related to the man might first begin with wider discussions of the stress of life and maintaining perspective about what is important.

6. *Deconstruct masculinity, acknowledge masculine stereotypes, and challenge them directly.*

The systematic deconstruction of masculinity involves two related skills. First, it involves the actual deconstruction talk of masculinity throughout the counselling process. Here such questions as "What kind of man do you think you are expected to be?" or "I would like to challenge some of the traditional beliefs about what men should and shouldn't be. Do you think you can hear them?" are useful. Counselling thus concerns itself with wider meta-discussions of the stereotypes of masculinity and the pressures to conform.

The second skill involves teaching men to deconstruct the prevailing ideology regarding masculinity on increasingly sophisticated levels. This may begin by basic observation regarding masculine stereotypes (e.g., humorous masculine traits), and proceed to more personal and less obvious ways, in which the client reinforces masculine roles both in himself or in his family (e.g., catches himself shutting off his son's tears). Here the male is taught to render conscious what was previously unconscious and catch the ways in which he enacts and enforces masculine stereotypes in his everyday life.

7. *Recognize the difficulty that men have attempting to make change.*

Often men's attempts to change can go unnoticed, are minimized, or attacked for being poor attempts. It is important to recognize the efforts that men are making to improve. Often, especially early on, his lack of awareness may lead to superficial and often frustratingly small attempts at change. But for many traditional men, change is very threatening as it shakes their security and challenges their perceptions of themselves on many levels. Change therefore needs to be recognized as a very difficult undertaking and any progress that occurs needs to be celebrated and reinforced.

Also, men can become easily defensive, and this needs to be addressed carefully to avoid the risk of alienation. Such statements such as "I know you are on the hot seat here" can acknowledge their efforts and difficulties. In this way the gains that men make, however small, are recognized and the difficulties they experience are acknowledged and kept from becoming overwhelming problems and, as a consequence, excuses for quitting.

8. *Explicit empathy and acknowledgment for their feelings of loss and grief.*

There has been much literature that suggests that men have difficulty dealing with loss and have trouble grieving successfully. Therefore, explicitly empathizing with the grief that men feel in their lives helps them to acknowledge and connect with these emotions and understand more about who they are. The counsellor starts with the assumption that many men carry around a deep and abiding sense of loss, which they have difficulty recognizing and dealing with effectively. Acknowledging the loss and empathizing with their pain helps them recognize the need to address grief in their lives.

9. *Provide a positive interpretation of their intentions.*

It is important not to portray masculinity as all negative, something that needs to be "overcome." Likewise, it is important to see many of the failed efforts that men have made in their relationships as misguided attempts to do well rather than reflecting malice or selfishness. For men, it is essential to acknowledge that usually the intentions of an action are good even when demonstrating insensitivity or inflicting hurt. Often the approach that is useful is one in which men are usually trying to do the right thing, but are often following poor advice.

Frequently, the stance that is taken with traditional males is one of distrust, skepticism, and judgment. Many men feel chronically misunderstood and in many respects this reflects their actual experience. Instead, the preferable approach is to acknowledge their efforts and intentions while encouraging them to continue seeking the best means possible to achieve their desired goals.

10. *Insist on their ability to change.*

Finally and most importantly, it is necessary to insist that men work hard to make change and break away from traditional thinking. For example, it is not sufficient that men simply curb violent behaviour, yet fail to address their perspectives and beliefs that encourage and perpetuate violence in relationships. Insisting that men are actually able to make change and strongly encouraging them to think of change in broader and deeper terms will ensure lasting and more meaningful progress.

CONCLUSION

Undoubtedly there has been a great deal of change in respect to gender roles over the last few decades. However, much of this change has been centred around redefining the roles of women. Men, particularly working-class men in rural and northern towns, have not typically been the focus of interest or intervention. Rather, men have often been seen as clinging defensively to a patriarchal social structure and unwilling to change. One of the great ironies of social work and other helping professions is that it is primarily informed by male-dominated theory and research, yet has done such a poor job of understanding and engaging men to make real change in their lives. This fact and the bias toward an urban emphasis in theory and research has meant that men in smaller cities and towns are a large and often problematic population that has gone virtually unacknowledged.

This chapter suggests that traditional masculinity remains a dominant force in the lives of men in rural and northern communities. It is a force that is also strongly associated with the perpetuation of violence, as well as many other serious social problems. However, more recently there has been fascinating and significant work in the area of masculinity research. Men who are very traditional in their gender role no longer have to be seen as difficult or intractable clients. Instead, social work practitioners in rural or northern settings need to be innovative and aware of the contextual and gender role pressures on men. Helping men to make significant change in their lives and the lives of their families is indeed an important and emerging field, and perhaps one of the only ways in which some of our most severe social problems will be successfully addressed.

NOTES

1. Brooks et al. (1995); Miedzian (1991); Johnson (1997); Segal (1997); Connel (1987).
2. O'Neil et al. (1995); McCreary (1994); Good et al. (1995); Mintz et al. (1990).

REFERENCES

Antonucci, T. C. & Akiyama, H. (1987). An examination of sex differences in social support among older men and women. *Sex Roles*, 17, 737–749.

Brooks, G. R. (1990). Post-Vietnam gender role strain: A needed concept? *Professional Psychology: Research and Practice*, 21, 18–25.

Brooks, G. R. (1995). *The centerfold syndrome*. San Francisco: Jossey-Bass.

Brooks, G. R. & Silverstein, L. S. (1995). Understanding the dark side of masculinity: An interactive systems model. In R. F. Levant and W. S. Pollack (eds.), *A new psychology of men*, pp. 280–333. New York: Basic Books.

Burda, P. C. & Vaux, A. C. (1987). The social support process in men: Overcoming sex-role obstacles. *Human Relations*, 40, 31–44.

Cheatham, H. E., Shelton, T. O., & Ray, W. J. (1987). Race, sex, casual attribution, and help-seeking behavior. *Journal of College Student Personnel*, 28, 559–568.

Cochran, S. V. & Rabinowitz, F. E. (1996). Men, loss and psychotherapy. *Psychotherapy*, 33(4), 593–600.

Connell, R. W. (1987). *Gender and power*. Palo Alto: Stanford University Press.

David, D. & Brannon, R. (eds.). (1976). *The forty-nine percent majority: The male sex role*. Reading: Addison-Wesley.

Dunk, T. W. (1994). *It's a working man's town: Male working-class culture*. Montreal: McGill-Queen's University Press.

Eisler, R. M. (1995). The relationship between masculine gender role stress and men's health risk: The validation of a construct. In R. F. Levant and W. S. Pollack (eds.), *A new psychology of men*, pp. 207–225. New York: Basic Books.

Eisler, R. M. & Skidmore, J. R. (1987). Masculine gender role stress: Scale development and component factors in the appraisal of stressful situations. *Behavior Modification*, 11, 123–136.

Fischer, A. R. & Good, G. E. (1997). Men and psychotherapy: An investigation of alexithymia, intimacy, and masculine gender roles. *Psychotherapy*, 34(2), 160–170.

Goleman, D. (1995). *Emotional intelligence*. New York: Bantam.

Good, G. E., O'Neil, J. M., Stevens, M., Robertson, J. M., Fitzgerald, L. F., Debord, K. A., Bartels, K. M., & Braverman, D. G. (1995). Male gender role conflict: Psychometric issues and relations to psychological distress. *Journal of Counseling Psychology*, 42, 3–10.

Harrison, J. (1995). Roles, identities, and sexual orientation: Homosexuality, heterosexuality, and bisexuality. In R. F. Levant and W. S. Pollack (eds.), *A new psychology of men*, pp. 359–382. New York: Basic Books.

Hudson, L. & Jacot, B. (1991). *The way men think: Intellect, intimacy, and the erotic imagination*. New Haven: Yale University Press.

Johnson, A. G. (1997). *The gender knot: Unraveling our patriarchal legacy*. Philadelphia: Temple University Press.

Levant, R. F. (1992). Toward the reconstruction of masculinity. *Journal of Family Psychology*, 5, 379–402.

Levant, R. F. (1996). The new psychology of men. *Professional Psychology: Research and Practice*, 27, 259–265.

Levant, R. F. & Kopecky, G. (1995). *Masculinity reconstructed*. New York: Basic Books.

McCreary, D. R. (1994). The male role and avoiding femininity. *Sex Roles*, 31, 517–531.

Messner, M. A. (1992). *Power at play: sports and the problem of masculinity*. Boston: Beacon.

Miedzian, M. (1991). *Boys will be boys: Breaking the link between masculinity and violence*. New York: Doubleday.

Mintz, L. B. & O'Neil, J. M. (1990). Gender roles, sex, and the process of psychotherapy: Many questions and few answers. *Journal of Counseling and Development*, 68, 381–387.

O'Neil, J. M. (1981). Patterns of gender role conflict and strain: Sexism and fear of femininity in men's lives. *Personnel and Guidance Journal*, 60, 203–210.

O'Neil, J. M., Good, G. E. & Holmes, S. (1995). Fifteen years of theory and research on men's gender role conflict: New paradigms for empirical research. In R. F. Levant and W. S. Pollack (eds.), *A new psychology of men*, pp. 164–206. New York: Basic Books.

O'Neil, J. M., Helms, B., Gable, R., David, L., & Wrightman, L. (1986). Gender Role Conflict Scale: College men's fear of femininity. *Sex Roles*, 14, 335–350.

Pleck, J. H. (1981). *The myth of masculinity*. Cambridge: MIT Press.

Robertson, J. M. & Fitzgerald, L. F. (1992). Overcoming the masculine mystique: preferences for alternative forms of assistance among men who avoid counselling. *Journal of Counseling Psychology*, 39(2), 240–246.

Segal, L. (1997). *Slow motion: changing masculinities, changing men*. London: Virago.

Tolson, A. (1977). *The limits of masculinity*. New York: Harper & Row.

Chapter Nine

GROUP TREATMENT IN NORTHERN ONTARIO FOR MEN WHO ABUSE THEIR PARTNERS

Larry Cheblovic and Keith Brownlee

Domestic violence is a pervasive and serious social problem with profound and far-reaching effects. According to Statistics Canada's 2004 seventh annual *Family Violence in Canada: A Statistical Profile* report, data from a subset of ninety-four police departments shows that approximately one-quarter (27%) of the victims of violent crimes in Canada were victims of family violence. The Statistics Canada 1994 *Violence against Women Survey*, found that three in ten women currently or previously married in Canada have experienced at least one incident of physical or sexual violence at the hands of a marital partner, and one-third of women who were assaulted by a partner feared for their lives at some point during an abusive relationship. A far greater number of marital partners are reported to experience other types of abuse such as verbal, emotional, economic, or other forms of threatening behaviours.

In a city the size of Thunder Bay, Ontario, with a population of 117,000, it is estimated that approximately 8000 women fall within the category of being physically or sexually assaulted at the hands of a marital partner. The extent of this violence and the resulting injuries sustained by women suggests that for many women the "sanctuary" of the home is a dangerous, violent, unsafe place. Clearly, a concerted and comprehensive response is required to address this very serious issue.

The women's movement of the 1970s increased the level of awareness of domestic violence. As a result, a network of services and programs evolved to address domestic violence. This broader network of services included not only the development of shelters for the protection and safety of women who were victims of abuse, but also the development of group treatment programs for men who batter their partners. Group treatment for abusive men is one approach commonly utilized to alleviate this difficult and complex problem. The primary objective of working with abusive men is to eliminate or reduce the level of domestic violence, and to provide safety for their partners. Group treatment is viewed as a preventative measure, as well as an important area of study in the treatment of domestic violence.

ORIGINS OF GROUP TREATMENT FOR MEN WHO BATTER

Group work has long been recognized as an acceptable modality for a variety of treatments. Over the past two decades, psychologists and social work practitioners have increasingly focused attention on providing group therapeutic interventions for treatment of men who abuse (Health Canada, 1998).

The first known organization in the world to develop a group treatment for men who batter emerged in Boston in 1977. At that time, a group of eight men who were supportive of the women's shelter movement came together to form a men's group called "Emerge." Women activists were frustrated with the high incidence of violence when women returned home from the shelter. In other instances, men were known to move from one relationship to another, perpetrating violence. Following the establishment of "Emerge," several hundred group treatment programs developed in North America for abusive men (Edleson et al., 1992).

Group treatment programs for men who batter emerged in Canada in the early 1980s. In 1981 there were only four such programs in Canada, increasing to thirty in 1984. By 1993 there were 124 treatment programs with the largest percentage located in Ontario. In a more recent publication, the National Clearinghouse on Family Violence reported that in 1998 there were 201 treatment programs listed in Canada (Health Canada, 1998).

THE EFFECTIVENESS OF GROUP TREATMENT FOR MEN WHO BATTER

Treatment programs for men have expanded rapidly in the past two decades and considerable attention has focused on evaluating the effectiveness of such programs. One of the most frequently asked questions in this area of study is, "Does group treatment for men make a difference in reducing or eliminating violence?"

Numerous research studies have been completed indicating that overall, treatment programs for men are effective in eliminating or reducing the level of violence toward female partners.[1] Overall, research studies have shown group treatment to be effective in ending violence among 59 to 84 percent of program completers over short follow-up periods (Edleson et al., 1990).

A great deal of caution needs to be exercised in interpreting any of these research findings. For the victims of domestic abuse, the aforementioned research results are not intended to raise false hopes. Treatment for men who batter is a very individual process and consequently may result in some men ending their abusive behaviours, while others do not. In many cases, women remain in the relationship once the male batterer commenced attendance in a treatment program. Providing an optimistic view of treatment programs may jeopardize the victim and in some cases place the victim in greater danger.

A number of methodological limitations are associated with the aforementioned research findings; namely, the lack of any experimental control groups, and the difficulty in obtaining reliable measures of reporting violence. In some research studies, police reports and partner's reports were obtained, while in others, only the men's reports were obtained. Utilizing men's reports of violence may understandably lead to under-reporting of violence. Typically, women report considerably more violence, although it may be under-reported because divulging such information may also in some cases put the woman at greater risk for violence. Finally, the selective nature of these research studies does not allow for generalizability of research findings. Considerable attention has focused on evaluating the relative effectiveness of group treatment for men who batter. The degree of group structure and the length of group treatment vary and have been a frequent source of debate. Research findings reveal that brief, structured educational group programs are the most effective in helping batterers end their violence and threats of violence (Edleson et al., 1990).

First Step Program

The First Step Program is a group educational treatment program originating in Thunder Bay in 1984 and administered through the Catholic Family Development Centre, which is a member agency of Family Services Ontario. The aim of the program is the elimination of male violence toward female partners. It is estimated that to date the program has provided services to over 900 men. The target population consists of men who are physically, verbally, or sexually abusive toward their female partners and referrals are primarily received through the court system, local agencies, or self-referral. The program is twenty-four weeks in length consisting of weekly group meetings for approximately two hours. Group composition usually consists of eight to ten participants with two groups operating concurrently. Admission to the group is open-ended, which enhances accessibility for service by avoiding a waiting period.

We will now consider various aspects of group treatment as they pertain to the First Step Program, and will include a brief description of program values and objectives, group facilitation, and intervention beginning with the initial phase of assessment.

ASSESSMENT: THE INITIAL PHASE OF INTERVENTION

The initial phase of intervention begins with a process of assessment, which usually takes one or two sessions on a one-to-one basis. Essentially, the purpose of assessment is to gather sufficient information to: (1) develop an understanding of the nature, frequency, and severity of violence; (2) to evaluate the level of safety or danger the partner may be experiencing; and (3) to evaluate the suitability of the client for participating in group treatment. In addition, some strategies for avoiding further violence will be discussed during this initial assessment phase.

One approach widely utilized in preventing an escalation of violence is employing a self-control plan, which consists of taking a "time out." This procedure requires the client to monitor the warning signals that commonly lead to an incident of violence. These arousal cues, or "red flags" as they are commonly called, may consist of physical or emotional sensations such as tightened muscles, clenching fists, or escalating anger.

During this "time out" period, the client may use several techniques to de-escalate and achieve a state of calm. By removing himself from the scene, taking a walk, and using positive self-talk, violence may be avoided. Developing an appropriate network of supports with whom to discuss a positive, non-violent plan of action is an additional tactic or approach for preventing violence.

Men are often observed seeking assistance following the occurrence of a crisis. The practitioner may be required to employ crisis intervention skills and to assess for the possibility of suicidal or homicidal tendencies. In the event of separation, partners are considered to be in a state of high risk for violence and the practitioner needs to ensure every effort is made to provide for their safety. Clients are required to provide consent for periodically contacting their partners to ensure they have a safety plan in place, and to familiarize themselves with relevant community resources. Program staff will continue to contact partners, with their consent, at any time if it is felt that women are at risk.

Program restrictions may at times disqualify an individual from attending group treatment. For example, an individual who is actively abusing alcohol or drugs may be requested to attend assessment or treatment for substance abuse, whereas an individual with serious psychological problems may be referred to receive attention through the appropriate mental health service agency. Once the alcohol/drug or the mental health problem has been addressed and the condition stabilized, the individual would be invited to participate in group treatment. In cases where the individual is not deemed to be appropriate for group participation, the practitioner may offer counselling on an individual basis. The primary consideration is always to assess and determine the most appropriate and beneficial form of treatment for the individual client while at the same time taking into consideration the needs of the group.

Group Participation

Participation in the program requires that men attend regularly, participate actively, report any incidence of violence, adhere to group confidentiality, and take precautionary measures such as removal of firearms from the house. Participants are informed that any intent or threat to kill or harm another person will be reported to police, and the potential victim will be notified or warned. In the event of child abuse, the proper authority would be contacted through Child and Family Services. If the participant is mandated to attend through the court system, the appropriate personnel—for example, the probation or parole officer—will be informed regarding the participant's attendance, his level of participation, and group progress, as well as any act of violent behaviour that constitutes a violation of the court order.

Group Intervention

A major emphasis during group intervention is a focus on the client's violent or abusive behaviours, which may include a full range of violent acts, from physical and sexual abuse to uttering threats and destroying property. Discussion regarding the first incidence of violence, the worst incident, and the most recent incidence of violence provides an opportunity for further exploring and investigating the nature of violence and the related issues. Physical abuse can involve pushing, grabbing, shoving, slapping, hitting, kicking, choking, punching, or using a lethal weapon. Sexual assault may involve any form of unwanted touching, including sexual intercourse and pressure to have sex in a way that is unacceptable to a woman. Destroying property or uttering threats such as punching walls or breaking furniture is a potent form of abuse particularly in a context where the abuse victim previously encountered physical abuse. Various forms of emotional or psychological abuse that serve as a means of controlling the victim are also identified. Yelling, name-calling, controlling her social activities or her financial matters are examples of some of the forms of abuse that are examined. Specific and personal identification of abusive behaviours is seen as being an important strategy throughout the treatment process, and all forms of abuse are treated as a method of dominating and controlling the victim. Physical abuse is observed as always being accompanied by emotional/psychological abuse and, in the cycle of violence, emotional/psychological abuse frequently escalates to physical abuse in an attempt to dominate and control the victim.

Group intervention is seen as being the most effective means of dealing with men who use violence to control their partners. Sakai (1991) states that "for treating domestic abusers, group intervention seems to work more effectively than does individual counselling" (p. 537). Group participants have frequently been observed to challenge each other in striving to attain a change in their attitudes and actions. The makeup of the group, which is comprised of older and newer members, facilitates the opportunity for constructive feedback. As an example, one group member may confront another member who may be blaming or minimizing his actions. Yet again, when one individual is not focusing on himself or not taking responsibility for his own actions, the group members may assist that individual to change his focus or demonstrate how he can effect positive change by taking personal responsibility. The group setting also allows for each participant to feel that he is not alone in his struggle to deal with his abusive behaviours. The ability to relate and to identify with each other is made possible through the group setting.

Group Facilitation

The group is facilitated by a male practitioner with the assistance of a female facilitator when available. The presence of a female facilitator is seen as having a therapeutic advantage and allows men the opportunity to practise responding to a female in a non-violent, respectful manner. A female facilitator is also recommended in that she is able to provide a woman's perspective in relation to violence. This also provides an opportunity for modelling respectful behaviour between the male and female facilitator.

The client/practitioner relationship is a significant feature in helping the client achieve a non-violent, non-abusive lifestyle. The initial intake and assessment sessions provide the stage for this relationship. The role of the practitioner is to engage the client in an open and honest dialogue pertaining to his violent and abusive acts toward his partner. Achieving a workable relationship is critical to helping the client become accountable for his actions. Employing a hostile, interrogative, or judgmental approach will only serve to further enhance the client's denial of his abusive actions and refusal to engage or participate in the treatment process. The practitioner may be challenged in supporting the client, while not excusing or minimizing his actions. Likewise, it may be difficult to confront the client without destroying his openness and his willingness to change. Treating the client as a worthy human being and utilizing a respectful, non-aggressive approach, while not condoning any violent behaviour, is considered to be the most effective way of promoting positive change while also acting as a model of acceptable behaviour.

Program Values

A fundamental premise of the First Step Program is the belief that violence is a tactic of power and control and is unacceptable in any form, whether it is physical, psychological, sexual, or emotional. Violence against women is related to societal structural factors and, moreover, is a contravention of basic human rights. Increasing the safety of women is a fundamental objective of the First Step Program.

Violence is seen as a personal, intentional choice, and the intent of violence is to exert power and control over another individual. Fundamental to the program is the belief that each individual is responsible and accountable for his or her own actions and behaviours. Violence is a choice, and men are encouraged to change by realizing that they have the power to choose.

Violence is also considered to be a learned behaviour: what is learned can be unlearned. Again, the responsibility for unlearning violent or abusive behaviours and relearning alternative non-violent, non-abusive behaviours is the responsibility of each individual. It is also believed that every individual has the capacity to be non-violent and the ability to assume responsibility for a non-violent lifestyle. It is the responsibility of the practitioner to assist the client in reaching this optimal level of functioning.

Finally, a foundation of the First Step Program is that all individuals are worthy of dignity and respect. As such, each program participant is treated in a respectful manner. It is believed that witnessing a respectful approach will serve to provide a model of behaviour and demonstrate an alternative non-abusive manner of interacting with others. In this way, the practitioner is viewed as being a role model for teaching non-violent, non-abusive forms of behaviour. The challenge for the practitioner is to accept the individual as being worthy of respect while at the same time not condoning his violent, abusive behaviours and maltreatment of others.

The following section will examine various aspects of working with men in a group treatment program for violence who display a resistant and reluctant attitude toward treatment. The intent is to shed some understanding and provide some suggestions to aid the practitioner in enabling a positive and productive experience for group participants.

Working with the Reluctant Client

It is estimated that approximately 60 per cent of men who attend treatment programs for abusive behaviours are court-mandated. The differences between the mandated client and the client who is attending voluntarily are usually quite apparent. Initially, the mandated client is generally observed focusing his attention outwardly and blaming his partner for her actions, or blaming the court system for his predicament. The voluntary client, on the other hand, usually demonstrates a desire for change and a capacity to focus on himself openly and honestly, which is seen as a prerequisite for invoking positive changes. This dichotomous dynamic inevitably presents an ongoing challenge for the practitioner. With the reluctant client, the practitioner may initially find it very difficult to focus on the client's abusive or violent behaviours.

It is imperative for the practitioner to understand that a client may have a valid reason for his reluctance to participate in a group setting. For many of these participants, attending a setting with other men and being expected to reveal their abusive behaviours, their related beliefs and feelings, and their cognitive processes is a foreign experience. Sharing their personal stories and focusing on themselves are rare, atypical experiences for them, in contrast with their common experience of looking outward to blame others for their circumstances, and mistrusting even the practitioner.

The resistant client is often seen by the practitioner as being disruptive, negative, and harbouring an attitude of victimization. Invariably the group facilitator may be fearful that this negativity and disruptive attitude may infiltrate the entire group. However, the opposite may sometimes occur. Mark had just commenced group treatment, having been court-mandated to attend. During his second group session he explained how his partner always "pushed his buttons," and how he is paying the price for merely pushing her away during an argument. Mark went on to exclaim that it was not his choice to attend group treatment. The group facilitator saw this as an opportunity to acknowledge Mark's feelings about not having chosen for himself to attend. At that point, Brian (another group member) spoke up and explained that he had felt the same way when he first began attending group treatment. He went on to state that the group had "helped him to look at things in a different way. I needed to look at myself and start thinking about my actions and how they affect other people instead of blaming other people for my actions." Another group member offered his thoughts. Joe had been attending for several months and stated, "I spent five years in lock-up for always blaming other people for pushing my buttons, never took responsibility for any of my actions and all that crap just kept me going back to jail." Joe went on to explain the level of power and violence in a penitentiary in the form of domination and sexual abuse. "You want to end up there, just keep blaming everybody else for your troubles."

This positive feedback from other group members in group treatment is a powerful influence on group peers. Mark received a clear message of the benefits of group treatment and the consequences of continuing his negative, abusive, and self-destructive behaviours. In this example the benefits of having newer and older group participants is evident. The influence of peers has frequently been observed as being a powerful influence for the newer group member.

Developing a relationship with the client is a critical aspect of group treatment. "There can be no successful psychotherapy with these men without an alliance, but they immediately present us with a priori stance of anti-alliance"

(Shay 1997, p. 505). Shay further states that "an alliance must be built delicately, gingerly and gradually. This alliance is built step-by-step by conversing in the language of the client and by creating an experience which operates against shame, against humiliation, against premature vulnerability and exposure, and against higher expectations than can be met by the client" (p. 505).

Provision of a safe environment is critical in promoting effective treatment. The First Step Program is facilitated in such a way as to have a high positive regard and respect for each individual while at the same time demonstrating an attitude of non-acceptance for any violent, abusive behaviour. Developing a safe environment while at the same time confronting group members in a productive manner is a challenging task for the group practitioner.

Men have been frequently observed to enter a treatment program in a very apprehensive, anxious, and resistant manner. Mandated clients, in particular, perceive group treatment as a form of punishment and harbour feelings of inadequacy, failure, and a fear of exposure. Caplan et al. (1995) describe a rather conflicting dichotomous circumstance for men in group treatment, stating that:

> On the one side lies the desire for a "second chance" through learning new ways to behave, but on the other side lies a vision of being mortified in the presence of a group of men through coerced humiliating admission of failure and inadequacy. Treatment for batterers requires an environment where clients feel reassured enough to talk casually but candidly about themselves. Effective treatment engages these men in non-defensive conversations about their behaviours and life experience (p. 34).

To achieve the desired goals of treatment, it is imperative for the helping professional to model appropriate behaviours and to create a trusting environment that is emotionally safe. An atmosphere of openness, mutual support, and safety can facilitate positive behavioural changes.

Conversely, non-constructive confrontation in the form of judgmental, condescending, sarcastic, or pejorative remarks may produce a non-communicative or defensive response from group participants.

The primary safety component in a treatment group for batterers is a high positive regard for each client. Clients must feel that no matter what they have done in the past, they will be treated with respect within the group. Any intervention that the client perceives as an attack might trigger defensive responses that impede the progress of treatment. The client's inability to express what is really going on will eventually sabotage the treatment and possibly put his partner at further risk (Caplan et al., p. 35).

Oliver Williams (1994) reaffirms the notion of a safe environment when he states that "men who batter will be able to confront their violent behaviour in a group treatment environment only, if it engenders mutual support, trust, vulnerability and sharing" (p. 95). Developing this environment is clearly the role of the professional practitioner.

The following statements made by group members reflect the importance of a safe environment. One member says, "I enjoy the group I am with, especially their honesty. Talking to somebody about what I have gone through has helped me to be more aware of my problems and to make some necessary changes." Another client comments that, "I have been given a lot of support and hope about controlling my anger and abusive behaviours and I feel not alone any more." A feeling of safety facilitates the expression of one's thoughts and feelings without fear of rejection, punishment, or humiliation. The creation of a safe group treatment environment also serves as a model of behaviour for men who have identifiably exhibited threatening, abusive behaviours, and who create unsettling and unsafe environments within their own family setting.

Recognition of abusive behaviours, an admission of wrongdoing, and taking responsibility for one's abusive and violent behaviours are integral components and fundamental requirements in the process of ending violence. It is important, however, for the practitioner to recognize that these are foreign skills for the newcomer. Men commonly present in group in a defensive fashion, displaying denial, blame, and minimization of their actions. Recognition, admission, and taking responsibility for one's violent and abusive actions toward their partner is often a novel experience for men initially attending group treatment. In working with men who batter, Clow et al. (1992) observe that assuming "responsibility for choice and control was a major new awareness for participants" (p. 98).

What is often perceived by the practitioner as resistance is simply a lack of skills on the part of the client to adapt to positive changes. Denial, minimization, and blame are defences that the client has learned to use to protect himself, and which usually have been a part of the client's makeup for some time. These same defences prevent the client from making positive, constructive changes. The practitioner requires specialized skills in helping the client overcome these defences. Providing a safe environment for group participants is conducive to helping men develop an understanding that they alone are responsible for choosing either abusive, violent actions or non-abusive, non-controlling actions.

David was court-mandated to attend group treatment and initially expressed considerable resistance and reluctance to participate. After attending for two months, he made this comment during one group session. "I have learned that I need to take ownership for my actions and that I am responsible and only I decide my behaviours." David went on to explain that the group had helped him to see things in a different way, to identify his abusive behaviours, and to take responsibility for changing his hurtful actions toward others. Provision of a safe environment is conducive to contributing to these positive changes.

One final element deserves mention in working with men who are violent with their partners and who resist group treatment. Violent men are commonly perceived as having a total disregard for the damaging effects of their abusive behaviours. In working with men who are resistant to treatment, Shay (1997) discusses the notion of offering empathy in tolerable doses. He states, however, that "empathic interventions that sound pitying increase humiliation rather than diminish it" (p. 510).

Within the context of working with men who are violent, empathy is defined as having a regard for the feelings of the victim and a recognition of the damaging effects of violence. Within the group setting, it is clearly apparent when a group participant achieves the ability to empathize with his partner. At this stage of recovery, the male abuser goes from blaming, minimizing, and denying to recognizing his own abusive behaviour, to taking responsibility for his actions and recognizing the hurt and damage he has caused another person. In this context, the ability to empathize is imperative in achieving a lifestyle of non-violence.

The batterer may have neither awareness of, nor practice in, the social skill of empathy. As the client develops this skill in group treatment, and as he develops trust in the safety of the treatment group, he may risk the discomfort of empathizing with the recipient of his violent behaviour. Accepting the feelings of fear, pain, confusion, and outrage in his intimate partner is an uncomfortable experience for the batterer, for it can arouse within him strong feelings of guilt and shame. However, empathizing with his partner's feelings is an essential part of his recovery (Caplan et al., 1995, p. 42).

Browne et al. (1997) have also commented on the ability to empathize, stating that "changes made out of increased awareness and empathy last a lot longer and generalize a lot better than changes made out of fear of humiliation"(p. 268).

Modelling empathy, providing empathy to group participants in tolerable doses, and helping the client to develop the ability to empathize is a challenging aspect of group treatment. Understanding and empathizing with the client helps the client to understand and empathize with his partner's feelings of fear, anger, and pain.

The aim of group treatment is for the practitioner to provide an effective and efficient program delivery system that is responsive to client needs, and to ensure that best practices and procedures are followed in assisting men to eliminate violent behaviours. Working with reluctant clients presents the practitioner with added challenges. The ingredients of successful group treatment for men who are violent are complex and multifaceted. An array of strategies contribute to ending violence. Providing a safe environment for group treatment, however, is critical in helping men develop positive alliances with the practitioner and other group members, and ultimately in helping men end violent behaviours and develop attitudes of respect and equality toward female partners.

SOME NORTHERN CONSIDERATIONS

The First Step Program is a geographically isolated service in northern Ontario. The nearest group treatment for violent men is located in Kenora to the west and in Sault Ste. Marie to the east. Each of these locations is approximately a day's drive from Thunder Bay. This geographic isolation presents a variety of issues in the delivery of treatment services for violent men, the most obvious of which is a lack of accessibility. Men residing in the rural areas of northern Ontario are neither able to access nor benefit from these services. The result is evidenced in a perpetuation of domestic violence and the subjugation of female partners.

The perpetuation of violence operates on at least three different levels and has serious implications for all three: the individual, the family, and the community. Violence is a drain on numerous social institutions, some of which include the judicial system (judges and lawyers, social service workers, probation officers, health care workers, and police officers). It has been estimated that, on a national level, the cost of domestic violence is in the $4.2 billion range (Department of Justice Canada, 2002).

Men who are violent in northern rural areas are dealt with primarily through the justice system without any recourse for rehabilitation. Judges, lawyers, probation workers, and police officers are the primary agents in dealing with violent men particularly in northern fly-in areas. In the case of men who are incarcerated, the penal system becomes a major player in dealing with the criminal aspect of violence.

The level of services for men who batter in northern rural areas is inadequate and insufficient. In the northern fly-in settlements, there are no provisions for group treatment for violent men. A number of alternatives need to be explored in order to bolster these services for abusive men in northern rural communities.

One option is to provide a program of outreach to northern rural areas. Smaller communities that lack resources often look to larger urban centres for specialized services. Providing an intermittent treatment program for violent men is more beneficial than no level of service at all.

Developing a comprehensive community-based program for the treatment of violent men may be another option for consideration. A community approach would involve a variety of partners, including women advocates, police officers, the judicial system, and counselling services for violent men. In northern Aboriginal communities, the method of counselling may be culturally adaptive to include ceremonial practices such as healing circles, smudging, sweat lodges, and the medicine wheel. The First Step Program is attended by a significant number of Aboriginal men; however, in terms of numbers, they are the minority. Although every attempt is made to provide a culturally sensitive approach, it may be both impractical and impossible to provide a traditional cultural approach. Within the Aboriginal community, healing circles, utilizing the medicine wheel, and smudging are traditional methods used in healing ceremonies. It is not known if the lack of these traditional healing ceremonies has negatively impacted the efficacy of treatment services.

Developing some strategies for providing safety for women in isolated areas is not an easy task. Providing a safe shelter for women may involve having the violent male removed from the community or in some cases having to remove the victim of violence from the community. Specialized training for police officers in domestic violence situations would be an important factor, particularly in the northern isolated regions. A comprehensive community approach requires that all the community players adhere in a collaborative and co-operative approach in reducing the level of violence and providing safety for victims of violence.

Providing a residential group treatment program for men during incarceration is seen as being a third viable option in helping men to eliminate their violent and abusive behaviours. Violent men who have been removed from their homes and incarcerated may, however, return to their rural community following discharge from prison. The shortcoming of this recommendation is that a large percentage of violent men are never sentenced to a period of incarceration.

What is known is that within a larger metropolitan centre such as Toronto, there are a variety of treatment groups that allow for ethnic-specific groups (i.e., Asian, Latin, Black, as well as North American Caucasian groups). Provision of culturally appropriate treatment groups is beneficial in that it allows for incorporating socialization characteristics specific to particular ethnic groups.

A procedural policy within the First Step Program has been to request that program participants remove any firearms from their premises while participating in the program. This precautionary safety measure takes on a new meaning in northern communities, particularly with the Native population. Hunting and trapping have long been known to be an integral component of Aboriginal lifestyle. In this context, a firearm is viewed as a tool for hunting and therefore a tool for providing sustenance for the family. This example of cultural diversity illustrates the necessity of being aware of cultural differences within the group setting.

Respecting the confidentiality of group participants is another issue that affects the provision of services within a northern rural setting. On occasion, group participants commenced treatment only to discover that associates, friends, or other family members were also attending the same group session. In other instances, men may have been previously intimate with a girlfriend or partner of another group member. In such cases where personal boundaries overlap, there is a threat to confidentiality, which may affect the group members' ability to share openly and participate freely in the group process. In the First Step Program where there are two groups running concurrently, this circumstance may be readily resolved by offering the participant the opportunity to attend another group. In smaller communities, where there is only one group program, this dilemma could not be so readily resolved.

Public figures and other business personalities who have been mandated to attend group treatment present yet another issue related to confidentiality. Fear of exposing their actions and losing public favour creates added reluctance for these men to participate openly in group treatment. Issues related to confidentiality seem to be intensified in smaller rural northern communities.

Lack of resources is yet another aspect of group treatment in northern communities that affects the quality and effectiveness of group treatment. Group facilitators are more isolated and thereby may experience a diminished level of support. The ability to network with co-workers is not present and workshops and other training sessions are not only less available but also more costly to attend in larger urban centres. More options are available not only for group participants in larger urban centres but also for group facilitators in terms of support, training, and other related resources.

CONCLUSION

In recent years, provincial courts, which deal exclusively with domestic violence, have been established in parts of the province of Ontario. These courts are seen as acting proficiently and in a timely fashion in matters related to domestic violence. It is believed that there are currently eight such courts in the province; however, most are located in larger urban centres, such as Toronto and Ottawa. Domestic violence courts are non-existent in the northwestern part of the province. As a result, court proceedings are frequently delayed, which in some cases may put the female victim of violence at further risk.

A police officer is frequently the first person to arrive at the scene of a domestic violence occurrence. As such, they play an important and critical role in apprehending the perpetrator, laying charges, and providing some level of support and protection for the victim. Lack of policing resources is particularly evident in some northern rural areas and specifically in northern fly-in areas where there may be a total absence of policing services. In such cases, the victim of violence may be forced to fend for herself or continue to live as a victim of violence.

Providing safety for victims of domestic violence is a difficult task, particularly in the vast regions of northern Ontario and the outlying Aboriginal communities or in other jurisdictions within and outside of Canada. Safety, however, is a basic fundamental human requirement and as such it must not be abandoned in the face of logistical difficulty. In addition to shelters for abused women, group treatment for abusers is a significant addition to strategies of prevention, or at least reduction, of domestic violence in northern and rural communities.

NOTE

1. Edleson et al. (1985); Farley et al. (1988); Russell et al. (1997); Palmer et al. (1992); Purdy et al. (1981); Halpern (1984); Edleson et al. (1985); Hawkins et al. (1985); Dutton (1986); Hamberger et al. (1986); Rosenbaum (1986); Waldo (1986); Douglas et al. (1987); Leong, Coates et al. (1987); Edleson et al. (1990).

REFERENCES

Browne, K. O., Saunders, D. G., & Staecker, K. M. (1997). Process-psychodynamic groups for men who batter: A brief treatment model. *Families in Society: The Journal of Contemporary Human Services*, 78(3), 265–271.

Caplan, T. & Thomas, H. (1995). Safety and comfort, content and process: Facilitating open group work with men who batter. *Social Work with Groups*, 18(2–3), 33–51.

Clow, D. R., Hutchins, D. E., & Vogler, D. E. (1992). TFA Systems: A unique group treatment of spouse abusers. *The Journal for Specialists in Group Work*, 17(2), 74–83.

Department of Justice Canada. (2002). Family violence: A fact sheet from the Department of Justice Canada. Available at www.canada.justice.gc.ca/en/ps/fm/familyvfs.html#topdoc.

Douglas, M. A. & Perrin, S. (1987). *Recidivism and accuracy of self-reported violence and arrest*. Paper presented at the Third National Conference for Family Violence Researchers, University of New Hampshire, Durham.

Dutton, D. G. (1986). The outcome of court-mandated treatment for wife assault: A quasi-experimental evaluation. *Violence and Victims*, 1, 163–175.

Edleson, J. L., Miller, D. M., Stone, G. W., & Chapman, D. G. (1985). Group treatment for men who batter. *Social Work Research Abstracts*, 21(3), 18–21.

Edleson, J. L. & Syers, M. (1990). Relative effectiveness of group treatments for men who batter. *Social Work Research Abstracts*, 26, 10–17.

Edleson, J. L. & Tolman, R. M. (1992). *Intervention for men who batter*. Newbury Park: Sage.

Farley, D. & Magill, J. (1988). An evaluation of a group program for men who batter. *Social Work with Groups*, 11(3), 53–65.

Halpern, M. (1984). *Battered women's alternatives: The men's program component*. Paper presented at the meeting of the American Psychological Association, Toronto.

Hamberger, L. K. & Hastings, J. E. (1986). Personality correlates of men who abuse their partners: A cross-validation study. *Violence and Victims*, 1(4), 323–341.

Hawkins, R. & Beauvais, C. (1985). *Evaluation of group therapy with abusive men: The police record*. Paper presented at the meeting of the American Psychological Association, Los Angeles.

Health Canada. (1998). *Canada's Treatment Programs for Men Who Abuse Their Partners*. Ottawa: National Clearinghouse on Family Violence.

Leong, D. J., Coates, C. J., & Hoskins, J. (1987). *Follow-up of batterers treated in a court-ordered treatment program*. Paper presented at the Third National Family Violence Research Conference, University of New Hampshire, Durham.

Palmer, S. E., Brown, R., A., & Barrera, M. E. (1992). Group treatment program for abusive husbands: Long-term evaluation. *American Journal of Orthopsychiatry*, 62(2), 276–283.

Purdy, F. & Nickle, N. (1981). Practice principles for working with groups of men who batter. *Social Work with Groups*, 4(3/4), 111–122.

Rosenbaum, A. (1986). Of men, macho, and marital violence. *Journal of Family Violence*, 1(2), 121–130.

Russell, R. & Jory, M. K. (1997). An evaluation of group intervention programs for violent and abusive men. *The Australian and New Zealand Journal of Family Therapy*, 18(3), 125–136.

Sakai, C. E. (1991). Group intervention strategies with domestic abusers. *Families in Society: The Journal of Contemporary Human Services*, 72(9), 536–542.

Shay, J. (1997). "Okay I'm here but I'm not talking!" Psychotherapy with the reluctant male. *Psychotherapy*, 33(3), 503–513.

Statistics Canada. (1994). *Violence against women survey*. Ottawa: Housing, Family and Social Statistics.

Statistics Canada. (2004). *Family violence in Canada: A statistical profile 2004*. Ottawa: Canadian Centre for Justice Statistics.

Waldo, M. (1986). Group counselling for military personnel who battered their wives. *Journal for Specialists in Group Work*, 11, 132–138.

Williams, O. J. (1994). Group work with African American men who batter: Toward more ethnically sensitive practice. *Journal of Comparative Family Studies*, 25(1), 91–103.

Chapter Ten

ADULT SURVIVORS OF CHILDHOOD SEXUAL ABUSE: A Mixed-Gender Therapy Group

Darlene Olimb

Group therapy as a treatment modality for adult survivors of childhood sexual abuse is widely suggested.[1] Searching the literature reveals a significant contribution with regard to group treatment for female survivors and a small, but growing, aggregate regarding similar treatment for male survivors. Almost unanimously, authors discuss homogeneous groups in their treatment approaches and designs. This chapter offers a framework for a mixed-gender group treatment approach to the psychological consequences of childhood sexual abuse that persist into adulthood.

The most commonly identified long-term effects of sexual abuse in childhood include: deep-seated guilt over the abuse; mistrust of others; social isolation; fear and anxiety; intense feelings of rage and loss; chronic feelings of low self-esteem and inadequacy; sexual dysfunction; dissociative symptoms; and manifestations of post-traumatic stress disorder (Knight, 1993).

Although certain aspects of long-term effects on the psychological functioning of male and female survivors are different, both sexes experience common issues. In a study comparing the psychosocial maladjustment of adult males and females who were sexually molested as children, Hunter (1991) found that both male and female abuse victims demonstrated considerably greater dysfunction across multiple measures of adjustment compared to control groups of non-abused subjects. There are some significant differences, but the similarities are much greater (Davis, 1990).

RATIONALE FOR A MIXED-GENDER THERAPY GROUP

The mixed-gender therapy group model was developed to serve clients in a small rural community in northwestern Ontario. Unique conditions affecting northern social work practice have been discussed elsewhere and will not be repeated in this chapter. It is, however, important to comment on several aspects of context in working with adult survivors of childhood sexual abuse in rural communities in the north. The dynamics of shame, secrecy, and isolation are significant restraints for disclosure of the abuse to a social worker who may know the client or the client's family in the community. It is even more difficult for that client to consider attending a group in which the individual is likely to encounter people who are known in other capacities such as neighbour or co-worker.

The same dynamics may have operated throughout the individual's childhood, thus allowing the abuse. The social worker must carefully choose and prepare each prospective group member. To place them in such an atmosphere before they are able to handle it would be counter-productive and possibly harmful (Knight, 1997).

A second issue facing the social worker in the rural northern community is that of person-power. A northern social worker has to be especially resourceful where agency and professional mandates may be broad, the sorts of problems encountered may be novel, resources may be scarce, and needs are great (Graham, 1996). With regard to group therapy for adult survivors of childhood sexual abuse, co-therapists are recommended both to manage the emotionally draining nature of work with the group and to support one another.[2] Agency resources in northern rural communities are minimal with low staff–client ratios. In this case two staff with high numbers of cases constituted the mental health staff of the agency. In addition there were no male social workers available to work with the male sexual abuse survivors.

Typically, caseloads consisted of a wide variety of mental health issues: the staff was required to play a range of roles. Brownlee et al. (1997) note that this diversity of practice roles contrasts with the specialized roles and, therefore, the depth of knowledge that is possible in an urban centre. Access to consultation and outside expertise require considerable time and financial expenditure on the part of service providers who develop a focused treatment approach. The client population similarly faces the constraints of time, travel, and finances. There is, in addition, a tendency for northern workers to develop interest areas and, subsequently, to see a higher proportion of clients with similar problems in the area of interest (Brownlee et al., 1997). In addition to reading extensively and practising in one field, the author attended workshops conducted by specialists, including Mike Lew, Ph.D. (Victims No longer), Yvonne Dolan, M.A. (Resolving Sexual Abuse), Karen Saakvitne, Ph.D. (Transforming the Pain), Bill Brodovsky, M.S.W. and Libby Yager, M.S.W. (Helping Couples and Families: Healing from Sexual Abuse), and Terryl Atkins, M.F.A. (Fundamentals in Art Therapy) to gain outside expertise in preparation for leading the mixed-gender therapy group for adult survivors.

GROUP DESIGN AND PREPARATION

The social worker is responsible for the creation and design of the group. Criteria for type of group, composition, structure, timing, assessment, goal-setting, programming, evaluation, and termination require thoughtful planning as empirical research on group therapy for survivors of severe childhood abuse is sparse (Scott, 1999). In a review of the literature concerning individual and group therapy for survivors of childhood sexual abuse, Cahill et al. (1991) describe various types of group treatment, including short-term, time-limited approaches, open-ended groups, and self-help groups.

The selected, mixed-gender therapy group adhered to the short-term time-limited model consisting of twenty three-hour sessions held weekly. The major purpose of the group was to provide education and therapeutic support within a clearly structured environment. Clients usually feel nervous about joining a group that will focus on memories that they may have suppressed for years. If the group has a foreseeable end, clients may feel more able to make the short-term commitment (Gil, 1990).

GROUP COMPOSITION

Composition of the mixed-gender group presents several issues for consideration, including previous therapy, adjustment prior to the group, supports outside the group, behavioural and personal characteristics, history of victimization, and the goodness of fit among members. The latter is especially important in terms of balance between men and women. An imbalance in the number of men and women in the group could increase maladaptive interactions such as blaming and care-taking.

The process of selecting candidates for the group consisted of completion of a screening questionnaire and a pre-group screening interview with the group leader. A second interview included a spouse or significant other chosen by the candidate. This step was included in the selection process due to limited resources available to candidates in the northern rural community as well as expressed interest of the clients in using the minimal support network that was available to them. Ultimately, the six-member group included three men and three women ranging in age from forty to fifty-five years. All members were married with children, had jobs in the community, were currently receiving, or had recently received, individual therapy, and were motivated to participate in the group experience.

GROUP STRUCTURE

Structure refers to the planned, systematic, time-limited interventions used to help clients change in desired directions (Toseland et al., 1995). Each session requires structure in the interest of personal safety and maximizing participation of group members. It is important to state clearly what the format for sessions will include and to stick to the format. Trust is a salient issue for survivors of childhood sexual abuse. The client expects to be betrayed, while setting the stage and opportunity for the betrayal, thus validating the basic belief that people cannot be trusted (Bradley et al., 1989). When the social worker maintains consistency with the format of sessions, issues of trust and personal safety begin to be repaired.

Guidelines and norms for the group are concerned with confidentiality, boundaries, and aspects such as start and end time, breaks, and permission to leave the room temporarily should group content become overwhelming to a member. While it remains the responsibility of the worker to establish confidentiality and boundary guidelines, the author encouraged the mixed-gender group to develop other norms. Although many ground rules are common among different groups, each group needs to ensure that its ground rules fit its unique identity (Crowder, 1993).

USE OF TIME AND TIMING

Timing as an aspect of group structure is pertinent in two areas: the number and length of each group session and the use of time during the session. The latter relates to the format of group sessions, including check-in, education, discussion, and closing. The mixed-gender group met in twenty sessions held weekly and the time allotted for each session was three hours, including a fifteen-minute break. It is generally held that each group member have time to speak. Individuals were required to participate, however minimally they chose, at check-in and at closing. Participation in discussion was more flexible with a "pass" option. Survivors are reluctant to reveal their true feelings and true selves to others and, like most individuals, approach the group with a mixture of fear and anxiety (Knight, 1997). It is the responsibility of the social worker to promote participation in discussion while respecting the hesitation of members to speak. Cohesiveness in the group develops as survivors risk sharing their stories and quiet members become empowered to speak as they listen to those who bravely take the initiative.

ASSESSMENT

Assessment of group process is ongoing throughout the life of the group. In a mixed-gender group one can expect certain themes to emerge, including differential communication styles, dissimilar expressions of anger, relationships with the opposite sex, and the possibility of flirtation and/or sexual tension. While it is easy to get caught up in the content of the group, it is the responsibility of the social worker to observe and gently confront behaviours that impair the group process.

In a group that includes men and women there is a tendency for women to talk less, talk primarily to the men, share less personal information, and be less involved in the discussion when men are in a group. On the other hand, men have been found to be more personal and self-disclosing in a group that contains both men and women (Knight, 1993). The social worker's gender and behaviour can be problematic if the worker adheres to gender-based expectations. However, if the social worker is sensitive and relatively bias-free the difficulties can be worked through. Appropriate modelling by the social worker is a crucial component in guiding the group's behaviour.

Suppression of emotions is a common characteristic among adult survivors of childhood sexual abuse and represents a difficult area of group work. With growing awareness of differential power, childhood losses, and lifelong effects of childhood sexual abuse, survivors can typically access their buried anger. Generally men are more able to express their anger while women can express other emotions such as sadness. The mixed-gender group affords an opportunity for vicarious experience of emotion for both sexes. Female members who grieve about their lost innocence and lost sense of self and self-worth are modelling appropriate behaviour for their male counterparts. Male members who vent their anger over their victimization are voicing the unspoken sentiments of the female participants (Knight, 1993).

Impaired relationships with the opposite sex is perhaps the primary issue clients identify as problematic. Individuals frequently present at mental health agencies with marital and relationship concerns; childhood sexual abuse is frequently disclosed later in the counselling process. Sometimes clients are unaware of the connection between childhood sexual abuse and current dissatisfaction with intimacy and sexuality in their relationships. A number of authors have discussed the impact of childhood sexual abuse on intimacy and sexuality.[3] The mixed-gender group is a social unit in which members inevitably act out dysfunctional relationship patterns.

Male survivors struggle with strong feelings of inadequacy and question their masculinity. They fear women, often defending against this through generalized feelings of suspicion, mistrust, and resentment. Female survivors harbor intense feelings of rage toward men, and are frightened by them (Knight, 1993).

In a study of psychosocial maladjustment, Hunter (1991) found that male and female child sexual abuse victims displayed less satisfaction in their intimate relationships. Another study found that males and females significantly differed with respect to the effect of early sexual experiences on current sexual attitudes and relationships, with females assigning more negative quality to these experiences (Fritz et al., 1981).

Relationship problems experienced by members of the mixed-gender group support the theory that childhood sexual abuse negatively affects the quality of marital relationships. What is lacking in the literature is information about parent–child relationships. Members of the mixed-gender group identify difficulties in parenting, including fear for the safety of their children, protective behaviours that often become control issues (especially as children enter adolescence), and a decreased ability to communicate their concerns to children because of the secrecy survivors have maintained about their own childhood victimization. Males describe a tendency to encourage sons toward physical fitness and sports, hoping that physical prowess would protect the boys. Males describe closer emotional relationships with daughters, with whom they could "let down their guard" and relate effectively. Females tended to be vigilant concerning their daughters' friends and activities, monitoring schedules and arrangements anxiously. Females indicated they were more relaxed about their sons' involvement with individuals and activities. Both sexes describe doubt and confusion about expressing physical affection toward their children. Due to the discovery in-group of the extent of the negative consequences of their childhood sexual abuse, members discussed the need for parenting skills support.

Sexual abuse of children is not about sexuality; it is violence perpetrated by an individual with more power toward an individual with less power. The inescapable fact is that the violence occurs in a sexual manner, thereby causing considerable damage to the sexual being of the survivor. Deighton et al. (1985) note in the agency's groups that members who were either married or involved in significant heterosexual relationships all report emotions ranging from extreme fear to disgust with sexual contacts (because any sexual contact might trigger mental flashbacks to childhood). Sexual dysfunction among sexual abuse survivors is widely reported in the literature.[4]

The mixed-gender group identified sexuality as an issue, but members were reluctant to talk about specifics. The author initiated discussion through an educational component focusing on healthy sexuality. Members responded positively to this approach, which led from intellectual discussion to individual concerns regarding their past and current sexuality. Although the potential for seductive behaviours among members existed, in actuality it was not an issue that is presented in this particular group. The need to control others, and the perception of self and others as sexual objects is a common pattern among sexual abuse survivors as a result of arrested sexual development. Contrary to expectations, the mixed-gender group members treated each other respectfully, maintaining good boundaries. Members exhibited nurturing, rather than sexualized behaviour toward each other. Knight (1993) reports members' interactions with one another may reflect another pattern frequently observed among survivors, which is their tendency to completely separate emotional intimacy from sexual intimacy.

GOAL SETTING AND CONTRACTING

Goal setting is an important functional aspect of group work in that goals can be measured and progress in the group therapy can be assessed. Goals can be thought of as individual and collective undertakings. Goal setting can be accomplished over the first two group sessions with the social worker assisting in the development of realistic, measurable goals. The highest priority is to offer an experience that will empower the clients to move beyond their preoccupation with the incest event (Bradley et al., 1989).

The mixed-gender group developed individual goals, including: the ability to sleep through a night without disrupting nightmares, relief of depression, development of healthy sexuality, relinquishing debilitating anger, confronting the abuser(s), and creating healthy family relationships. The group goals were to place the abuse experience(s) into perspective as a childhood tragedy and to move from surviving to thriving.

TERMINATION

Termination is often a painful, anxiety-evoking concept for survivors of childhood sexual abuse. Often relationships are not formally or appropriately terminated (Bradley et al., 1989). Members need to be well prepared for termination. In actuality termination begins at the onset of group therapy when the structure and format of the group are developed. In addition, termination occurs with each group session. Several sessions prior to termination, the social worker should address issues that clients identify such as fear of facing the world alone, new memories that result in a setback, resistance to closing and requests for more sessions, and a wavering self-confidence. These issues can be worked through in the last few sessions with sensitivity and compassion.

Reluctance to terminate in the mixed-gender group focused on the issues identified above and on the expressed need of members for continued identification with a community of survivors. Group members proposed the idea of continuing to meet as a self-help group. Good self-help groups offer many benefits to members. In consideration of access to a group facilitator in a nearby community, the author agreed to assist in the transition from therapy group to self-help group. Collaboration with the facilitator employed at a Sexual Abuse Centre in another northern community facilitated the transition and allowed a definitive ending with the group therapy social worker and a new beginning with resources outside of the mental health agency.

The final meeting ended with a celebration ceremony. The event included a meal and attendance of family members. Group members had previously discussed a desire to share aspects of their childhood experience with their children; members decided to conduct the sharing in a group format as they felt more comfortable and supported with others present. It was thought that initial disclosure in this manner was believed to provide a springboard to further discussion outside of the group.

EVALUATION OF THE GROUP EXPERIENCE

Evaluation is a process that occurs throughout the group experience and includes evaluation of group process, worker effectiveness, and programming. Evaluation is a naturally occurring aspect of termination and planning for formal evaluation as part of the closing session of the group allows members to reflect on their subjective experience within the group. Evaluation can be either written or verbal, providing feedback and information with which to improve future group therapy efforts.

In the case of the mixed-gender group, verbal evaluation of the twenty-week group treatment transpired at the closing celebration. Members' narratives simultaneously informed about the pain of the childhood sexual abuse, long-term effects, healing during the group experience, and hopefulness for the future. One male member explained how the feelings he had had prior to the group experience—that female physiology made it more "normal" for a female to be sexually abused than a male—had changed, because females in the group allowed him to see that the long-term effects of sexual abuse were similar for both sexes (despite differential physiology). A female member asserted that prior to the group experience she viewed all males as threatening and dangerous; the opportunity to listen to men who had been wounded in childhood facilitated a change in attitude that reflected compassion toward them.

PROFESSIONAL CONCERNS

To reiterate, it is generally recommended that groups for adult survivors of childhood sexual abuse use co-therapists, both to manage the intense work done in this type of group and to support each other. Crowder (1993) declares aspects of work with survivors, such as members' attempts to split the workers into good therapist and bad therapist, transference and counter-transference, and vicarious traumatization, require good teamwork and supervision.

Vicarious traumatization is the transformation of the therapist's or helper's inner experience as a result of empathic engagement with survivor clients and their trauma material (Saakvitne et al., 1996). Vicarious trauma is an occupational hazard. While an extensive knowledge base exists on the psychological consequences of traumatic experiences for victims, less attention has focused on the enduring psychological consequences for therapists who had exposure to the traumatic experiences of victim clients (McCann et al., 1990). Agencies have an organizational responsibility to recognize that vicarious trauma is a natural consequence of the work and to support trauma workers through provision of effective supervision, continuing education, caseloads that balance trauma survivors with less intense cases, and opportunity for professional networking among trauma workers in a geographical area. Individual workers need to be aware of their vulnerabilities and monitor themselves for signs of vicarious trauma, including changes in their beliefs, in their inner sense of balance, and in their sensory experiences. Social workers are notoriously poor with regard to self-care, despite advice and encouragement directed at clients to take care of their physical and psychological well-being. It is essential for trauma workers to strive for awareness and balance in their professional and personal lives.

Professional networking is difficult for social work practitioners in northern rural and remote communities because of isolation and long distances between communities with poor roads, especially during winter months. Agencies must balance the cost of travel and time away from work with the need to support trauma workers in their employment. A creative professional networking strategy, developed by trauma workers in three northern communities, was endorsed by their respective agencies. Monthly meetings rotating among the three communities afforded trauma workers a venue for support, ongoing education, and collaboration to address vicarious traumatization.

CONCLUSION

This chapter presents an innovative and powerful form of therapy for adult survivors of childhood sexual abuse, a group therapy format that includes both women and men. The realities of northern social work practice preclude recommended venues for group work with survivors, including homogeneous groups led by a same-sex worker. Advantages of the mixed-gender group prove unique in addressing the long-term effects of childhood sexual abuse, most notably relationships with the opposite sex. This chapter has also identified parenting as an area for further study.

NOTES

1. Bradley & Drews (1989); Deighton & McPeek (1985); Dolan (1991); Gil (1990); Scott (1999).
2. Bradley & Drews (1989); Deighton & McPeek (1985); Gil (1990); Scott (1999).
3. Bass & Davis (1988); Crowder (1993); Deighton & McPeek (1985); Dolan (1991); Gil (1990); Knight (1993); Scott (1999).
4. Bradley & Drews (1989); Cahill et al. (1991); Crowder (1993); Dolan (1991); Forward & Buck (1978); Fritz et al. (1981); Hunter (1991); Knight (1993); Singer (1989). Therapists must be prepared to sensitively deal with anything that is shared in order for the conflicts and issues of guilt be resolved (Bradley & Drews, 1989, p. 71.)

REFERENCES

Bass, E. & Davis, L. (1988). *The courage to heal*, rev. edn. New York: HarperCollins.
Bradley, T. T. & Drews, J. R. (1989). Group treatment for adults molested as children. *Social Work with Groups*, 12(3), 57–75.
Brownlee K. & Delaney R. (1997). Developing our own: Inside versus outside expertise in northern social work practice. In K. Brownlee, R. Delaney, & J. R. Graham (eds.), *Strategies for northern social work practice*, pp. 14–25. Thunder Bay: Centre for Northern Studies, Lakehead University.
Cahill, C., Llewelyn, S. P., & Pearson, C. (1991). Treatment of sexual abuse which occurred in childhood. *British Journal of Clinical Psychology*, 30, 1–12.
Crowder, A. (1993). *Opening the door: A treatment model for therapy with male survivors of sexual abuse*. Ottawa: National Clearinghouse on Family Violence.
Davis, L. (1990). *The courage to heal workbook: For women and men survivors of child sexual abuse*. New York: Harper & Row.
Deighton, J. & McPeek, P. (1985). Group treatment: Adult victims of childhood sexual abuse. *Social Casework*, 66, 403–412.
Dolan, Y. (1991). *Resolving sexual abuse*. New York: W. W. Norton.
Forward, S. & Buck, C. (1978). *Betrayal of innocence*. Markham: Penguin.
Fritz, G. S., Stoll, K., & Wagner, N. N. (1981). A comparison of males and females who were sexually molested as children. *Journal of Sex & Marital Therapy*, 7(1), 54–59.
Gil, E. (1990). *Treatment of adult survivors of childhood abuse*, 2nd end. Walnut Creek: Launch Press.
Graham, J. R. (1996). A practical idealism: A theoretical values conception for northern social work practice. In R. Delaney, K. Brownlee, & M. K. Zapf (eds.), *Issues in northern social work practice*, pp. 95–103. Thunder Bay: Centre for Northern Studies, Lakehead University.

Hunter, J. A. (1991). A comparison of the psychosocial maladjustment of adult males and females sexually molested as children. *Journal of Interpersonal Violence*, 6(2), 205–217.

Knight, C. (1993). The use of a therapy group for adult men and women sexually abused in childhood. *Social Work with Groups*, 16(4), 81–93.

Knight, C. (1997). Critical roles and responsibilities of the leader in a therapy group for adult survivors of child sexual abuse. *Journal of Child Sexual Abuse*, 6(1), 21–37.

McCann, L. L. & Pearlman, L. A. (1990). Vicarious traumatization: A framework for understanding the psychological effects of working with victims. *Journal of Traumatic Stress*, 3(1), 131–149.

Saakvitne, K. W. & Pearlman, L. A. (1996). *Transforming the pain*. New York: W. W. Norton.

Scott, W. (1999). Group therapy for survivors of severe childhood abuse: Repairing the social contract. *Journal of Child Sexual Abuse*, 7(3), 35–55.

Singer, K. I. (1989). Group work with men who experienced incest in childhood. *American Journal of Orthopsychiatry*, 59(3), 468–471.

Toseland, R. & Rivas, R. (1995). *An introduction to group work practice*, 2nd edn. Boston: Allyn and Bacon.

Chapter Eleven

POLICE RESPONSES TO FAMILY VIOLENCE IN A NORTHERN COMMUNITY: Some Implications for Policy

Julie Woit, Keith Brownlee, Rod Brown, and Roger Delaney

The police have a key role in assisting families in crisis with domestic violence situations.[1] However, controversies have surrounded police responses to domestic violence.[2] This controversy is perhaps related to police attitudes toward family violence, role ambiguity when intervening in a domestic violence situation, and confusing departmental policy.[3] Moreover, co-ordination difficulties between police services and social work services have been identified by Hechler (1988), who reports that social workers tend use co-ordination strategies to bring about change while police tend to enforce the law through confrontation. In a similar vein, Saunders (1988) believes that the basic differences in belief systems between police and social workers must be addressed and worked on prior to initiating co-ordinated activities.

Trute et al. (1994) explore issues associated with co-ordinating child sexual abuse services in rural communities. Because they were interested in philosophical differences between members of key professional groups in a co-ordinated service, they developed empirical measures to explore professional attitudes toward intervention, in other words, a means of measuring professional ideology. In terms of the differences between police attitudes and other human service professionals, they found significant differences in three areas. First, in terms of the "seriousness of the issue," police scored significantly lower than child welfare workers; this suggests that police believe child sex abuse to be less traumatic than other professionals. Second, police scored significantly lower than child welfare workers and mental health workers in terms of prioritizing treatment over punishment; this suggests that police officers view treatment as being less effective than punishment. Finally, overall the police scored significantly lower than child welfare workers, suggesting that they are less likely to identify many different types of perpetrators and their families who are involved in child sexual abuse. They conclude that these attitudinal differences must be addressed in order for effective co-ordination to exist. An interesting fact from this study is that there was no significant difference between female and male police officers on these three issues. However, it is important to emphasize that families can benefit directly from a positive encounter with the police (Brown, 1984; Jaffe et al., 1978).

This chapter describes efforts made in Thunder Bay, Ontario, to improve police responses to domestic violence and to make their interventions more successful/helpful to the families and individuals involved. We believe that our experience with these efforts raise important considerations for integrated responses to family violence.

The authors involved the Thunder Bay Police in a study with two aims in mind. First, the idea was to investigate how women who experienced domestic assault would perceive the service provided by the police under two conditions of police response; and second, whether the different police responses would influence the number of women seeking social services. In the first police response, existing orders were to be followed, which directed officers to leave a card (Domestic Violence Referral Card) of support and counselling services available to victims. The second police response involved initiating a call to the local Physical and Sexual Assault Centre to request their immediate on-site services on behalf of the victim. This option was chosen because research has shown that women in domestic violence situations often do not initiate contact with social service agencies, and that if the police initiate the contact on their behalf it often leads to the most effective response (Caputo et al., 1986; Finn, 1985; Parnas, 1971). It was anticipated that the involvement of the Domestic Violence Response Team would lead to a perception of the support provided by the police as being more helpful and that it might lead to an increased use of local counselling and support services by the women.

The study included 102 women who were victims of domestic violence and who sought assistance from community service providers. The small size of the community made it possible to include almost all community service providers in the project. All the shelter houses (shelters are specifically mandated to provide a place of safety for victims of domestic assault) and secondary community service agencies (agencies mandated to provide counselling to adults in general) agreed to participate in the data collection.

A Client Participation Questionnaire, consisting of seven brief questions, was used. The questions included whether the police were called during the last incident of family violence and, if not, the reasons for not calling them; the month the incident occurred; whether the Domestic Violence Response Team was called and, if not, the reasons for not calling them; whether the team's efforts were helpful to the individual; and finally, whether the police interventions were helpful.

The Sexual and Physical Assault Centre agreed to have a worker respond to a call from the police if that service was required following a domestic incident. This worker would be a member of their Domestic Violence Response Team, and would make a site visit. The Police Department agreed to implement the two response conditions and to make available the police computer network.

Three separate Routine Orders, or Directives, were issued by the Chief of Police. In accordance with customary procedures the uniformed officers received these orders through the computer network. The first order re-established an existing order that directed officers to leave the Domestic Violence Referral Card with the victim during investigations. As noted above, this card listed a variety of resources and support available in the community. The second order was a repeat of the first given again after one month, restating the same directive, to ensure full participation. The officers were directed to leave the card and when clearing the occurrence to inform the Communications Centre of this intervention. The order to inform the Communications Centre was necessary to track whether the card was being left. The third directive, issued to the officers in the same manner, identified the background of this study, and the procedures involved in contacting the Domestic Violence Response Team. The order directed the police to actively initiate the referral. Although the initiative was expected to be taken by the police at this point, it should be noted that once contact had been made with the Domestic Violence Response Team the client was in no way pressured to accept services or maintain contact after the first visit.

An unexpected finding emerged from the project. Very few officers indicated in their occurrence report that the card had been left, and fewer officers contacted the Domestic Violence Response Team. The routine orders to the police officers did not mention that this intervention had to be acknowledged in the clearing remarks to the Communications Centre; thus, occurrence narratives on the Ontario Municipal and Provincial Police Automative Cooperative (OMPPAC) were reviewed to determine whether or not the police officers were requesting the services of the Domestic Violence Response Team.

It became evident from this information that many calls that should have been designated as "domestic violence" were identified under "assault involving family members" for which the Domestic Violence Response Team did not have to be notified. The results showed a significant decrease, $X2 = 5.09$, $df = 1$, $p<.02$, in the designation of the category of domestic violence. This raised a question with regard to internal communications and policy surrounding the entry and categorizing of the violent incident. As a result a second study was carried out to examine internal police communications and to describe the front-line constables' "relationship" with the information communication system that governs their daily professional performance.

The participants for the study were drawn from the Thunder Bay Police Services. Although a request was made to be allowed to randomly select a number of uniformed officers to participate in a qualitative study, permission was not granted for this procedure and twelve officers were selected, by their supervisor, to participate. The officers ranged in age from twenty-five years to forty-five years and numbers of service years ranging from two to nineteen years. Ten male and two female officers were interviewed.

The researchers elected to conduct individual interviews with the twelve officers while they were on active patrol duty. A decision was made, following informal conversations with officers, to manually record, versus audiotaping, the conversation with the officer. The manual recording of the content appeared to be perceived as less threatening to the officers. The manual recording created difficulties in clearly recording verbatim.

A semi-structured questionnaire with seven questions was used. Four of the questions addressed the issues of internal communications, specifically standing orders and directives. One question addressed differences between sexual assault and domestic violence investigations. Another question explored police perception of auxilliary social work support services and the last question explored police perceptions of individual values and attitudes affecting work performance.

The researchers hoped to gain additional insights, through these questions, into how the individual officer processes communications that directly influence his/her daily conduct. Through these final three questions, the researchers hoped to gain insights into the issue of individuality and, further, what has been previously referred to here as the "individual discretion" of the uniformed officer, and how individual views and values influence his/her intervention.

During the interview process, the officers shared their views on a number of items. A seemingly high degree of comfort was achieved between the officers and the researcher, facilitating the officer's expression of views on a number of items. These included frustration and discontent toward present role and performance demands, and the perceived lack of support from administration and, further, from the community.

Once the interviews were completed, the data was reviewed separately by two researchers to increase the reliability of individual objective analysis. Each written transcript was then directed back to the respondent to review. When time and opportunity allowed, a direct contact was made with the respondent; otherwise, due to one researchers studying abroad, a note was left with the transcript, asking the respondent to review the transcript and to make any corrections, deletions, or additions to the recording as necessary. This was to ensure that the officer felt that s/he had been accurately represented. As well, given the inability to record verbatim, the transcription at times appeared "choppy" as sentences were incomplete (the topic of conversation often ranged from topic to topic). In providing the respondents the transcripts to review, validity is supported by ensuring agreement between researcher and informant (Smith et al., 1994). The officers were provided with a contact person from within the Police Services who would ensure that the transcripts were returned to the researchers and who also maintained their anonymity. One implication of leaving the transcript was the officer did not have the opportunity for "face-to-face" contact with the researcher. However, given the uniformed officer's busy work schedule, leaving the transcript to review at his/her opportunity may have been a suitable alternative.

The responses for each question were summarized and condensed into specific themes. The researchers then reviewed and compared the analysis of each question, condensing the data even further to form central categories. This process follows the format outlined within ethnographic content analysis, in which the researcher "begins with a discovery-oriented ethnographic design to generate descriptive categories and theoretical concepts directly from detailed descriptions from a group of people (i.e., informants) from within a particular setting of interest" (Atkinson et al., 1989, cited in Smith et al., 1994).

From the reviewed transcripts, three central categories of concern emerged. Following the review of the categories additional officer perceptions will be highlighted.

1. Too many directives.

Officers' comments on the excess of directives include the following; " ... so many, impossible to keep track of," " ... literally hundreds of routine orders," and "so many orders to read, it's tough to concentrate on any." With the excessive numbers of orders, officers explained how they were not provided with sufficient time to review them. This is evident in the following remarks: " ... issued poorly, not enough training on Standing Orders, thrown on computer and not enough time to study them," and " ... never provided time to review it; there is no form to ensure the Constable reads it." Officers further called for the need to simplify the Orders, such as "simplifying Orders, so everything is outlined" and "Directives in e-mail are/can be 5 pages long, 90% of the e-mail gets F6'd" (discarded).

2. Criticism of e-mail.

Comments made throughout the interviews reflected further discontent with the manner in which the orders are communicated via computer services. The following reflects these concerns; "OMPPAC terrible way of communicating info ... " and " ... seems logical how they are doing it now but not efficient ... I can't suggest a better way." Officers also disliked the lack of "face-to-face" contact between supervisors and constables: "E-mail ...

absolutely not [efficient], don't use to full advantage; can't replace face-to-face contact."

3. *Lack of respect for uniformed body by senior administration.*
Statements consisted of concern for the division between administration and constable: "Lack of respect for front line officers from administration." There were also comments regarding uniformed officers not being consulted prior to the issuing of a directive. These comments include the following: " ... if I voice something to administration, I feel like I'm hitting my head against the wall ... " and, "more input (required) from persons who the directives are directed to .... "

Officers' perceptions on other topics will be analyzed briefly here. All twelve officers involved in the study considered that the directives they received were followed to some degree. Comments on this subject included: "To a large extent they are followed, police procedures adhered to as best as possible"; "I would say they're [officers] following the idea or perception of what's being wanted but are not following by the letter": "Like any organization you have people who follow and the rebellious few who don't"; and "I think basically we follow them [directives], in general we know that if we don't we can be charged under the Police Act."

There was an equal division between respondents as to whether the two types of assaults, domestic and sexual, elicit different responses, with the differences reflecting some officers' beliefs that differences exist in the investigations. Officers' statements on the differences between the two investigation procedures include the following: "sexual assaults, so many different levels of seriousness, take more time to investigate; takes time to take a proper statement"; "sexual assault and assault are different offences, the sex assault victim has a clearer understanding of what is the police role, [whereas in a] domestic role of police not so clear"; and "domestic [assault] is easier to investigate; both parties are present; a lot of sexual assaults [victims] don't know the identity [of the assailant]." Statements on the similarities between the two investigation procedures included the following: "I don't do much that is different; treat it as an assault basically the same way, take a report, talk to witnesses, if possible arrest the accused"; "basically they are both serious criminal investigations warranting interviews with victims and witnesses ... " and, "no less of an investigation done between them; every report and incident is different—some investigations are short."

When the respondents were asked whether personal values influenced the officer's performance, seven officers believed that they did: " ... officers attending to calls can be bringing their experiences into it; it's part of being human"; and, "I would say yes, can't get away from that; ... past incidents/people can influence an officer, that's part of life, just like how the victim views us." Five respondents believed officers' personal values did not influence their performance. One statement that supports this view is as follows: "most of us are extremely professional, we may have these thoughts but they aren't let out during the call."

Hanewicz (1985) identifies three approaches toward the issue of "discretion." The first is the legal approach. "This approach to discretion is probably the oldest .... Americans have had a tendency to look to the law for solutions to social and personal problems (phrases like 'Let's make a law against it' and 'Sue the bastards!' get their bite from their truth). Consequently, it is only natural that we should expect the law to take care of the discretion problem" (p. 44). An example of the legal approach, on a local level, is the directive from the Solicitor General, which orders that criminal charges shall be laid in all domestic assault situations. The statement reported by the researchers referring to the threat of charges being laid under the Police Services Act, if charges are not laid in a domestic assault, is an example of the legal approach to discretion.

The second approach is the organizational approach. Hanewicz (1985) points out that within this approach, " ... more attention should be directed to the organizational environment of policing, where administrative policies and regulations are formed to guide the day-to-day activity of police officers. This second approach emphasizes the role of the chief administrator in shaping the world of discretion" (p. 45). According to Goldstein in *Policing a Free Society* (cited in Hanewicz, 1985), " ... the result of distinguished academic and administrative experience sets out the responsibility of police administrators to provide clear guidance to police officers in handling the wide array of discretionary situations they encounter .... As a general rule, police administrators have not adequately taken on this responsibility" (p. 45). Obstacles to providing this clear guidance are reflected in the comments of this study's participating officers' such as, " ... lack of face to face contact" [with supervisors], "too many directives," and the "inability to retrieve messages easily." A second issue under the organizational approach is the belief that police administrators perceive they understand the profession better than others. Statements by participating officers further suggest a perception that the administration believes itself to understand policing better than front-line officers. Comments made earlier regarding the lack of respect for uniformed body by senior administration certainly reflect this.

The last approach is the behavioural approach, which involves a "detailed dissection of the daily police role ... it begins where discretion is exercised by individual police officers, and works its way to other perspectives as insights warrant" (Hanewicz, 1985, p. 46). The researchers identified values and ethics of officers in making daily decisions, which reflects this more phenomenologically based approach. The officers' comments, which state that values and attitudes did influence their practices, could warrant further exploration.

Following the analysis of the officer statements, the officers' were contacted once again to review the central categories, and were asked to indicate if they agreed with the analysis. Several officers responded, and participated in providing additional feedback. Often, the officer added information to the already existing central categories substantiating what was already said or, in one case, informing the researcher that some additional new training had been provided (which this particular officer believed was beneficial).

RECOMMENDATIONS

In conclusion, the following recommendations are offered for consideration based upon the issues that emerged from the interviews with the police officers.

- Explore the possibility of Thunder Bay Police Service developing a system that allows input from front-line officers into the formation of standing orders and directives.
- When standing orders and directives are formulated, ensure they are concise, clear, and direct.
- Officers need ample time to review orders at the beginning of their shift, especially after extended time off. Officers also would appreciate important and ongoing orders to be posted in an accessible location where they can be reviewed on occasion. Two suggestions provided by participants included leaving the directive in the lunch-room or the recording room.
- A system could be developed in which officers must sign that they have read and understood the directives that apply to them. This system would generate discussion between front-line officers and their immediate supervisors regarding controversial directives. Additional training sessions may be both necessary and beneficial to ensure understanding of the directives.
- Administration should take a leadership role in acknowledging positive job performance by front-line officers. Gandy (1967) found that police officers will seriously limit discretion if they believe their decision may have a negative consequence on their record in the department or may result in discipline for making poor judgments. Acknowledgment that co-ordination is valued and will not reflect poorly on the officer in the event of a mistake will increase the likelihood of their using discretion and working with other agencies.
- Canvassing of front line-officers to discover their training needs will assist the in-service training officer in completing an effective training schedule.
- The researchers support the view of Hanewicz (1985) in the "need to improve upon the training and related preparation of police officers for

the responsibility and dynamics of discretion" (p. 51). Moreover, the need to understand the ideology that drives police services, and to work to minimize basic belief differences between the police and other stake holders in co-ordinated services is also essential (Trute et al., 1994).

In closing, one question posed to the officers dealt with their perceptions of how personal values and attitudes influence performance. Over half of the responding officers believed that personal values and attitudes influenced how officers respond to occurrences. Since it is very difficult, if not impossible, to alter an individual's personality or long-standing attitudes, it is essential that hiring practices be developed and maintained to ensure that each candidate has the values and ethics consistent with protection and service. Professional suitability inventories may be one tool utilized by hiring committees to explore comprehensively this significant issue. Individuality is difficult for bureaucracies to accommodate. Hanewicz (1985) states, " ... psychology may help us to understand what people are capable of, and what they cannot do too often if they are to remain mentally and physically healthy" (p. 51). The researchers believe that personality inventories that examine stress management styles and work performance in adverse conditions, when given to candidates during the hiring process, would provide insight as to how candidates would exercise discretion in the execution of policing duties.

NOTES

1. Bae (1981); Berk et al. (1980); Jaffe et al. (1978); Pence et al. (1989); Waaland et al. (1985).
2. Cannings (1984); Cohn (1987); Homant (1985); Lavoie et al. (1989); Oppenlander (1982).
3. Caputo & Moynihan (1986); Parnas (1971); Smith (1987).

REFERENCES

Bae, R. P. (1981). Ineffective crisis intervention techniques: The case of the police. *Journal of Crime and Justice*, 4, 61–82.

Berk, S. & Loseke, D. (1980). "Handling" family violence: Situational determinants of police arrest in domestic disturbances. *Law and Society Review*, 15, 319–345.

Brown, S. E. (1984). Police responses to wife beating: Neglect of a crime of violence. *Journal of Criminal Justice*, 12, 277–288.

Cannings, M. (1984). Myths and stereotypes—Obstacles to effective police intervention in domestic disputes involving a battered woman. *Police Journal*, 57(1), 43–56.

Caputo, R. K. & Moynihan, F. M. (1986). Family options: A practice/research model in family violence. *Social Casework: The Journal of Contemporary Social Work*, 67, 460–465.

Cohn, E. G. (1987). Changing the domestic violence policies of urban police departments: Impact of the Minneapolis experiment. *Response to the Victimization of Women and Children*, 10(4), 22–24.

Finn, J. (1985). The stresses and coping behavior of battered women. *Social Casework: The Journal of Contemporary Social Work*, 66, 341–349.

Gandy, J. (1967). The exercise of discretion by the police. Unpublished D.S.W. thesis, Faculty of Social Work, University of Toronto.

Hanewicz, W. B. (1985). Discretion and order. In F. A. Elliston & M. Feldberg (eds.), *Moral issues in police work*. Totowa: Rowman and Allanfeld.

Hechler, D. (1988). *The battle and the backlash*. Lexington: Lexington Books.

Homant, R. J. (1985). The police and spouse abuse: A review of recent findings. *Police Studies*, 8(3), 163–172.

Jaffe, P., Thompson, J. K., & Paquin, M. J. (1978). Immediate family crisis intervention as preventative mental health: The family consultant service. *Professional Psychology*, November, 551–560.

Lavoie, F., Jacob, M., Hardy, J., & Martin, G. (1989). Police attitudes in assigning responsibility for wife abuse. *Journal of Family Violence*, 4, 369–388.

Oppenlander, N. (1982). Coping or copping out: Police service delivery in domestic disputes. *Criminology*, 20, 449–465.

Parnas, R. I. (1971). The police response to domestic violence. In L. Radzinowicz and M. E. Wolfgang (eds.), *Crime and Justice: The criminal in the arms of the law*, vol. 2. New York: Basic Books.

Pence, E., Duprey, M., Paymar, M., & McDonnell, C. (1989). *The justice system's response to domestic assault cases: A guide for policy development*. Duluth: Minnesota Program Development.

Saunders, E. (1988). A comparative study of attitudes toward child sexual abuse among social work and judicial system professionals. *Child Abuse and Neglect*, 12, 83–90.

Smith, D. A. (1987). Police response to interpersonal violence: Defining the parameters of legal control. *Social Forces*, March, 767–782.

Smith, T. E., Sells, S. P., & Clevenger, T. (1994). Ethnographic content analysis of couple and therapist perceptions in a reflecting team setting. *Journal of Marital and Family Therapy*, 20, 267–286.

Trute, B., Adkins, E., & MacDonald, G. (1994). *Coordinating child sexual abuse services in rural communities*. Toronto: University of Toronto Press.

Waaland, P. & Keeley, S. (1985). Police decision making in wife abuse: The impact of legal and extralegal factors. *Law and Human Behaviour*, 9(4), 355–366.

Chapter Twelve

HISTORICAL AND SOCIAL INFLUENCES ON VIOLENCE IN ABORIGINAL FAMILIES

Michelle Derosier and Raymond Neckoway

INTRODUCTION

In recent history many Aboriginal Peoples have begun to provide their account of the centuries-old relationship with the dominant society, an historical relationship that was, at times, very destructive and full of suffering and devastation. Aboriginal Peoples' history has been documented by non-Aboriginal peoples, attempting to portray a nation about which they knew little or nothing.

The tragic effects of colonization on Aboriginal Peoples over the centuries is now being more widely recognized, and perhaps, more importantly, validated. Hundreds of years of colonization and forced assimilation have eroded a traditional Aboriginal way of life, culminating in poverty, depression, alcoholism, suicide, and violence across generations. Emma LaRocque (1994) refers to colonization as "a process of encroachment and subsequent subjugation of Aboriginal peoples since the arrival of Europeans. From the Aboriginal perspective, it refers to loss of lands, resources, and self-direction and to the severe disturbance of cultural ways and values" (p. 73).

LaRocque (1994) also makes the connection between colonization and the racism that is still prevalent between Aboriginals and mainstream society. The historical view of Aboriginal Peoples being "savages" and "squaws" may not be as prevalent today; however, subtle remnants of these derogatory labels can arguably still be felt by many Aboriginal Peoples. She states that "Colonization and racism go hand in hand" and that:

> Racism has provided justification for the subjugation of Aboriginal Peoples. While all Aboriginal people are subjected to racism, women further suffer from sexism. Racism breeds hatred of Aboriginal peoples; sexism breeds

hatred of women. For Aboriginal women, racism and sexism constitute a package experience (LaRocque, 1994, p. 74).

Many Aboriginal Peoples, today continue to suffer a sense of cultural loss, as well as disruption to their cultural norms and values. The impact of colonialism, in particular with the experience of residential schools, continues to resonate in current Aboriginal life. The losses that Aboriginal Peoples, have suffered have been great. Many generations of cultural evolution have brought changes in the roles, values, and traditions of our people, which have caused us to lose pride in our history. These changes have created confusion, at times even chaos, in Aboriginal communities, evident in behaviours such as alcoholism, suicide, and widespread violence.

Despite the turmoil and consequential effects of the past, we see a tremendous healing journey taking place within many Aboriginal communities across Canada. Aboriginal Peoples are working hard in many different arenas (i.e., health, justice, child welfare, and education) by utilizing both traditional and Western approaches to guide communities toward wellness for the generations to come.

HISTORICAL CONTEXT

Violence and aggressive behaviour can be traced back throughout history. History provides examples of violence in all societies, particularly against women and children. It would be inaccurate and unreasonable to say that there was no violence within traditional Aboriginal communities. However, many have suggested that violence was not as prevalent and widespread as it has become in the last several decades. There are historical accounts that support the notion that equality, respect, and harmonious living between the sexes were valued parts of traditional Aboriginal life (Hart, 2002). Unfortunately, the values of respect and harmony between the sexes appear to have eroded over time. Several studies have been conducted that support this statement. One such study, completed in 1989 by the Ontario Native Women's Association (cited in Royal Commission on Aboriginal Peoples, 1996a), found that eight out of ten Aboriginal women in Ontario had personally experienced family violence. Of those women, 87 per cent had been injured physically and 57 per cent had been sexually abused.

Egalitarianism was common for traditional Aboriginal society, in contrast to the patriarchal European society of the time. An example of the power difference between men and women can be understood when discussing the "rule of thumb." Historically in European society, a man could legally beat his wife with a rod no thicker than his thumb. Clare Brant (1990) also makes reference to this rule when discussing Native ethics: "the permissiveness and non-interference that Native men practiced with regard to their wives and children was a source of puzzlement to early settlers who applied the 'rule of thumb' to beating their own family members as a means of 'keeping them organized and disciplined' (p. 3). Brant (1990) also describes the ethic of non-interference as "a behavioral norm of North American Native tribes that promote positive interpersonal relations by discouraging coercion of any kind, be it physical, verbal, or psychological" (p. 535).

The centrality of the traditional Native "ethics," which were once an essential part of harmonious community living, appears to be less prevalent than it was in the past. LaRocque (1994) makes a correlation between the erosion of traditional Native ethics and values, and the current status of Aboriginal women. More specifically, she attributes the diminishing status of women to the progression of colonialism. "Prior to colonialism, Aboriginal women enjoyed comparative honour, equality and even political power in a way European women did not at the same time in history" (p. 73). She further states that:

> Many, if not the majority, of Aboriginal cultures were originally matriarchal or semi-matriarchal. European patriarchy was initially imposed upon Aboriginal societies in Canada through the fur trade, missionary Christianity and government policies. Because of white intrusion, the matriarchal character of Aboriginal spiritual, economic, kinship, and political institutions was drastically altered. (p. 73–74)

In matriarchal societies, in contrast to patriarchal ones, the mother is at the head of the family, clan, or tribe; final decision-making power rests with her or possibly with other older females in this kind of organization. It is imperative to understand that this system was particular to certain cultural groups, and that this is not meant to reflect a "Pan-Indian" organizational structure.

There are a variety of causes of violence in any society, and the problem of violence cannot be addressed with any singular explanation. However, many authors make a link between systemic racism and colonialism, and the inequality of, and subsequent breakdown in, colonized societies (Memmi, 1991). The breakdown of colonized societies implies the weakness and inferiority of the colonized rather than the effects of colonization. Warry (1998) makes reference to the continuing systemic racism in Canada, which he feels still exists today, when he states, "Aboriginal people feel this racism in many ways—when searching for a job, when in school, through subtle images in text or television. Racism continues to restrict individual and collective achievement" (p. 30). This is important to mention when looking at the cycle of violence within

Aboriginal communities. For Aboriginal individuals who leave their communities to escape violence, racism faced in an urban centre is an additional barrier. When faced with racism their hope may be diminished and the return to the cycle of abuse may appear to be the only option.

Also discussed within the literature on violence in Aboriginal communities is the notion of the normalization of violence. There has been a lack of positive role models within the many communities that have been inundated with violence across generations. Many Aboriginal communities are small and close knit and, for some, violence has almost become the norm. McGillivary (cited by Proulx et al., 2000) refers to this normalization of violence within isolated communities as a major barrier to protecting women and children. He states that "denying that violence is taking place, or defining it as natural, cultural, or inevitable continues to perpetuate the violence and complicates the system's response to it" (p. 4).

While family violence in Aboriginal communities shares many characteristics with Canadian society at large, the Royal Commission on Aboriginal Peoples (RCAP) states that:

> Family violence in Aboriginal communities is distinct, however, in that the unbalanced power relationships that structure the lives of Aboriginal people are not found primarily in the relationships between men and women. The imbalance lies in the powerlessness of Aboriginal people relative to society as a whole, including the social institutions that dominate every aspect of their lives, from the way they are educated and the way they can earn a living to the way they are governed (RCAP, 1996c, Vol. 3, Ch. 2).

The imbalance described above continues to be observable within Aboriginal communities. Aboriginal Peoples, in some communities, still suffer what has been referred to as "Third World Conditions." Poverty, high unemployment rates, lack of adequate housing, and overcrowding are issues Aboriginal communities continue to face. With the erosion of a traditional economy and the lack of employment opportunities within Aboriginal communities, members find themselves reliant on government programs to provide for their families. The scarce employment opportunities in Aboriginal communities are hardly enough to provide for the community as a whole. In Aboriginal communities the limited work that is available is often granted to women. Brant (1990) makes reference to this, stating "the little work which does exist on many Native reserves such as community health representatives, child protection workers, cleaning staff, and secretarial work, is often awarded to women" (p. 251). The increased tendency for women to work outside the home has also been recently linked in the literature as another cause for domestic violence:

The Indian men, however, unemployed and idle are constantly humiliated by having their families being supported by the welfare system. A power struggle ensues when the Native woman is the breadwinner and the exercise of intimidation and violence may be the last resort of the down trodden warrior (Brant, 1990, p. 251).

Some of the damaging long-term psychological conditions such as shame and humiliation have been mentioned throughout the literature on Aboriginal violence. Memmi (1991) reveals how the economic, social, educational, legal, and political structures are all designed to benefit the colonizers. This would apply to policies relating to employment, the ability to trade or set up businesses, the use of property as collateral, and so on. These policies have been developed to the detriment of Aboriginal communities in their inability to compete with municipalities for business development and investment. This creates conditions of poverty and dependence.

Another concern that is mentioned within the literature is a process that is referred to as "internalization." Adams (cited by LacRoque 1994) states: "as a result of disintegrative processes inherent in colonization, Aboriginal people have subconsciously judged themselves against the standards of white society, often adopting the White Ideal, which entails 'internalizing' or believing—swallowing the standards, judgments, expectations and portrayals of the dominant white society" (p. 74). Authors[1] have provided documentation regarding the negative stereotypes and the externally enforced descriptions of themselves, which have created feelings of shame and rejection not only of themselves but also of Aboriginal Peoples in general. Warry (1998) also refers to internalization as "cultural stress" when he states: "the internalized effect of colonialism and post-colonialism, and racism, which leads individuals to question their personal self worth and value of their own culture" (p. 145).

RESIDENTIAL SCHOOLS

All across Canada many Aboriginal Peoples are beginning to tell "their" stories. As the stories of the past unfold, the atrocities that lie within a dark history are revealed. Many of these stories are filled with the suffering and devastation that has long been ignored.

Conceivably one of the most devastating occurrences in recent history has been the attempt of the Canadian federal government to "civilize" and "assimilate" Aboriginal children through "education." Aboriginal children across Canada were removed (at times forcibly) from their home communities and placed into residential schools. "The schools, 80 of them at the high point, were the centerpiece of the assimilation strategy" (RCAP, 1996a, Vol. 1, Part 2, Ch. 6). Some of the residential schools were situated far from their communities, making it difficult for parental or family visits (in some schools parental visits were not permitted). Children were separated from their families for months at a time and, in some cases, did not see their families again.

> The common wisdom of the day that animated the educational plans of church and state was that Aboriginal children had to be rescued from their "evil surroundings," isolated from parents, families and community, and "kept constantly within the circle of civilized conditions" (RCAP, 1996a, Vol. 1, Part 2, Ch. 10).

While in the residential schools, some children with siblings at the same school were not permitted to communicate with each other, especially in their native tongue and children were often punished for speaking their language. Knockwood (1992) provides an example of what would take place if the children at the residential school at Shubenacadie, Nova Scotia, were caught speaking their native tongue: "when little children first arrived at the school we would see bruises on their throats and cheeks that told us that they had been caught speaking Mi'kmaw. Once the bruises began to fade, we knew they'd stop talking" (p. 98).

Many Aboriginal Peoples relate the shame and humiliation directly back to their experiences in residential schools. Knockwood (1992) states: "many students remember the systematic humiliation which they suffered at least as vividly as the pain. More than three decades after the school's closing many students still feel a sense of violation and shame" (p. 91). Some Aboriginal Peoples refer to the shame and humiliation as being worse than the physical beatings. Many Aboriginal Peoples feel that shame and humiliation is a direct result of the racism, oppression, and colonization. While others make reference to specific incidences that created this shame, such as being publicly shamed and humiliated in the residential schools for bedwetting, the humiliating public inspections of the female students' underwear, and humiliation of sexual abuse. Some of these experiences can be found in the testimonies of students who attended the Shubenacadie residential school in Nova Scotia (Knockwood, 1992) and many personal testimonies throughout the Royal Commission on Aboriginal Peoples Report (1996a, 1996,b, 1996c).

Aboriginal Peoples were systematically deprived of their language, culture, and spirituality. This systemic deprivation is described by the Royal Commission Report on Aboriginal Peoples: "it was through language that children received their cultural heritage from parents and community. It was the vital connection that civilizers knew had to be cut if progress was to be made. With the growing silence would come the dying whisper of Aboriginal cultures" (1996a, Vol. 1, Part 2, Ch. 10).

For many Aboriginal children who attended residential schools, sexual, physical, and emotional abuse was widespread. Many children, while attending residential schools, were subjected to multiple forms of abuse for many years. When many of these children left the residential schools and became adults, they were left with minimal parenting skills and years of experiencing and observing violent behaviours. In accordance with social learning theory (Bandura, 1973), individuals experiencing multiple forms and levels of abuse have learned to interact in violent ways. The intergenerational effects of the residential schools are also discussed in the Royal Commission Report on Aboriginal Peoples.

> The residential school led to a disruption in the transference of parenting skills from one generation to the next. Without these skills many survivors had difficulty in raising their own children. In residential schools, they learned that adults often exert power and control through abuse. The lessons learned in childhood are often repeated in adulthood with the result that many survivors of the residential school system often inflict abuse on their own children. These children in turn use the same tools on their children (RCAP, 1996a, Vol. 1. Ch. 10).

Many Aboriginal Peoples turned to alcohol as a means of coping with the pain, humiliation, and suffering from their past. For many years Aboriginal Peoples suffered in silent anguish as they reached for alcohol as a means to dull the pain, which in turn only created further problems within the communities. For some Aboriginal communities, alcohol abuse and suicide reached epidemic proportions. In a report prepared for the Aboriginal Healing Foundation in 2003, Corrado et al. (2003) state that:

> In addition to the cultural damage to Aboriginal societies effected by the residential school system, it is estimated that 85 per cent of the Aboriginal clientele in drug and alcohol treatment programs today have been in residential schools. Moreover, it is argued that the high levels of various psychological problems facing Aboriginal people, including depression, family violence and breakdown, mental health problems and specific self-destructive behaviors such as suicide are the direct result of the abuse by Aboriginal Peoples in the residential school system (p. 12).

In the early 1980s, a healing movement began to correct the damages being done by what was thought of as primarily an alcohol problem. "The earliest initiatives focused on addressing the pernicious pattern of alcoholism that was destroying so many lives" (Solicitor General of Canada, 2002, p. 4). "As more and more individuals began to experience success in dealing with their alcoholism, it gradually became clear that alcohol and drug abuse was only the "tip" of a very large and complex "iceberg, the bulk of which remained hidden beneath the surface of community life" (Solicitor General of Canada, 2002, p. 5).

In residential schools children were taught not to cry, and developed a loss of feeling and/or learned inappropriate ways of expressing feelings. Phil Fontaine, the 1992 Grand Chief of the Assembly of Manitoba Chiefs and former residential school student, challenged the norm of "don't talk" by stating:

> The residential school experience had serious negative consequences for many of our people who have suffered in silence for too long. It is time to take the first step and let others know they are not alone in their suffering. No matter how painful, the stories of our people must be told and heard. Through sharing our past we can begin to heal ourselves, our communities, our people as we look to a better tomorrow (RCAP, 1996a, Vol. 1, Ch. 10).

Clare Brant (1990), an Aboriginal psychiatrist, described the residential school system for Native Peoples as "a greasy blot upon the history of Canada." He further states that:

> Many communities, reserves and villages were totally denuded of children between the ages of four and sixteen for ten months of the year. The children were subjected to separation and loss from their parents, intimidation, physical beatings and sexual abuse. When they returned to their communities and became parents, they applied the same childrearing practices they had learned at the boarding schools (p. 3).

Corrado et al. (2003) cite the Law Commission of Canada, which report "the devastating effects of the residential school systems on Aboriginal families and communities has been so pervasive that some believe that this school system could have only been part of a larger campaign of cultural genocide" (p. 12).

Another causal link within the literature on violence in Aboriginal communities is what is referred to as the "sixties scoop." The term "sixties scoop" was coined, suggesting the random apprehensions of Indian children (Timpson, 1995, p. 530). This mass apprehension took place during the 1960s and 1970s, and placed Aboriginal children into non-Aboriginal foster care and adoptive homes throughout Canada, the United States, and some countries in Europe. Proulx et al. (2000) refer to this as a continuation of colonization. They state that residential schools and foster care placements took children away from their families and communities, creating a significant upheaval in the lives and development of Aboriginal women and children. According to Proulx et al. (2000), the "shame of being Aboriginal was instilled, as assimilation became the primary lesson taught in these institutions. Young minds were exposed to norms and values that further removed them from their community" (p. 16).

Once more, children were removed from their families and community. This maintained the continual disruption of Aboriginal life. "In the Canadian literature, Hudson and Mackenzie (cited in Timpson, 1995) frame the child welfare system's relationship to Native Peoples within the colonial relationship. The relationship between the child welfare system and Native Peoples was one of cultural colonialism" (p. 531). The child welfare system, along with the residential school system, stripped Aboriginal children, adults, and Elders of the experience of being family members, and hindered the formation of bonds that are essential to healthy community development.

Spirituality was another central aspect of Aboriginal life that was severely disrupted. The gradual erosion of Aboriginal spirituality can be traced back to the outlawing of traditional Aboriginal ceremonies by the Canadian federal government in the 1880s. An example of this can be found in the Royal Commission Report (1996a, 1996b, 1996c), which describes the 1884 and 1885 outlawing of the potlatch and sundance ceremony (two separate spiritual ceremonies of the coastal and plains culture respectively). The government even criminalized certain Aboriginal spiritual practices: "Participation in the potlatch was made a criminal offence, and it was also illegal to appear in traditional costume or dance at festivals" (RCAP, 1996a, Vol. 1, Part 1, Ch. 6). The government viewed the spiritual practices and traditions of Aboriginal Peoples as obstacles to assimilation rather than a vital aspect of Aboriginal life that contributes to the overall health and well-being of the individual, family, and community. Graveline (1998) underlines this point:

> "A universal sense among native people exists in regard to spirituality and that it coexists in all aspects of life. It is not separate but integral, it is not immutable, it is not replaceable, it resides in the essence of the person, and it is not always definable. It is in the community and among the people, it needs to be expressed among the people" (p. 53).

TRADITIONAL EDUCATION

It is important to note that the Aboriginal traditions and teachings presented within this paper are limited in scope when compared and viewed within the vast, holistic nature of traditional Aboriginal life. It is imperative to take a glimpse into the traditional way that Aboriginal Peoples have educated the young while strengthening the familial bonds that are the foundation of their life. All family members took part in this process: it has often been stated that it takes a whole community to raise a child. "Aboriginal pedagogy, our own world-view and teachings, served the need's of Aboriginal people for thousands of years before the arrival of a new and dominant pedagogy" (Stiffarm, 1998, p. 29). Aboriginal Peoples from all tribes across North America have always had a unique relationship to the land. In this unique relationship, which was built on respect, all human beings, the natural environment, and the supernatural are interconnected. Aboriginal Peoples do not see the natural environment and the supernatural as being apart from us, but rather as an extension of our being. "Everything in the universe is a part of a single whole. Everything is connected in some way to everything else. It is therefore possible to understand something only if we can understand how it is connected to everything else" (Bopp et al., 1984, p. 26). Not only was this unique understanding and respect necessary for the survival in the natural environment, but it also served as part of the intricate learning processes of Aboriginal life. This learning process was continual, and therefore took place at every stage of life. The responsibility of transmitting this knowledge was seen as the responsibility of the community as a whole. Cajete (1994) describes:

> The living place, the learner's extended family, the clan and tribe provided the context and source for teaching. In this way, every situation provided a potential opportunity for learning, and basic education was not separated from the natural, social, or spiritual aspect of everyday life. Living and learning were fully integrated (p. 33).

This learning process instilled in members a sense of responsibility, a sense of productivity, and an overall sense of connection. Haig-Brown (1988) further illustrates this learning process:

> The methods used to teach skills for everyday living and to instill values and principles were participation and example. Within communities, skills were taught by every member, with Elders playing an important role. Education for the child began at the time he or she was born. The child was prepared for his role in life whether it be, hunter, fisherman, wife, or mother. This meant that each child grew up knowing his place in the system .... Integral to the traditional education system was the participation of the family and community as educators (p. 37).

Within traditional Aboriginal societies men and women respect one another and are aware of their clearly defined roles within the community. This is described by Martha Flaherty of the Inuit Women's Association of Canada in 1993:

> There is agreement that women were traditionally responsible for decisions about children, food preparation and the running of the camp. While clear divisions of labour along gender lines existed, women's and men's work was equally valued. If a woman was a sloppy sewer, her husband might freeze; a man who was a poor hunter would have a hungry family. Everyone in the camp worked hard and everyone had a specific role based on their age, gender and capabilities (RCAP, 1996d, Vol. 4, Ch. 2).

Part of the learning process was passed down orally, usually through storytelling by the Elders in the community. It was the Elders who passed on the knowledge of ancestors through storytelling, along with the values and traditions of the tribe. Storytelling included the myths and legends of the Aboriginal community. Stories also provided teachings to community members about creation, plants, medicines, animals, and birds, as well as morality, which showed the Aboriginal Peoples the path to follow in life's journey.

> Elders are respected and cherished individuals who have amassed a great deal of knowledge, wisdom and experience over the period of many years. They are individuals who have also set examples, and have contributed something to the good of others. In the process, they usually sacrifice something of themselves, be it time, money, or effort …. Elders, Old ones, Grandfathers, Grandmothers don't preserve the ancestral knowledge. They live it (RCAP, 1996d, Vol. 4).

The well-being of Aboriginal individuals and communities is also being achieved in many areas through the incorporation of Western and Traditional approaches to healing. Many Aboriginal Peoples recognize the valuable healing methods of both societies. Several programs within Canada have found that the integration of both healing methods are effective. While an integrative healing process has been identified as being helpful, the helping relationships that are built on respect and understanding of our past and present realities are found to be most effective.

Moving Forward

It is apparent that Aboriginal Peoples in Canada are still suffering from the effects of colonialism, the residential school system, the child welfare system, and other forms of institutionalization. However, an increasing number of concerned individuals are working toward reversing the effects of a history that has contributed to widespread violence within Aboriginal communities. It is widely recognized that healing must take place within all areas of Aboriginal life in order for real change to occur.

Despite current efforts to eliminate violence within Aboriginal communities, many tendencies still exist within Aboriginal families. One of these barriers resides with individuals who have not worked toward healing themselves. The healing must start with individuals as they strive to undo the effects of racism, colonialism, and discrimination. Hart (2002) makes reference to individual healing where he states: "helpers begin in the helping process by addressing themselves. They prepare themselves to help others by establishing and maintaining an awareness of their own emotional, mental, spiritual, and physical well-being" (p. 105).

Alcoholism, solvent abuse, and drug addiction have been identified by many as major barriers to eliminating violence. Many Aboriginal Peoples who are working toward healing Aboriginal communities recognize that the addiction must be overcome before true healing can begin.

Reconnecting to our spiritual self is another element that will facilitate in the healing process:

> In Aboriginal Traditional forms, the spiritual infuses a person's entire existence within the world. A spiritual connection helps not only to integrate our self as a unified entity, but also to integrate the individual into the world as a whole. Spirituality is experienced as an ongoing process, allowing for the individual to move towards experiencing connection—to family, community, society and Mother Earth (Graveline, 1998, p. 55).

To facilitate this spiritual connection, many Aboriginal Peoples have incorporated traditional healing practices, such as the sweat lodge ceremony, pipe ceremony, cleansing ceremony, and the use of traditional medicines. In a report prepared for the National Aboriginal Health Organization, Hill (2003) stresses the importance of traditional ceremonies and practices to Aboriginal well-being:

> Traditional ceremonies and spiritual practices ... are precious gifts given to Indian people by the Creator. These sacred ways have enabled us as Indian people to survive—miraculously—the onslaught of five centuries of continuous effort by non-Indians and their government to exterminate us by extinguishing all traces of our traditional way of life. Today, these precious sacred traditions continue to afford American Indian people of all Nations the strength and vitality we need in the struggle we face everyday; they also offer us our best hope for a stable and vibrant future (p. 15).

Decolonization is another process that is recognized as a necessary step toward community healing.

The process of decolonization, according to Blaut, involves two parts. First, it is necessary to resurrect one's own history and to find out how it has contributed to the history of the world. Secondly, it is necessary to rewrite colonial history to show how it has led to poverty rather than progress (Graveline, 1998, p. 37).

Graveline (1998) goes on to further state that "Decolonization requires that we challenge the internalization of the structurally imposed reality of being victims and being inferior" (p. 40).

By educating both Aboriginal and non-Aboriginal people to understand how colonization and systemic racism have affected the lives of Aboriginal communities across Canada, we may begin to bridge the gap between ourselves and our relationships to others. Furthermore, by understanding how the roles, values, and norms of a once egalitarian society have been disturbed, this may address the wrongfully internalized shame felt by many Aboriginal Peoples.

In conjunction to learning our history, many feel it necessary to explore the interrelated traditional teachings and values that are said to have been with us since time immemorial. "A return to traditional teachings and beliefs may renew or instill a sense of identity, thereby increasing self worth and self efficacy" (Proulx et al., 2000, p., 105).

> Healing is a developmental process aimed at achieving balance within oneself, within human relationships and between human beings and the natural and spiritual world. The concept of healing in Aboriginal communities focuses on well-being rather than sickness. It focuses on moving the population toward wholeness and balance. It includes all levels of the community from individual to nation and embraces politics, economics, patterns of social relations and the process of cultural recovery (Solicitor General of Canada, 2002, p. 44).

Violence in Aboriginal communities needs to straddle the responsibility of the individual in perpetuating the violence and the role racism, colonization, and residential schools have played in socializing violence in Aboriginal communities.

NOTE

1. Brant (1990); LaRocque (1994); Warry (1998).

REFERENCES

Bandura, A. (1973). *Aggression: A social learning analysis.* Englewood Cliffs: Prentice-Hall.
Bopp, J., Bopp, M., Brown, L., & Lane Jr., P. (1984). *The Sacred Tree.* Lethbridge: Four

Worlds International Institute For Human And Community Development.

Brant, C. C. (1990). *A collection of chapters, lectures, workshops and thoughts.* Native Mental Health Association of Canada.

Cajete, G. (1994). *Look to the mountain: An ecology of Indigenous education.* Asheville: Kivaki Press.

Corrado, R. R. & Cohen, M. I. (2003). *Mental health profiles for a sample of British Columbia's Aboriginal survivors of the Canadian residential school system.* The Aboriginal Healing Foundation.

Graveline, J. F. (1998). *Circle works: Transforming Eurocentric consciousness.* Halifax: Fernwood.

Haig-Brown, C. (1988). *Resistance and renewal: Surviving the Indian residential school.* Vancouver: Tillicum.

Hart, A. M. (2002). *Seeking Mino-Pimatisiwin: An Aboriginal approach to helping.* Halifax: Fernwood.

Hill, M. D. (2003). *Traditional medicine in contemporary contexts: Protecting and respecting indigenous knowledge and medicine.* Ottawa: National Aboriginal Health Organization.

LaRocque, D. E. (1994). *Violence in Aboriginal communities.* Winnipeg: Department of Native Studies, University of Manitoba.

Knockwood, I. (1992). *Out of the depths: The experience of Mi'kmaw children at the Indian Residential School at Shubenacadie, Nova Scotia.* Lockport: Roseway.

Memmi, A. (1991). *The colonizer and the colonized*, 2nd edn. Boston: Beacon Press.

Proulx, S. & Perrault, S. (2000). *No place for violence: Canadian Aboriginal alternatives.* Halifax: Fernwood.

Royal Commission on Aboriginal Peoples (RCAP). (1996a). *Report of the Royal Commission on Aboriginal Peoples.* Vol. 1. *Looking forward, looking back.* Ottawa: Indian and Northern Affairs Canada.

Royal Commission on Aboriginal Peoples (RCAP). (1996b). *Report of the Royal Commission on Aboriginal Peoples.* Vol. 2. *Restructuring the relationship: Part One.* Ottawa: Indian and Northern Affairs Canada.

Royal Commission on Aboriginal Peoples (RCAP). (1996c). *Report of the Royal Commission on Aboriginal Peoples.* Vol. 3. *Gathering strength.* Ottawa: Indian and Northern Affairs Canada.

Royal Commission on Aboriginal Peoples (RCAP). (1996d). *Report of the Royal Commission on Aboriginal Peoples.* Vol. 4. *Perspectives and realities.* Ottawa: Indian and Northern Affairs Canada.

Solicitor General of Canada. (2002). *Mapping the healing journey. The final report of a First Nation Research Project on Healing in Canadian Aboriginal Communities.* Ottawa: Solicitor General Canada.

Stiffarm, Lenore A. (1998). *As we see: Aboriginal pedagogy.* Saskatoon: University Extension Press, University of Saskatchewan.

Timpson, J. (1995). Four decades of literature on Native Canadian child welfare: Changing themes. *Child Welfare*, 74(3), 525–546.

Warry, W. (1998). *Unfinished dreams: Community healing and the reality of Aboriginal self-government.* Toronto: University of Toronto Press.

Chapter Thirteen

MINO-YAA-DAA: HEALING TOGETHER

Cyndy Baskin

INTRODUCTION

Family violence within Canada's Aboriginal communities, both on- and off-reserve, is more prevalent than in the rest of society. Even so, comparatively little has been written and published about this topic. Aboriginal Peoples assert that family violence is a direct result of the colonization process, which continues to affect many families and communities.[1] For the most part, the combination of the criminalization of family violence and Western methods of intervention and treatment have not helped the situation. In fact, Aboriginal Peoples often report being revictimized by these processes.[2] Additionally, many communities continue to view the professions of law enforcement and social work as an extension of the colonizing process by many communities, perceiving them to be agents of social control rather than of social change.

The problem of family violence within Aboriginal communities must be approached in a way that is both community-controlled and culture-based. Such an approach must be holistic in nature and, therefore, needs to include interventions that centre on community awareness, healing processes for the entire family, and an alternative to the present Western-style criminal justice system.

This chapter will explore issues related to family violence within Canada's Aboriginal population, as well as Aboriginal perspectives on culture-based approaches to family violence interventions and healing. I was part of a specific program, which I will discuss at length as an example of a community-controlled, culture-based approach to healing the effects of family violence.

Aboriginal Peoples tend to introduce themselves and begin relationships before they move into any task. Thus, I will now locate myself.

I am of Mi'kmaq and Irish descent. My spirit name translates as "The Woman Who Passes on the teachings" and I belong to the Fish Clan. Originally from New Brunswick, I have lived in Toronto for several years. As a social worker, I have developed, implemented, and trained other Aboriginal service providers in family violence healing programs for fifteen years. Currently, I am an Assistant Professor in the School of Social Work at Ryerson University and a Ph.D. candidate at the Ontario Institute for Studies in Education/University of Toronto. I am straight, able-bodied, lower middle class, a survivor of family violence and the mental health system, a partner, and a mother.

I am choosing to consistently use the term "Aboriginal" throughout this chapter. It is my understanding that this term includes all of us—status, non-status, Métis, those of mixed blood, and Inuit. It is important to me that I be inclusive.

CULTURE-BASED INTERVENTION

Given the historical context of family violence in Aboriginal communities, it is understandable that many Aboriginal Peoples do not use mainstream services and programs to help them with their situations. Specific reasons for this have been cited as:

- racism within agencies
- fear of losing one's children
- fear of being revictimized
- needs not being met (services not being family-focused or culturally relevant)
- services appear fragmented (different needs are isolated, not treated holistically) (Baskin, 2002; Frank, 1992; Health Canada, 1996).

In addition, Aboriginal Peoples have been portrayed in white North American literature and popular culture in both negative and stereotypical ways. These often both promote and condone violence against Aboriginal women, thereby making it difficult for them to reach out to white people for help. Racism by both individuals and mainstream systems promote violence through a differential response and treatment of Aboriginal peoples (Bruce, 1998).

Programs that are based upon the culture and traditions of Aboriginal Peoples and that involve Aboriginal methods of healing have a much greater chance of succeeding than do programs developed and managed by non-Aboriginal agencies. In keeping with the principle of Aboriginal self-government, it is the right and responsibility of Aboriginal communities to take control of family violence interventions. The movement toward Aboriginal self-determination, which is rooted in community-based responsibility, action, ownership, and empowerment, needs to be respected and supported. Aboriginal communities must have the jurisdiction, legal responsibility, and financial resources to determine their own local priorities, standards, and organizational capacities to address all aspects of family violence interventions. This includes community-based healing for all of its members.

For Aboriginal Peoples, the concepts of healing—rather than merely responding to incidents of violence—and the focus on wellness demand a strategy that is different from the current responses to family violence. There is a contradiction between the Aboriginal solution, which seeks harmony and balance among individuals, the family, and community, and the mainstream one, which is crisis-oriented, punishes the abuser, and separates the family and community (Maracle, 1993).

Recovering positive Aboriginal identities will contribute to healing within Aboriginal communities. Aboriginal Peoples cannot look outside their cultures for their self-image. Aboriginal traditional values, especially in the area of relationships, carry the instructions for healing. Aboriginal traditional healing works for Aboriginal Peoples because in dealing with family violence, it involves more than the removal of harmful behaviours. It involves the building of healthy relationships within families and communities by:

- focusing on self-esteem and self-worth as Aboriginal Peoples
- offering support
- using symbols that engage the senses and the gifts of the earth to heal rather than only words
- teaching respect for the self, family, community, and the earth
- taking the focus away from an individualistic approach to the situation
- balancing the four aspects (psychological, physical, emotional, and spiritual) of the person, so she/he can use all of her/his resources
- promoting ways of achieving harmony and integration within (Vancouver Native Education Centre, 1991)

MINO-YAA-DAA

Analysis regarding the impacts of colonization on Aboriginal Peoples and understandings about culture-based approaches went into the development and implementation of a family violence intervention program for an urban Aboriginal community of about 300 people. I was involved in all aspects of the program, which ran from 1995 to 2000. I became the co-ordinator of the program and, with other service providers, facilitated all of the circles and other activities for women, children, and men.

Early in service implementation, women and children attended a circle together to give the program an Aboriginal name. As most of the community members who attended were Ojibway, a name was chosen in this language—"Mino-Yaa-Daa"—which means "healing together."

The Mino-Yaa-Daa Program offered services to children on a rotating basis according to age. It is important that children feel special, so the facilitators need to be supportive and encouraging. This is why work with children included activities such as learning the responsibilities of caring for sacred objects, lighting the fire and smudging, which provided self-confidence as Aboriginal Peoples. The relationship between children and facilitators is also important. Developing trust, security, and a safe environment were major principles of the program. Children also require firm, but caring and consistent, guidelines in order to feel safe and to be able to set appropriate boundaries with other. Respect for the needs of children and their ownership of the circle was another major principle of the Mino-Yaa-Daa Program. Thus, the children themselves, rather than the facilitators, set most of the boundaries or rules for the circle and the consequences for breaking them.

All of these factors created an accepting, non-judgmental atmosphere where children could share their stories and feelings about their experiences of family violence, knowing that what was said in the circle stayed in the circle (with the exception of child protection issues, of course). In doing so, they learned that they were not alone, that they were not the cause of their parents' behaviours, and that breaking the silence helped to change how they felt about themselves.

Activities for the children's circles were developed around the goals and objectives of the program. These included:

- developing self-esteem and a positive Aboriginal identity
- expressing feelings appropriately
- seeking safety in the home and the community
- letting go of self-blaming attitudes around issues related to family violence
- developing healthy ways of coping with problematic situations
- resolving conflicts without violence
- incorporating traditional teachings, values, and practices in their lives
- finding effective means of communication

Other components of the services for children included:

- learning Elders' teachings
- engaging in spiritual ceremonies such as the sweat lodge and Full Moon
- observing cultural responsibilities such as fire-keeping and medicines preparation

- case conferencing with other agencies and service providers
- contacting parents

A major purpose of the Mino-Yaa-Daa Program's services for women was to bring the community's women together. Only through women joining together can the disempowering silence around issues related to family violence be broken. By coming together in a circle, women learn that they are not alone and that their situations and feelings were similar to others'. They learned how to trust, take risks, and both give and receive support, thereby building relationships and a community of empowered women. This can be achieved only by coming together in a circle—it cannot happen through individual counselling or therapy.

As with children, women also need a safe place of their own in order to express their needs and concerns and begin the healing process. Therefore, the women negotiated their own boundaries for the circle to suit their needs for safety and comfort. The most important boundary for the circle was confidentiality, which was respected by both facilitators and participants. All community women were invited and welcomed into the program. There were no prerequisites—abstaining from alcohol and drugs (except when coming to the circle, of course), being currently involved in an abusive relationship, living a traditional lifestyle—in order to attend. A member did not even have to talk if she didn't want to!

The circle implemented both culture-based and some Western healing practices (as long as these were compatible with the values of Aboriginal cultures). Medicines for smudging, sacred objects for holding, and traditional teachings on the topics raised in the circle were always available, but not requisite. They were offered as a matter of personal choice for each woman.

Within the circles, participants and facilitators addressed the following areas:

- developing self-esteem and a positive identity as Aboriginal women
- developing healthy relationships with children, partners, and community members based on non-victimization
- identifying, expressing, and appropriately releasing feelings
- finding healthy, empowering coping behaviours
- learning self-care
- removing stigmas and labels
- letting go of past experiences that interfere with today
- resolving conflicts
- appreciating the values, beliefs, and healing practices of Aboriginal cultures
- making decisions and planning for the future
- role modelling

Two important elements were emphasized in the women's circles. The first was to focus on the tools that women learned in the circles, and then implement them in their daily lives. It was important for the circle to have practical value. The second focus was the need for women to support each other and to develop friendships outside of the program. This was important to create Aboriginal cultures' value of interdependency, which emphasizes how everyone has gifts and resources inside them as well as the natural ability to help others. Incorporated into all program services for women was Aboriginal cultures' belief in the healing powers of laughter. We had fun!

Other services offered to women by the Mino-Yaa-Daa Program included:

- sweat lodge ceremonies
- Elders' teaching circles
- Full Moon ceremonies
- individual crisis intervention sessions upon request

In order to fulfill the program's goals and objectives of developing a community, culture-based approach, it was crucial to implement an educational and healing process for the men of the community as well. Eradicating violence toward women cannot be done without men changing their abusive behaviours and attitudes. In addition to the circles, all of the other services that were offered to children and women were also offered to the community's men (except Full Moon ceremonies). The Full Moon ceremony is a ceremony for women and girls where they celebrate the gifts of womanhood and offer prayers for their loved ones and themselves. Since the Full Moon ceremony includes oral teachings, readers who wish to know more about the ceremony may wish to speak to Aboriginal Peoples such as Traditional Teachers/Elders.

The principles and values of the circles for children and women, such as confidentiality (with limitations, of course, in order to ensure the safety of women and children), ownership, and the negotiation of boundaries were extended to the men's circles as well. The facilitators of the men's circles were both a man and a woman. This was an important aspect of both the message and the role modelling emphasized by the program. The facilitators symbolized equality and respect between men and women, and there was a strong recognition of the roles and responsibilities of both according to Aboriginal cultures. The female facilitator was often asked by participants to discuss circle topics from the perspective of an Aboriginal woman. In addition, participants valued the building of a relationship with a strong woman who usually took the lead in circle facilitation and in confronting the men on abusive behaviours. Both facilitators participated in the men's sweats and Elders' teaching circles. The Elders for the men's component of the program were also both a man and a woman, again stressing equality between the two and the valuable learning that comes from female teachers.

Two principles lay at the foundation of the program's services for men: non-judgment and accountability. In order for men to understand and change abusive behaviours, they must feel safe enough to open up about them. Although abusive actions were seen as wrong, men were never viewed as "bad people." The second principle stressed that circle participants were responsible for their actions and accountable to those they had hurt, their families, and the community. This is in keeping with Aboriginal cultures' view of justice.

Within the circles, facilitators and participants addressed the areas that were covered in the women's circles as well as the following:

- identifying physical, psychological, spiritual, and emotional abuse
- understanding the attitudes around controlling and abusive behaviours
- understanding issues of power and control
- breaking the cycle of violence
- learning the origins of family violence
- making amends to their partners, families, and community for the abuse
- learning the roles and responsibilities of men according to Aboriginal cultures
- dealing with issues of substance abuse
- finding appropriate ways of dealing with anger and other powerful emotions

The men's component of the Mino-Yaa-Daa Program was also one of the ten recognized Partner Assault Response Strategy Programs in Toronto, that are supervised and funded by the Ministry of the Attorney General. It was the only Aboriginal-focused program on the roster. This meant that it was the only Aboriginal program that could accept men who went through the specialized domestic violence courts.

In addition to these services, the Mino-Yaa-Daa Program also included community healing. This involved community members' participation in the following ways:

- attending Elders/Traditional Teachers' teaching circles
- attending educational workshops on issues related to family violence, community responsibility, and community healing
- attending feasts and socials
- attending sweat lodge and Full Moon ceremonies
- attending workshops on drum-making, singing, and dancing
- attending cultural events focused on children and youth

- developing and implementing of a community watch safety program
- participating in demonstrations
- facilitating of a four-day community healing conference that included a special ceremony to commit to ending family violence

In order to assess the impact of the Mino-Yaa-Daa Program on its participants, an evaluation process was built into the development of the program. An evaluation was conducted at the end of each year. This evalution included assessment of the following goals:

- attitudes around issues related to family violence
- responses to specific services, topics, and activities
- cognitive and behavioural changes in relating to others and coping with problem situations
- increased safety
- recommendations for changes in future services

The methodologies of the evaluation included:

- a questionnaire on attitudes around issues of family violence completed by each participant at the beginning and end of service implementation
- weekly reports completed by program facilitators on each service area
- evaluation form on degree of satisfaction with services
- interviews with participants conducted by an independent researcher
- interviews with family members of participants conducted by an independent researcher

Over the years, evaluations indicated that children consistently reported that they learned problem-solving techniques as well as how to improve their own safety. With the researcher, they discussed that they "learned what to do when a person approached [them] to try to take [them] away" and what to do when parents were fighting. They pointed out that in the circle they had discussed issues of self-blame when violence occurred within their families.

Children explained in the interviews that when a violent incident occurs, "even though some people tell [them] not to call the police, [they] know it is best to call them." They also explained that they knew to leave the violent situation and go to another adult's home, where they would be safe. Some children recommended that "it helps to stay calm [in such situations] and to get someone that can help."

All of the parents reported positive changes in their children following circle attendance, including both improved relations with their children and ability to problem solve. They described their children as "being more mature," "able to teach others about the medicines," "more confident," "feeling special," "more outgoing," "able to talk more," "having a greater interest in the culture and traditions," and "proud of who they are." Some parents noted specific changes in how their children were relating and dealing with feelings and problems. These changes were described as "closer relationships" with parents, "expressing their feelings honestly" with them, "suggesting ways to work out situations at home," and "speaking up about what [they] want."

Parents added that they were receptive to these changes in their children because they had a positive effect on family relationships. Some commented that they were "able to correct unfair responsibilities placed on children," that they had begun to "smudge together as a family," they saw their children "speaking to [them] and other adults with respect," and that they "participated in solving problems at home as a family."

In the women's programming, a participant expressed that attending an Elders' teaching circle provided by the program helped her to relate the traditional teachings to her life; through this she gained an improved understanding of a difficult situation she was undergoing. Another woman explained how the program helped her to clarify her values and beliefs so that she was better able to provide direction to her children. A third woman spoke about how she had grown much closer to family members and had been able to "deal with a lot of hard issues" with them because of what she had learned in the circles.

Participants of the women's circle also commented that their experiences helped them to work through issues with their partners, to be able to talk more openly, to set clear boundaries with others, to unlock issues connected to their past, be more assertive, and to deal with confrontation in healthy ways. Most discussed how they came to understand that the violence toward them was not their own fault, and as such they gained the confidence to leave abusive relationships, and had begun to implement self-care in their lives.

All participants of the men's programming indicated that they were able to give and receive support within the circle, and some noted that they were able to support participants outside of the circle as well. When asked by the researcher to address how participants of the men's circle were dealing with anger rather than becoming violent, all provided examples of "expressing it in a healing way, so I won't hurt someone or myself." Examples included "loud screams in a pillow," "hitting a pillow or punching bag," "talking to someone I can trust," "going for a walk," "exercising," "smudging," "deep breathing," and "crying because sometimes after the anger, there's sadness."

Men's circle participants stated that they used what they learned in the circles in their lives. One participant related that he incorporated the techniques and teachings from the circle "all the time and it works daily." Another reported that if he did not use what he had learned, "I wouldn't even be able to handle getting to the bus stop." A third related that he was "making a punching bag" similar to the one used in the circles. Another indicated that he thought issues over carefully, incorporating what he had learned from the circle, and then he talked to his partner. A fifth participant indicated that "I'm a very angry person, so I have to use what I learned quite frequently. To heal, you have to apply it, work on it all the time."

Most participants in the men's circle commented that attendance in the Mino-Yaa-Daa Program helped them in their relationships with partners. For some, this meant eventually accepting that the relationships were not going to continue, but that they needed to carry on with their responsibilities as fathers. Others stated that they worked more with their partners in recognizing exactly what the problems were and in dealing with them, they talked more with their partners, and they spent more time at home with their families. They generally described their relationships with their families as "improved," "better," and "more healthy." Some indicated that family members had begun to tell them they saw positive changes in them.

It seems participating in the Mino-Yaa-Daa Program was a success for all who attended. However, both participants and staff identified several struggles connected to the program such as:

- lack of financial and human resources
- geographic location in the far east end of Toronto, which made it difficult for many people to access
- uncooperative relationships with the justice system such as the police, judges, probation and parole officers, and crown attorneys
- disrespect for Aboriginal cultural practices from other systems like child welfare and medicine, and other programs providing therapy and education to male abusers
- no commitment from any funding source for an ongoing program

In the six years that the Mino-Yaa-Daa Program ran, to the best of my knowledge, only one participant reoffended by assaulting his partner. No mechanisms were built into the program evaluation to track ex-participants over the long term. However, as Aboriginal Peoples tend to develop relationships that last beyond formal programs, I know from personal, ongoing contact with past participants that a great many of them have moved on to more happy, successful lives. As far as I know, all of the women and their children stayed together. A few women are now attending university, some are working at Aboriginal agencies as helpers to other women, two have returned to their reserve communities to work on family violence interventions, while others are singing in women's hand drum groups and dancing at pow wows. Some left their abusive partners and never returned while others reunited with their partners when the partners had changed for the better. The men who were involved went on in similar ways as the women. Two of these men are now my friends: they're in healthy relationships, one has his own business while the other has a baby, and both come to my house and play with my son.

These friendships speak to what I wrote on earlier about not sacrificing men who have been perpetrators of family violence and about how violence is learned behaviour that can be unlearned. This also speaks to Aboriginal values around community responsibility and inclusiveness of all. Regardless of what Aboriginal Peoples may or may not do, they are all a part of our community. Each person has value and gifts to share with everyone else. Each person has inherent worth. The healing process brings all of this out of people so that we may engage with them as their true selves. Obviously, I know this to be true or I would never bring these men around my precious (and highly protected) child.

CONCLUSION

It is impossible to understand the current context of family violence in Aboriginal families and communities without an awareness of the history of colonization in Canada and present-day systemic racism. With this understanding comes a deeper appreciation of why dominant society's solutions to these social problems do not usually help and how the responsibilities and control of Aboriginal self-government within our communities have a far greater chance of success. A culture-based and community-controlled approach that focuses on holistic services is the choice of most communities today. We must be mindful, however, that this approach means listening to all voices and addressing the concerns and safety issues of those voices.

Another area of significance is that Aboriginal service providers, educators, and researchers need to begin to document, evaluate, and publish our good work on culture-based family violence healing programs. We have so much to share with each other about the struggles and the successes; those of us who are privileged have a responsibility to mentor others in carrying out the work, and we have ways of knowing and healing that are valuable to all humankind. I leave you with this appeal.

NOTES

1. Brownridge (2003); Bruce (1998); Chapin (1994); Durst, MacDonald & Parsons (1999); Fiddler (1991); Frank (1992); LaRocque (1994); Maracle (1993); Ontario Native Women's Association (1989).

2. Baskin (2002); Bruce (1998); Frank (1992); Hamilton & Sinclair (1991); Health Canada (1996); O'Donnell (2000).

REFERENCES

Baskin, C. (2002). Holistic healing and accountability: Indigenous restorative justice. *Child Care in Practice*, 8(2), 133–136.

Brownridge, D. A. (2003). Male partner violence against Aboriginal women in Canada: An empirical analysis. *Journal of Interpersonal Violence*, 18(1), 65–83.

Bruce, L. (1998). A culturally sensitive approach to working with Aboriginal women. *Manitoba Social Worker*, 30(2), 1, 8–10.

Chapin, D. (1994). *Peace on earth begins in the home*. Duluth: Mending the Sacred Hoop.

Durst, D., MacDonald, J., & Parsons, D. (1999). Finding our way: A community needs assessment on violence in Native families in Canada. *Journal of Community Practice*, 6(1), 45–69.

Fiddler, S. (1991). *Genesis of family violence in Native society*. Toronto: University of Toronto, unpublished paper.

Frank, S. (1992). *Family violence in Aboriginal communities*. Toronto: University of Toronto, unpublished paper.

Hamilton, A. C. & Sinclair, C. M. (1991). *Report of the Aboriginal justice inquiry of Manitoba*. Winnipeg: Province of Manitoba.

Health Canada. (1996). *Family violence in Aboriginal communities: An Aboriginal perspective*. Ottawa: Health Canada.

LaRoque, E. (1994). *Violence in Aboriginal communities*. Ottawa: Health Canada.

Maracle, S. (1993). Family violence: An Aboriginal perspective. *Vis-à-vis*, 10(4), 1 & 4.

O'Donnell, T. (2000). *Family violence project: Workshop report*. Toronto: Centre for Indigenous Sovereignty.

Ontario Native Women's Association. (1989). *Breaking free—A proposal for change to Aboriginal family violence*. Thunder Bay: Ontario Native Women's Association.

Vancouver Native Education Centre. (1991). *Training family violence workers*. Vancouver: Vancouver Native Education Centre.

LIST OF CONTRIBUTING AUTHORS

Michelle Aukema is a social worker with Child and Family Services, Winnipeg.

Cyndy Baskin is Assistant Professor of Mi'kmaq and Irish descent in the Department of Social Work at Ryerson University.

Karen Blackford was Associate Professor in the School of Nursing, Laurentian University. Sadly, Dr. Blackford passed away in 1999.

Rod Brown is a member of the Ontario Provincial Police and has worked in small rural communities.

Keith Brownlee is Professor in the School of Social Work at Lakehead University, and co-editor of the Northern Social Work Collection.

Larry Cheblovic is a graduate of Lakehead University and has worked as a volunteer social worker with the Thunder Bay Catholic Family Centre.

Diana Coholic is Assistant Professor in the School of Social Work at Laurentian University.

Roger Delaney is Professor in the School of Social Work at Lakehead University. He is a co-editor of the Northern Social Work Collection.

Michelle Derosier is of Aboriginal descent and a graduate student at the School of Social Work at Lakehead University.

Colleen Ginter is a social worker with Family Services Thunder Bay, and has extensive experience facilitating groups for Thunder Bay Catholic Family Centre.

John Graham is Professor of Social Work at the University of Calgary and Adjunct Professor of Social Work at Lakehead University.

Teresa Legowski is a social worker with the Sister Margaret Smith Centre for Addictions in Thunder Bay.

Chantal Morrison-Lambert is a social worker with the Children's Aid Association of Thunder Bay.

Raymond Neckoway is of Aboriginal descent, and is Assistant Professor in the School of Social Work at Lakehead University.

Darlene Olimb is a social worker with the Thunder Bay Catholic Family Centre and has had many years of experience working in small, remote towns.

Glen Schmidt is Associate Professor in the School of Social Work at the University of Northern British Columbia.

David Tranter is Assistant Professor in the School of Social Work at Lakehead University.

Susan van Yzendoorn is a social worker with the Kawartha Haliburton Children's Aid Society.

Julie Woit works in Thunder Bay as a private practitioner and as a consultant to the Thunder Bay City Police Force.